Managing Startups: Best Blog Posts

Thomas Eisenmann, Editor

O'REILLY®

Beijing · Cambridge · Farnham · Köln · Sebastopol · Tokyo

MANAGING STARTUPS: BEST BLOG POSTS

Thomas Eisenmann

Editor: Mary Treseler	**Cover Designer:** Randy Comer
Production Editor: Christopher Hearse	**Interior Designer:** David Futato
Copyeditor: Rachel Head	**Illustrator:** Rebecca Demarest

April 2013:   First Edition

Revision History for the First Edition:

2013-04-30:   First release

See *http://oreilly.com/catalog/errata.csp?isbn=9781449367879* for release details.

ISBN: 978-1-449-36787-9

[LSI]

Contents

Preface

Safari® Books Online

Note

Safari Books Online (*www.safaribooksonline.com*) is an on-demand digital library that delivers expert content in both book and video form from the world's leading authors in technology and business.

Technology professionals, software developers, web designers, and business and creative professionals use Safari Books Online as their primary resource for research, problem solving, learning, and certification training.

Safari Books Online offers a range of product mixes and pricing programs for organizations, government agencies, and individuals. Subscribers have access to thousands of books, training videos, and prepublication manuscripts in one fully searchable database from publishers like O'Reilly Media, Prentice Hall Professional, Addison-Wesley Professional, Microsoft Press, Sams, Que, Peachpit Press, Focal Press, Cisco Press, John Wiley & Sons, Syngress, Morgan Kaufmann, IBM Redbooks, Packt, Adobe Press, FT Press, Apress, Manning, New Riders, McGraw-Hill, Jones & Bartlett, Course Technology, and dozens more. For more information about Safari Books Online, please visit us online.

How to Contact Us

Please address comments and questions concerning this book to the publisher:

O'Reilly Media, Inc.
1005 Gravenstein Highway North
Sebastopol, CA 95472
800-998-9938 (in the United States or Canada)
707-829-0515 (international or local)
707-829-0104 (fax)

We have a web page for this book, where we list errata, examples, and any additional information. You can access this page at *http://oreil.ly/managing-startups*.

To comment or ask technical questions about this book, send email to *book questions@oreilly.com*.

For more information about our books, courses, conferences, and news, see our website at *http://www.oreilly.com*.

Find us on Facebook: *http://facebook.com/oreilly*

Follow us on Twitter: *http://twitter.com/oreillymedia*

Watch us on YouTube: *http://www.youtube.com/oreillymedia*

Foreword

Since 2009 I've been publishing an annual compilation on my blog, Platforms & Networks (*http://platformsandnetworks.blogspot.com/*), of what I deem to be the year's best posts by other authors about the management of technology startups. Readers have asked me to collect the posts in an ebook, so I was very happy when O'Reilly Media offered to do this. I was pleased, as well, to be able to donate my profits from the project to Endeavor Global (*http://www.endeavor.org/*), a terrific organization that supports entrepreneurship in emerging markets.

What I do. In my annual compilations, I've steered clear of news about product launches and funding rounds; likewise, I don't include posts that analyze trends in technologies or markets (e.g., big data, cloud computing, SoLoMo services). Instead, my focus has been on the management tasks that entrepreneurs must undertake when they search for a viable business model and then scale a startup. These tasks include the work done in the engineering, product management, marketing, sales, and business development functions. I pay special attention to ways in which functional managers leverage lean startup management practices. My compilations also cover a range of organizational issues; for example, dealing with cofounder tensions, recruiting and career planning, managing company culture, structuring the startup team, pacing the introduction of formal management systems and processes, working with the board of directors, and coping with the psychological pressures that inevitably confront entrepreneurs. Finally, I track developments in capital markets that are relevant to the management of tech startups; for example, the ebbs and flows of valuation bubbles and the proliferation of incubators and seed-stage funds.

Why I do it. I'm a business school professor who works closely with students aspiring to launch a startup or to work for one. My students are hungry for practical advice, and I've found that they learn a lot when I steer them to the wealth of insight available on the Web. As an educator, I feel fortunate to work in a field where practitioners are so eager to pay it forward by sharing their experiences and ideas. Over time, I started collecting posts for my own reference, and for sharing with my students. It was a natural step to curate these posts and publish the compilations.

I discovered that there was interest in the lists that I'd curated in the broader entrepreneurship community.

How I do it. Readers of my blog have asked how I pick the posts for my annual compilations. There's no science in my approach: I don't use an algorithm that tracks traffic or social media mentions. Rather, I regularly read a few dozen blogs —mostly written by entrepreneurs and venture capitalists—and I follow links to other posts that look interesting. My criterion for flagging a post for future reference is simple: did I learn something that seems worth passing on to my students or to current entrepreneurs? When I publish my compilation, I ask readers to suggest other posts that I've omitted, and I always get some great additions. I'm sure, however, that I've missed plenty of posts that deserve to be included, and I apologize to their authors.

I want to thank all of the individuals who gave permission to have their work republished here. The generosity of the startup community is amazing, and these posts are invaluable to those of us who teach and coach aspiring entrepreneurs.

—Tom Eisenmann, Editor

PART I

Lean Startup

How We Fooled Ourselves into Delaying Our Startup's Launch

Vinicius Vacanti (http://viniciusvacanti.com/)

I remember reading the first few pages of Steve Blank's book, *The Four Steps to the Epiphany* (*http://amzn.to/four-steps-epiphany*), and thinking two things:

- This is not exactly a page-turner.
- This is a really smart way of thinking about startups.

Soon after, I started attending the Lean Startup meetup (*http://www.meetup.com/lean-startup/*) in New York and reading Eric Reis's writings (*http://www.amazon.com/The-Lean-Startup-Entrepreneurs-Continuous/dp/0307887898/ref=ntt_at_ep_dpt_1*). I was a believer.

One of the main principles is to release an early prototype of your idea to potential users to get their feedback.

But, despite being all in on the Lean Startup movement, we didn't do that.

Why Didn't We Release an Early Prototype?

Our current idea, Yipit (*http://yipit.com/*), would find all the deals happening in your city (sample sales, happy hours, retail discounts) and would send you an email with the best seven, based on your interests and your location.

It would have taken us just a week to launch an early prototype.

We could have measured success based on whether people opened and clicked on the emails. We could have manually created the emails with deals we found and used MailChimp (*http://mailchimp.com/*) to send them out. There was no need to build any tech infrastructure.

But we came up with all sorts of excuses why we just couldn't release an early version.

Six painful months later, we finally put out the product. It didn't work—which was okay. What was not okay was realizing that our excuses for not releasing earlier were all wrong.

The Excuses We Came Up With

The bright side is that six months later, when we iterated Yipit into a daily deal aggregator, we learned to ignore the excuses and released a prototype in three days that took off right away.

Here are the excuses we made, and how we realized they didn't matter:

- **It wasn't good enough yet.** We thought manually sending deals wasn't good enough. We were guessing and didn't really know. It turned out that six months later, the automated version full of features wasn't good enough either. We could have learned why it wasn't good enough six months earlier and *spent that time actually trying to fix it.* Instead, we just guessed why it wasn't going to work, and guessed wrong.

- **We didn't want to give a bad impression to those early test users.** I can safely say that this doesn't matter. Those early test users just don't care. After we relaunched as a daily deal aggregator, we got exactly one email from a user saying they'd missed the sample sales. That's it. In fact, many of those early users enjoyed seeing our product develop.

- **It needed extra features.** We thought we had to have a web view, people had to specify where in the city they lived, it needed to have links to the source of where we found the deal.... None of these were right. We were guessing. Had we launched in a week, we would have quickly realized these features weren't going to make a difference.

- **It was going to take us a few months to build the tech backend.** We shouldn't have built it. We should have just used MailChimp to send the emails. For the next iteration of Yipit, we didn't build the backend (*http://viniciusvacanti.com/ 2010/12/20/the-shortcut-we-took-to-build-yipit-in-three-days/*). Users don't know what your tech backend looks like. Focus instead on getting the user experience right.

- **It needed to scale to accommodate hundreds of thousands of users.** No, it didn't. We weren't going to get hundreds of thousands of users. Not anytime soon. We should have just been worrying about getting our first 1,000 users (*http://vini ciusvacanti.com/2011/02/24/how-to-keep-your-first-1000-users/*).

- **Someone will see what we're doing and copy it.** If our idea had any merit, then there would have been at least 10 other groups of people out there also actively working on it. In fact, there were many groups of people working on a daily deal aggregator. But, because we launched in just three days, we were the first ones and got most of the press attention.

- **A potential investor will see it.** I'm not sure if any investors actually did see it. But even if they had, it's not a bad thing. Investors like to see the progress you make as a product and as a team (*http://www.bothsidesofthetable.com/2010/11/15/ invest-in-lines-not-dots/*).

- **TechCrunch will write about us when we're not ready.** They won't. We spent a bunch of time trying to get people to write about us, and they didn't. Also, in some crazy scenario where someone writes about our terrible prototype, I can safely say it won't matter in the long run. Startups succeed because they have a good product, not because they got good launch PR.

The Excuse I Didn't Admit

There's one more excuse I didn't talk about. *I was afraid it wouldn't work.*

I had quit my job. I had told my family and friends about the idea, and they were all telling me how much they believed in me. What if the idea was bad? What if I had to tell them it didn't work? What if I had to admit failure?

You have to fight this feeling. The best way I've come up with is to think of a startup as an experiment, not as a business (*http://viniciusvacanti.com/2012/01/23/ have-idea-for-a-startup-dont-launch-a-company-launch-an-experiment/*). Your early experiments are supposed to go wrong. Your goal is to find out what went wrong and iterate.

Lastly

For those of you that don't have an amazing excuse (like, you will be put in jail if you do this), please launch an early prototype. Not waiting to launch is, by far, the best advice I can give. Hopefully you'll listen more than we did.

2

How to Build It: Lean Prototyping Techniques for Hardware

Graeham Douglas (http://graehamdouglas.com)

After recently writing a blog post on my vision for the future of 3D printers (*http://graehamdouglas.com/2012/11/06/3d-printers-are-not-the-future-of-manufacturing/*), I wanted to expand more broadly on my thoughts on prototyping technologies, and particularly on rapid and lean prototyping for mechanical designs.

"Lean" started in the context of manufacturing automobiles, and has since been taken to describe prototyping and customer development for software startups. Many software/web startups do not win because of a science or technology invention. Instead, *user experiences and marketing are what drive success.* I think people are realizing that this can apply to hardware as well, and the increasing ease of prototyping is helping to drive the increase in hardware-based projects and startups such as those seen on the design section of the crowd-funding platform Kickstarter (*http://www.kickstarter.com/discover/categories/design*). Of course, hardware continues to have the challenge that production and distribution continue to be more difficult than for software.

I will outline here the tools and methods I use in prototyping hardware.

The Dollar Store

Duct tape, super glue, spray paint, and a dollar store full of imagination are possibly the best (and maybe least expected) prototyping tools. I'm a strong advocate of the super-alpha prototype: the more you can build quickly, the faster you can find what you don't know. It's also easier to get excited about a project when you have something tangible to show people (potential customers!).

Figure 2-1. Tons of inexpensive, easily modified parts (image courtesy Wikimedia Commons (http://commons.wikimedia.org/wiki/Main_Page))

Don't forget the spray paint, or finishing your prototype in general! A prototype that looks sketchy automatically throws off people you show it to. Civilians will discount even the best features of a prototype if it looks unprofessional, unfinished, and ugly. Amazon, electronics stores, and hardware stores are also great resources, especially once you have enough of an idea of what you are building that you can specify a specific part. Before that, quick, cheap, and convenient should be the main criteria for finding parts and materials.

Pen and Paper

Very quick calculations can prove your idea violates the laws of physics. Save yourself embarrassment and make sure that you are the one to do these calculations, not someone else (like an investor), and that you do them before you spend too much time on a project. Such calculations can also help you decide between design alternatives and optimize design choices.

Simple sketches can help you realize ideas and form them to guide physical prototypes. There are often a lot of different ways to build or do something. Having different ways on paper can help in deciding which direction to take. They can also express your ideas quickly to other people.

Computer Modeling

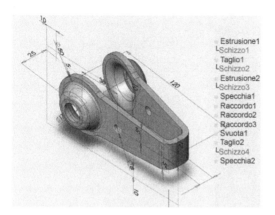

Figure 2-2. CAD model and development (image courtesy Nikola LK (http://commons.wikime dia.org/wiki/User:Nicola_L.K.) on Wikimedia Commons)

A tried-and-true method for professional mechanical designers, some computer aided design (CAD) programs have come down in price a lot recently. Alibre (*http://www.alibre.com/*) 3D CAD software, for instance, is about the same price as Microsoft Office Home and Business, and gives probably 70–80% of the functionality of professional design programs that cost over 10 times more. Entry-level CAD systems often don't have simulation applications to test the physics of parts, but some packages are available open source that do. Simulation also requires training to make reliable models.

I'm not sure why CAD isn't getting more publicity for maker, hacker, and hobbyist use—a physical model is often easy to make from a fully rendered CAD model. CAD models can be changed more easily and quickly, and at less cost. Design iteration time on CAD can be as quick as modifying software code.

However, if the final widget uses parts that interact with one another, a CAD model may not be able to prove everything works together. This is especially true for moving parts or embedded electronics.

2D Cutting

Figure 2-3. 75mm thick steel, cut by waterjet (image courtesy Fromthecorner (http://commons.wikimedia.org/wiki/File:Waterjet_Steel_75_mm.jpg) on Wikimedia Commons)

Waterjet and laser cutters etch or remove a pattern from sheet metal (and other materials). The sheet can then be folded or pressed to a 3D final shape. These can be very cheap and quick: for example, a small part could be made in as little as five minutes and at a cost of $5. The size of the machines makes them practical for anything from smartphone to laptop size, with exceptions either way for certain applications.

The machines are not common in people's houses, and take a bit of a different design approach: you have to think about your 3D project on a 2D sheet. Even if you don't have one in your house, there should be several companies that will be able to cut your part in even a small city.

Additive Manufacturing

The fancy name for "3D printing," additive manufacturing has become popular for hobbyists and the media. It is fascinating to watch a part grow in front of you, and a variety of metals, plastics, and rubberlike materials are available, but generally not on the same machine. Machines are also now small, cheap, and usable enough that they are no longer restricted to industrial use. Assemblies that would otherwise require several components can be built as a single part on a 3D printer. 3D printers allow for making parts that are impossible with other processes—for instance, parts with internal holes and voids. They also can be used to make quick, inexpensive tooling for molds to make parts from. A prototype can be made for $20–$100+, depending what it is.

CNC

Computer numeric control (CNC) usually refers to a milling machine that cuts a big chunk of metal (or other material) into a finished part. It was probably the first type of "prototyping machine," but is often used for production as well. Usually people don't have these in their houses (although the hobbyist and homemade CNC group seems to be growing), and CNC parts can be more expensive than other contracted parts. Usually parts are in the $150+ range.

Molding and Fiberglass

Figure 2-4. Carbon fiber aeroshell from a fiberglass mold, UBC Solar Car team (http://www.ubcsolar.com/)

Molding and fiberglass are great for making irregularly shaped parts or if you need several copies of the same part. There can be a lot more initial work to make a mold than other processes, but quick molds using hobbyist and film-industry materials can be made pretty quickly. Some chemicals involved in fiberglass and some molds are toxic and require gloves and/or ventilation. Materials can be quite cheap—$50–$100 is enough to make most small- to medium-sized parts—but they can require extensive time and labor to prepare. The above aeroshell for the UBC Solar Car is a large carbon fiber part (approximately 2m × 5m × 1m) and took about $2,500 for the materials and about 500 hours of labor.

Welding

Welding allows the joining of metal. It is useful for many different parts, including frames from metal tubes or making sheet metal into 3D parts. Like molding, there can be a lot of setup time in making jigs to hold parts in place when they are being welded. Spot welders are good for quickly joining metal pieces and require much less skill to operate, and they are particularly useful in joining 2D sheet metal projects that were cut with a waterjet or laser to make 3D parts. Often, glues are easier to use and will suffice for a prototype.

Arduino

Arduino (*http://www.arduino.cc/*) and other microcontrollers are an easy and cheap way to prototype and integrate electronics into a project. There are lots of examples and support for the platform: someone else has probably already solved the problem you are having and is willing to help. SparkFun (*https://www.sparkfun.com/*) and others have good sensors and other electrical accessories that work with Arduino and other platforms.

User Feedback

If making something for more than a few people to use, you have to talk to people you hope will use it. Doing live demos or letting potential users play with your prototypes is important. But it's also important who you pick to ask for feedback and how you let them use it. With this feedback, you can improve the next round of prototypes, until the project is ready. I expect there are many parallels to lean software development here.

HOW I (TRY TO) PICK PEOPLE FOR FEEDBACK

These are the qualities that I look for:

Open to change

If people are too happy with what they already have, they will be resistant to change. Even worse is if the users don't want to change but they think their bosses will force them to. These types of people will think of any reason your prototype won't work, and it can be tough to convince them differently. Try to take away Milton's stapler and he'll burn the place down (reference to the movie *Office Space*).

Will give a fair assessment

Like the above people who will only say negative things about your work, try to avoid people who will only say positive things. Your mother is not the person to get good feedback from, assuming she is supportive of everything you do.

Some people get excited about anything just for being new. Feedback from them can be motivating, but coaching and interpreting may be required to make the advice constructive.

Is sympathetic to how prototypes are

Most people are never exposed to how things are made. Stuff comes from Amazon or Walmart, and it better be perfect. If it breaks, looks ugly, sounds funny, or crashes, it's a bad product and the company that made it may never be trusted again. Unfortunately for people looking for feedback, it's hard to get enough feedback from people who are sympathetic to early versions.

These people need to have their hands held if you choose them for product feedback, as they are often disappointed with what you show them. You need to manage expectations and teach them what exactly your prototype is showing. If they understand the prototype is only testing a few features of a final product, they will be more understanding. These people are why spray paint and making your prototype look good are so important: for early-stage design, discussion should be about ideas and features, not distracted by aesthetics.

Summary

Prototyping is cheaper and easier than ever. In my opinion, a prototype for many Kickstarter-ready design projects could be made for $1,000 in parts and materials, and some for even $100. Like in software development, the larger investment is in time put in by the designers. Of course, several (or sometimes many) stages of prototypes are needed to arrive at a final design. Good user feedback is essential, and this feedback should guide making the next round of prototypes. It is an iterative cycle. *The key to making good products is making mistakes early and learning from them. This is best done through prototyping and getting user feedback.*

Acknowledgments

Many of my ideas and views on prototyping were formed in the University of British Columbia Mechanical Engineering program, and particularly from the design faculty. Some thoughts are inspired by work from the Center for Design Research group at Stanford and the Engineering Design Centre at Cambridge. Any of these groups are great places to look more in depth at these points.

3

How Many Metrics Do You Need to Run Your Startup?

Ben Yoskovitz (http://www.instigatorblog.com)

Answer: only one.

One of the concepts we're pushing hard in the Lean Analytics book (*http:// leananalyticsbook.com/*) is the *One Metric That Matters* (OMTM).

The idea is this: at any given time in your business there's one key metric you should be focusing on. Not two, or three, or four. Just one. And that one metric becomes the driving force for what you do, experiments you run, and decision making.

Picking the metric is hard. Drawing a line in the sand for your goals with the metric is even harder. But these are both important for achieving the levels of focus and speed required to succeed.

At GoInstant (*http://www.goinstant.com/*) we've been very analytical. We measure lots of different things, from overall usage, to specific feature success, to performance and scalability. But none of these are the *One Metric That Matters*. We're still working on how to define our OMTM, but ultimately GoInstant will be a huge success when most of the Web is co-browsable "out-of-the-box." That will mean more customers can get up and running with GoInstant more quickly. Everything we do has to make more of the Web and more of the elements of websites and web applications co-browsable. It's a huge challenge.

So GoInstant's OMTM, which is still a work in progress, is essentially a percentage of the Web that is co-browsable. Measuring that is tricky. There are lots of variables. We clearly can't test the entire Web. Nor is that really necessary. So we're building systems and developing processes for testing a smaller but significant list of websites, and a large array of web elements (think: all different types of forms, form fields, types of code, pop-ups, logins, interactive elements, and so on; basically the "building blocks" of the Web) as a proxy for "the entire Web." We test on a continuous basis and will invest more than most companies in testing because of the challenges in building GoInstant's technology.

What's Your OMTM?

Well, that depends on a number of things. Check out a previous blog post (from Lean Analytics) for more info: *http://leananalyticsbook.com/one-metric-that-matters/*. While you're there, please sign up for updates too.

In the meantime, here are some elements of the *One Metric That Matters* to keep in mind:

1. **It will change over time**. The OMTM isn't static. When you're focused on acquiring users (and converting them into customers), your OMTM may be around which acquisition channels are working best or conversion rate from signup to active user. When you're focused on retention, you may be looking at churn and experimenting with pricing, features, improving customer support, and so forth.

2. **It answers the most important question you have.** At any given time you'll be trying to answer a hundred different questions and trying to juggle a million things. You need to identify the riskiest areas of your business as quickly as possible; that's where the most important question lies. And the OMTM should be there to measure and answer that question.

3. **It has a clear goal**. A metric without a goal is largely useless. You need to draw a line in the sand that helps you understand whether you're achieving success or not. The *One Metric That Matters* needs a goal.

4. **It focuses the entire company**. The OMTM should be front and center, physically visible for everyone to see all the time. Think about putting the OMTM on a giant TV screen in your office, or somewhere that people will look multiple times per day. The *One Metric That Matters* drives focus by being ever-present, and reminds everyone of its importance and the work that has to go into improving it.

5. **It inspires a culture of experimentation**. Experimentation is key. Moving through the *Build-Measure-Learn* cycle as quickly (and as often) as possible is key to generating and amassing enough learning that you can start executing effectively in the right directions. You want to inspire and instill a culture of

experimentation throughout your organization—the *One Metric That Matters* can help.

Collecting lots of data in and of itself isn't the problem. Most startups do that. Unfortunately, that's what they focus on—collecting lots of data—instead of figuring out what matters. When you fall too far into the numbers you actually lose focus on what's important. Instead, pick a single number that matters above all others. Maybe you'll pick the wrong one, but at least you're making a decision, which is better than dying from indecision (*http://www.instigatorblog.com/indecision-kills-startups/2009/12/16/*).

The *One Metric That Matters* is both a concept and a tool for building an experimentation-first startup, focusing on measurable goals, improving clarity, and using analytics in the most effective way possible to achieve startup success.

4

The Lean Stack MVP—A Different Approach

Ash Maurya (http://www.ashmaurya.com/)

In a previous post (*http://www.ashmaurya.com/2012/06/the-lean-stack/*), I outlined the thought process behind the Lean Stack and provided a 3,000-foot overview of the toolset. A number of you inquired if the new tools would be integrated into LeanCanvas.com (*http://www.leancanvas.com/*). The answer is yes, eventually.

My earlier iterations (Lean Canvas layers (*http://www.ashmaurya.com/2012/06/the-lean-stack/*) and the feature Kanban board (*http://www.ashmaurya.com/2011/07/how-we-build-features/*)) were all done in software. On the surface, a web app seemed to be the best choice because we already had a large pool of users, and software should be fast and easy to change, right? Not quite. Looking back at those experiments, they took too long, cost too much, and created lots of needless waste—not counting hours dealing with UX issues, browser issues, and other defects.

Note

You can almost always find unconventional ways to accelerate learning and reduce waste that don't involve building the final solution you had in mind.

The very first Lean Canvas minimum viable product (MVP) was a blog post. The canvas was then refined over numerous workshops (through slides and paper exercises) before it was turned into software. While I considered applying the same approach here, running experiments is a more advanced and later-stage step that didn't naturally fit into my one-day workshops.

So I invented a new learning product—the Running Lean Bootcamp (*http://www.spark59.com/bootcamps/running-lean*). The idea behind the bootcamp was to go beyond the book (*http://runninglean.co/*) and one-day workshops, which typically are characterized by high activation but low follow-through retention. In other words, people leave the workshop very excited but fail to put these principles into practice because real behavior change is hard.

The bootcamp aims to tackle this problem by getting people to run lean on their products for the period of the bootcamp—with accountability and personalized coaching built into the program. We get to share (and experiment with) our latest practices, and the teams get to move their businesses forward—making it a win-win for both of us. The flow described below was refined through working with ~20 startup teams from the last bootcamp.

This time around I also decided to experiment with a physical MVP (using posters). This went against my grain because I am more of an abstract thinker. Even when I studied electrical engineering back in college, I was always the first one out of the simulation lab, but the last one out of the hardware lab. Despite my initial skepticism, using a physical MVP here was one of the best decisions we made.

Within a couple days, we had the posters designed, printed, and hung on a wall. Here's a picture of what early versions looked like:

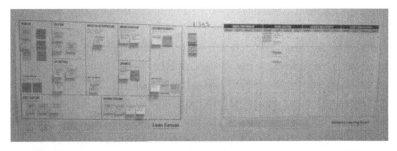

You'll notice there is no "Strategy and Risks" board in the top picture. That's because there wasn't one when we started. That board was the missing glue that was discovered accidentally as I was working with one of the startups. The second picture has a hand-drawn version of that board, which was eventually turned into a poster a few days later and rolled out to all the teams.

With software, we'd have had to go back and code for a few more weeks to get this working. In the physical world, the surrounding wall and post-its provided us with a blank canvas that could be repurposed for anything we wanted. This is just one example of the many liberties the physical boards afforded us throughout the process. Who says you can't iterate quickly with a physical prototype?

Let's walk through the actual flow next.

The Lean Stack Flow

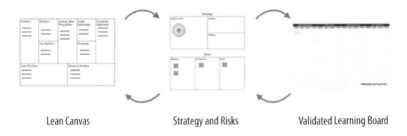

Lean Canvas   Strategy and Risks   Validated Learning Board

THE VISION—LEAN CANVAS

The first step of the process is still capturing the essence of your vision as a single-page business model diagram using Lean Canvas.

Lean Canvas

I have already written a lot about Lean Canvas (*http://www.runni ngleanhq.com/*), which I won't repeat here again. But I will share a common pitfall I've seen one too many teams fall into—the *analysis paralysis trap*.

Note

The goal of a Lean Startup is to inform our riskiest business model assumptions through empirical testing with customers—not rhetorical reasoning on a whiteboard.

Yes, over time your canvas should be correctly segmented, focused, and concise —and would probably even benefit from deep exploratory exercises like persona and customer flow creation. But achieving these goals on the first canvas is *premature optimization.*

Instead, initially focus your efforts on quickly moving through the Lean Stack layers and use the built-in feedback loop to prioritize the areas that need further development. For example, the most rewarding time for a deep dive into personas might be when you get to the build stage of your first experiment—which will probably be a problem interview.

THE STRATEGY—STRATEGY AND RISKS BOARD

With your vision documented, you then move on to the Strategy and Risks board. The goal here is to formulate an appropriate plan of attack—*one that prioritizes learning about what's riskiest above everything else.*

Lean Canvas   Strategy and Risks

Risk prioritization in a startup can be non-obvious. The best starting point is identifying gaps in your thinking and talking through them with formal and/or informal advisors.

Another great tool is studying preexisting analogs and antilogs. This is a conceptual framework introduced by Randy Komisar and John Mullins in their book, *Getting to Plan B (http://www.amazon.com/Getting-Plan-Breaking-Through-Business/dp/1422126692).*

> Note
>
> Analogs and antilogs essentially let you stand on the shoulders of others before you and see further by way of their lessons learned.

After studying a few analogs, some patterns might begin to emerge that help in formulating your implementation plan. For example, after 37signals's success with Basecamp (*http://basecamp.com/*), a number of companies applied their "build an audience through a blog, then follow with a web app" approach. Some succeeded, others didn't.

Note

While a strategy pattern cannot guarantee success, it can jump-start your journey.

THE PRODUCT—VALIDATED LEARNING BOARD

With your strategy and risks documented, you are now ready to move on to experiments.

| Lean Canvas | Strategy and Risks | Validated Learning Board |

Not surprisingly, the workings of this board raised the most questions. I'll just jump to the questions.

Question: How does one create a card for a product prior to conducting problem and solution interviews?

The product card is just a placeholder for the idea you plan to implement. All you need is a label to identify the idea or concept (which you can change later). It doesn't presuppose a solution definition or commitment to build it. The only time one could potentially struggle to find a suitable name is if one were randomly fishing for ideas to go implement. But even there, one could call this product "Random idea fishing expedition."

In practice though, by the time you get to this stage you've already got a pretty decent inkling of the problem, customer, and even possible solution. Instead of describing how to name your product, I should be expending more words trying to talk you out of prematurely naming your product—i.e., not spending precious cycles running domain name searches and designing logos for your "product."

Question: What is a minimum viable feature (MVF)? What is the relation to MVP? How does one know which one to use?

The product card is intended to capture "a unit of product" that is delivered to customers. The first "unit of product" you release to customers is your minimum viable product (MVP).

In my last post ("The Lean Stack—Part 1" (*http://www.ashmaurya.com/2012/06/the-lean-stack/*)), I was assuming a continuous deployment process like the one we use, where after the MVP we would deliver subsequent "units of product" as individual feature pushes. Given that not everyone deploys in that fashion, a more general label might have been to call it a *minimum viable release* (MVR), where the MVP is release 1.0 and a release can in turn be a single feature (MVP) or a collection of features.

In addition to the MVP and its follow-on MVRs, the product card can also be used to represent multiple related products on the same board. At Spark59 (*http:// spark59.com/*), we use a single Lean Stack to capture the many "tools, content, coaching" products we build.

Question: Can you explain the lifecycle of a product through the four stages on the board?

What I found after building a few products the lean way was that the process for going from idea to MVP is/should be the same as going from MVP to release 2.0, 3.0, etc. Otherwise, it's very easy to stop listening to customers and be led astray. That process is what I codified into the iteration meta-pattern shown on the board.

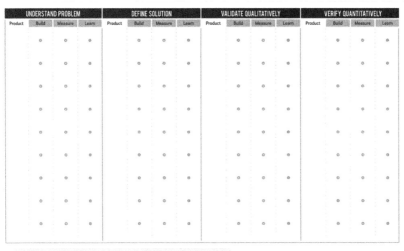

Validated Learning Board

At ideation, that process would involve:

1. Finding a problem worth solving by understanding the problem (and customers)

2. Defining a possible solution or MVP

3. Testing that MVP at small scale
4. Then scaling out

Subsequent releases follow similar stages:

1. Finding follow-on problems worth solving that justify the release
2. Defining possible solutions or features that make up the release
3. Testing the release at small scale using a partial rollout
4. Then verifying value through a full rollout of release

Question: Where do you capture product and experiment details?

The Kanban card is intended to visualize and communicate the flow of work. The face of the card is too small to hold all the details that go along with a product or experiment, so we only place the most critical pieces of information on each card:

- For a product, that would be an identifier (name) and exit criteria for the specific stage
- For an experiment, that would be an identifier (usually a short action-based name like "Run problem interviews") and a list of one or more falsifiable hypotheses
- For a risk or issue, that would be an identifier typically posed as a question, such as "Can we charge $100/mo for this product?"

If this were an online tool, opening a card would reveal more details. We implement this today using a separate one-page A3 report. A3 reports (named after the international paper size on which they fit) are extensively used at Toyota for various problem-solving initiatives that parallel a lot of similar challenges in a start-up. In my attempts to grok A3 reports, I uncovered another parallel between the four stages of the iteration meta-pattern above and the four stages of the Deming cycle (*http://en.wikipedia.org/wiki/PDCA*): Plan, Do, Check, Act (PDCA). But that's a whole other can of worms best left for a future post.

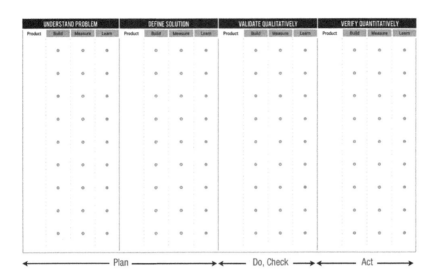

UNDERSTAND PROBLEM				DEFINE SOLUTION				VALIDATE QUALITATIVELY				VERIFY QUANTITATIVELY			
Product	Build	Measure	Learn	Product	Build	Measure	Learn	Product	Build	Measure	Learn	Product	Build	Measure	Learn
	○	○	○		○	○	○		○	○	○		○	○	○
	○	○	○		○	○	○		○	○	○		○	○	○
	○	○	○		○	○	○		○	○	○		○	○	○
	○	○	○		○	○	○		○	○	○		○	○	○
	○	○	○		○	○	○		○	○	○		○	○	○
	○	○	○		○	○	○		○	○	○		○	○	○
	○	○	○		○	○	○		○	○	○		○	○	○
	○	○	○		○	○	○		○	○	○		○	○	○
	○	○	○		○	○	○		○	○	○		○	○	○

←———————— Plan ————————→ ←——— Do, Check ———→ ←——— Act ———→

THE LEAN STACK IN ACTION

If you'd like to see a concrete case study, check out the video on my blog (*http://www.ashmaurya.com/2012/06/the-lean-stack-part-2/*).

NOW IT'S YOUR TURN

> *In lean thinking, a process is not something passed down [...] and set in stone, but rather a living product that is owned by the people doing the work.*

Where it goes from here is up to you!

5

Software Inventory

Joel Spolsky (http://www.joelonsoftware.com/)

Imagine, for a moment, that you've just come upon a bread factory for the first time. At first it just looks like a jumble of incomprehensible machinery with a few people buzzing around. As your eyes adjust, you start to see little piles of things that you *do* understand. Buckets of sesame seeds. Big vats of dough. Little balls of dough. Baked loaves of bread.

Those things are inventory. Inventory tends to pile up between machines. Next to the machine where sesame seeds are applied to hamburger buns, there's a big vat of... sesame seeds. At the very end of the assembly line, there are boxes and boxes of bread, waiting for trucks to drive them off to customers.

Keeping inventory costs money. Suppose your bakery has six 50-ton silos to store flour. Whenever they empty out, you fill them up. That means on the average day you have 150 metric tons of wheat flour in stock. At today's prices, you've tied up $73,000. Forever.

Inventory may have other costs too, like spoilage. Flour lasts for months, but the minute bread comes out of the oven it starts dropping in value; after 24 hours it's nearly worthless.

Why keep inventory at all? Because there are costs associated with running out of things, too. If sesame seeds take two days to order, and you run out of sesame seeds, you are out of the hamburger bun business for two days. Inventory provides a buffer that prevents any part of the process from stalling. There are modern algorithms to optimize how much buffer you need at every point (read up on Toyota's lean production system and the Theory of Constraints to get started).

Why should we care about any of this? The software production process has several major "inventory" accumulation points, itself. Stuff accumulates at those points and ends up wasting a lot of time and money.

"What? How is software like a factory?" you ask.

Think of product ideas as the raw material. Depending on your process, product ideas may go through several assembly line points before they are delivered as finished features to the customer:

1. A decision-making process (should we implement this feature?)

2. A design process (specs, whiteboards, mockups, etc.)

3. An implementation process (writing code)

4. A testing process (finding bugs)

5. A debugging process (fixing bugs)

6. A deployment process (sending code to customers, putting it on a web server, etc.)

(No, this is not "waterfall." No, it isn't. Is *not*. Shut up!)

In between each of these stages, inventory can pile up. For example, when programmers finish implementing their code (stage 3), they give it to a tester to check (stage 4). At any given time, there is a certain amount of code waiting to be tested. That code is inventory.

The "cost" of code inventory is huge. It might add up to 6 or 12 months of work that is stuck in the assembly line and not yet in customers' hands. This could be the difference between having a cutting-edge product (iPhone) or constantly playing catch-up (Windows Phone). It's nearly impossible to get people to buy Windows Phones, even if the iPhone is only six months better. A lot of markets have network effects, and being first has winner-take-all implications. So, getting rid of inventory in the development process can make or break a product.

Let's go over the three places most inventory accumulates:

Feature backlogs

Every product attracts new feature ideas, and you can't implement ideas as fast as you can think them up, so you write them down, and this list is called the feature backlog. A lot of the ideas in the backlog are bad ideas, and you may have only written them down to avoid hurting the feelings of the people who thought them up. Backlogs make everyone feel good.

The trouble is that 90% of the things in the feature backlog will never get implemented—ever. And every minute you spent writing down, designing, thinking about, or discussing features that are never going to get implemented is just time wasted. When I hear about product teams that regularly have "backlog grooming" sessions, in which they carefully waste a tiny amount of time and mental energy every day or every week thinking about every single feature that will never be implemented, I want to poke my eyes out.

Note

Suggestion: Do not allow more than a month or two of work to get into the feature backlog list. Once the backlog is full, do not allow new items to be added unless you remove existing items. Do not spend any time speccing, designing, or talking about backlog items: the backlog, in fact, should be seen as a list of things you are not allowed to talk about or work on.

The bug database

The bug database is obviously a great thing to have. Bug reports should be complete, accurate, and actionable. But I have noticed that in many real-world companies, the desire never to miss any bug report leads to bug bankruptcy, where you wake up one day and discover that there are 3,000 open bugs in the database, some of which are so old they may not apply any more, some of which can never be reproduced, and most of which are not even worth fixing because they're so tiny. When you look closely you realize that months or years of work has gone into preparing those bug reports, and you ask yourself, how could we have 3,000 bugs in the database while our product is delightful and customers love it and use it every day? At some point you realize that you've put too much work into the bug database and not quite enough work into the product.

Note

Suggestion: Use a triage system to decide if a bug is even worth recording. Do not allow more than two weeks' worth (in fix time) of bugs to get into the bug database. If you have more than that, stop and fix bugs until you feel like you're fixing stupid bugs. Then close as "won't fix" everything left in the bug database. Don't worry, the severe bugs will come back.

Undeployed features

There are still a lot of teams doing quarterly or annual releases, usually because their deployment process is expensive. Operating systems, or anything where software has to be installed by every user, is usually batched up.

This is one of the most expensive forms of inventory: unshipped feature inventory. It could be earning you money, but it's sitting on the shipping dock of your factory, while the guy down the street already has a product that does that exact same thing.

Sometimes, perniciously, you don't even feel the pain, because everyone on your team has been dogfooding the new version for months. I'm sure everyone at Microsoft has been happily using Windows 8 for a year now, so they don't really feel, on a day-to-day basis, the pain of OEMs trying to sell Windows 7 in a Mac OS X Lion world.

Note

Suggestion: Don't let completed features pile up in ways that don't make you money. Work on your deployment process so that you can get customers features in months rather than years. If you're already shipping monthly, figure out how to ship weekly. Keep pushing the bar on more and more frequent deployment of smaller and smaller changes.

So, where am I going with this? We've had all three kinds of inventory at Fog Creek: crazy long backlogs, overambitious bug databases, and features that got stuck for a year waiting for the next release to go out. All of these snuck up on us. I realized that we needed a system to constrain inventory so it doesn't build up.

My original idea was to make a product called *Five Things*. It was going to be a project manager where everybody was allowed to have five things assigned to them: two things they were actively doing, one thing that was "up next," and a couple more that they were planning. That exact design idea didn't go anywhere (but if you want to build it, go for it), but it did evolve into Trello (*https://trello.com/*).

Trello works great for a *reasonable* amount of inventory, but it intentionally starts to get clunky if you have too many cards in one list. And that's exactly the point: it makes inventory *visible* so that you know when it's starting to pile up.

If every day you look at your Trello board and see that there are 17 completed features that are totally ready to ship but that haven't shipped for some reason, you can go find the bottleneck and eliminate it.

And every time somebody suggests a crazy feature idea, you can look at the feature backlog, and if you realize it's just too long, you don't have to waste any time documenting or designing that crazy idea.

And hopefully, you'll spend less effort working on things that will never see the light of day. "Backlog grooming." Sheeeesh.

6

How to Get Out of the Building with the Validation Board

Trevor Owens (http://learni.st/users/trevor.owens)

Thousands of entrepreneurs, tech leads, UX practitioners, and product managers have downloaded the Validation Board (*http://leanstartupmachine.com/validation board/*) since its launch (*http://betabeat.com/2012/10/lean-startup-machine-validatio-board-test-your-startup-idea-eric-ries-trevor-owens/*). While the Validation Board process has been proven time and time again in our workshops (*http://leanstartupma chine.com/*), there's one aspect that might trip up the teams trying it out on their own: how to actually "get out of the building" and *run an experiment* on potential customers.

The first thing you should know is that there are Three Methods of Customer Validation, with increasing costs of execution. None of them involve writing code, which is even more expensive to execute.

We developed these methods at Lean Startup Machine (*http://leanstartupma chine.com/*) by observing techniques from hundreds of startup teams. Here's how to do them so you get real results.

Note

Required reading: "10 Things I've Learned" (*http://www.cindyalvarez.com/roundups/10-things-ive-learned*) by Cindy Alvarez.

1. The Exploration Method

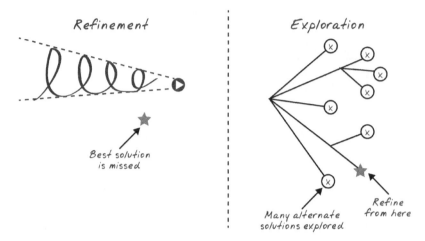

Exploration is based on ethnographic research (*http://en.wikipedia.org/wiki/ Ethnography*) techniques. The goal of exploration is to collect a lot of data on potential problem sets within a given industry or customer type, and to collect detailed stories about customer behavior.

TECHNIQUES (IN DECREASING ORDER OF COST AND QUALITY OF DATA)

- *Observation*: seeing the problem actually happen
- *Re-enactment*: attempting to simulate or re-create the problem
- *Interviews*: listening to the customer tell a story about the problem

Note

Required reading: "12 Tips for Customer Development Interviews" by Giff Constable (*http://giffconstable.com/2010/07/12-tips-for-early-customer-development-interviews/*).

FIVE BONUS TIPS FOR CUSTOMER DEVELOPMENT INTERVIEWS

- Always qualify the person you're talking to and make sure that person fits your customer hypothesis.
- The best question to start with is always, "Tell me the story of the time you did...."
- Never ask a question that starts with the word "would" (e.g., "Would you do X?" or "Would you pay for this?"). These are hypothetical questions that produce inaccurate data.
- Avoid confirmation bias by asking your team, "Could anyone disagree with this question?" The answer must always be yes.
- Avoid observer bias by withholding the facts of what you're testing or building (otherwise customers will reverse-engineer the questions). Even better is if customers don't even know it's an interview.

BAD QUESTIONS

- "Do you like [something everyone likes, e.g., music]?"
- "Do you have a problem with [insert too broad or too obvious problem]?"
- "Do you want more time and money?"
- "Do you wish you could have an [insert something awesome like a Porsche]?"
- Anything that has to do with your solution.

GOOD QUESTIONS

- "Tell me about the last time you...."
- "How are you currently solving [insert problem]?"
- "How/where did you search for a solution?"
- "If you could wave a magic wand and have anything you wanted, what would it look like?"

RECORDING DATA AND SCORING

Warning: If you don't record and score your data, it is as good as useless. You need to have a record for your team to access at any time when making a critical pivot. I recommend using Google Docs and sharing with everyone on the team. Unstructured data (notes) should be converted to a spreadsheet with structured data. My method is to list the different problem areas and rate the intensity of the problem from each customer's story from 0–3 stars. I also like Ben Yoskovitz's method for scoring problem interviews (*http://leananalyticsbook.com/scoring-problem-interviews/*).

AVOID A FALSE NEGATIVE/POSITIVE

Build rapport with your customers and dig deep into their stories and emotions. Keep asking why. Look for inconsistencies in case you're not being told the truth. Exclude any bad data from your sample.

2. The Pitch Method

The pitch method is about getting customers to give you a form of *currency*. This involves "pitching" them a specific solution (idea or low-fidelity mock-up) or benefit (the what without the how) before the product has been built. This is also known as *smoke testing*, a practice that has been used in retail and direct marketing for years.

FORMS OF PITCH

- Landing page
- Cold email
- Cold call
- Gimmick sign
- Fake ad
- Walking into a store and pitching the owner
- Kickstarter

FORMS OF CURRENCY

- Cash $$$
- Letter of intent
- Email addresses
- Paying with a tweet
- Taking a meeting
- Time
- Building something on your API

What people say and what they do are usually different, so collecting currency actually *proves intent*. Separating customers from their wallets lets you know that they are willing to change their behavior and/or pay for a solution.

3. The Concierge Method

The concierge method involves delivering your product through a physical service, handholding the customer. This method has also been referred to as "Wizard of Oz (*http://www.youtube.com/watch?v=NZR64EF3OpA*)"; i.e., faking the product with as little technology as possible. (In the movie the real Wizard is just a guy behind a curtain, pressing a button to turn on the flames.)

CONCIERGE TOOLS

- Email
- Physical labor
- Spreadsheets
- Open source software
- Cell phones

The goal of concierge is to make a small set of customers ecstatic with the proposed product before building it and marketing it to others. Food on the Table (*http://www.foodonthetable.com/*) scaled from 1 to 200,000 users this way. The first

20 customers they added one at a time, using email and a clipboard to deliver the value prop of the product.

We've seen teams validate in the pitch stage who *skip concierge* and end up *building the wrong thing*. This is because doing concierge is a critical step in understanding the "how" of a customer's problem.

PART II
Business Models

7

MBA Mondays: Revenue Models—Commerce

Fred Wilson (http://www.avc.com/)

Commerce has to be the oldest business model. Sell something to someone. Or maybe it was barter back then. In any case, ecommerce revenues topped $200b in the US in 2011 and are growing at close to 10% annually. Global ecommerce revenues are at least double that—maybe as much as $500b, depending on who you ask. So selling something to someone online is a big business and getting bigger.

Retailing is by far the largest component of the online commerce market. *Retailing* is buying a product at wholesale and selling it to the customer at a markup. Retailing involves inventory. You stock up on inventory so you can provide the goods quickly to the customer.

Amazon is the world's largest online retailer. Amazon's revenues in the past four quarters were approximately $55b. Clearly some of that revenue is non-retailing, but let's assume their retailing revenues are about $50b annually. They are roughly 10% of the global ecommerce market.

Retailing is a tough business. The difference between what you buy the product for at wholesale and sell it for at retail is called your *gross margin*. Amazon's gross margin ranges between 20% and 25%, depending on what time of year it is. The holiday quarter brings the lowest gross margins because retail makes up a larger percent of revenues. At Amazon's size, a 25% gross margin turns into a lot of money. But a smaller online retailer can really struggle at these margins. Let's imagine a retailer of bicycles on the Internet does $50m in revenues. That sounds great. But that means that only $10m to $12m a year actually stays in the business. The rest goes out to the bicycle manufacturers. And then the retailer has to pay for the website, the traffic acquisition, the staff to operate the business, and a lot more. Pre-tax margins for online retailers will typically be in the sub-10% range, often less than 5%. To put that in context, the bicycle online retailer that generates $50m in sales will keep a couple of million pre-tax at the end of the year. It's a business for sure, but not an easy one.

The reason that online retailing is so tough is that it is hard to differentiate one retailer from another. You want a new mountain bike? Go to Google and see what's out there.

Retailing has always relied on location to provide some margin protection. There is no "location" on the Internet other than search engine optimization. So gross margins online are going to be lower than they are in the real world. And on top of that, you have the capital outlays required to stock up on inventory and the markdown costs associated with getting rid of unsold inventory. And then there are the shipping costs, which increase the price to the customer unless you are willing to eat them.

I have never invested in online retailing. I don't like the economics of this business, even though it is a huge market.

Beyond retailing, there are a number of other ways to do commerce on the Internet. The next is *marketplaces*. Marketplaces are places where buyers and sellers come together to transact. Marketplaces have always existed in the offline world (*http://www.avc.com/a_vc/2009/12/thinking-about-etsy-in-the-san-telmo-markets.html*). It turns out that the Internet is a terrific place to create marketplaces. And they have much better economics. There is no gross margin for the marketplace operator, just a transaction fee. There is no inventory. There are no shipping costs. All of those costs are born by the seller. I have invested in quite a few online marketplaces. I love the economics of these businesses. I plan to write an entire post in this series on peer-to-peer business models and marketplaces will be a large component of that post, so I will move on.

One way to get past the gross margin and differentiation problem on the Internet is to make all the goods you sell yourself. This is called "vertically integrated retailing" and it is a growing trend in online commerce. A great example of this model is Warby Parker (*http://www.warbyparker.com/*), which makes and sells a line of fashion eyeglasses. Warby Parker has no stores (at least, it didn't when it started out). The Internet is its store. Vertically integrated retailing has better economics because your products aren't commoditized by Google and the other search engines. Customers seeking your products must come to your website to purchase them. But these businesses have other issues. Building a brand is tough, particularly from a standing start. Manufacturing, most likely overseas, can be a challenge. The capital costs remain high because you still need to stock up on inventory. And you can face markdowns if your stock-keeping units go out of style. Although I like this model much better than straight-up retailing, I have never invested in this model either. The Gotham Gal (*http://www.gothamgal.com/*) has made a few investments in this sector, though.

Another flavor of retailing is flash sales and daily deals. This is not a new concept on the Internet. There have always been clearance sales in the retailing world. But the Internet brings new tools to drive immediacy and rapid transactions. A French startup called Vente-Privee (*http://fr.vente-privee.com/vp4/Login/Portal.ashx*) brought the concept of the flash sale to the Internet over 10 years ago and it has been adopted widely across the globe, particularly in the past 5 years. Flash sales have better economics than traditional retailing. They are often acquiring the product at discounted prices. The inventory costs are lower because they blow out of the product quickly. And there is no competing for the buyer's loyalty on Google every day. Flash sales sites leverage mailing lists to bring their customers back again and again. The issue with flash sales is customer burnout. It is difficult to maintain a vibrant flash sale business over many years.

Auctions are another way to drive commerce online. eBay is the canonical company in this category. The nice thing about auctions is they leverage a set time frame to drive toward a clearing price. It is game of sorts and can be quite addicting and engaging. Auctions work particularly well in marketplaces where there are unique items to be bought and sold. eBay's gradual adoption of the "buy it now" model suggests that there are limits to the auction model at scale and that consumers prefer a straight-up retail model because of its simplicity. I suspect that auctions make up a substantially smaller percentage of online commerce revenues than they did 10 years ago.

The revenue model hackpad (*https://hackpad.com/EgXuEtSibE7#Web-And-Mobile-Revenue-Models-(final)*) includes a number of other forms of online commerce that I am not going to dive into in this post.

In summary, commerce represents the largest and most common online revenue model. But it is not an easy one to execute profitably. It lends itself to commoditization and margin compression in most cases, and the economies go to scale players like Amazon, eBay, and Walmart. While there has been substantial venture capital investment in this sector, particularly in recent years, it is not a sector that I like very much—other than marketplaces, which to me are really peer-to-peer businesses.

8

Freemium Pricing for SaaS: Optimizing Paid Conversion Upgrades

Rishi Shah (http://www.gettingmoreawesome.com/)

I've been building a new product and I'm almost ready to launch it. However, I'm having a really hard time figuring out the right pricing structure, so I'm going to analyze my favorite freemium Software-as-a-Service (SaaS) businesses.

Here is what I know I want:

1. A free plan. Since we are just starting out, I really want people to use the product for free (no credit card required). I'm okay with killing off the free plan later if it isn't working economically (existing free users would be grandfathered in).

2. It is a hosted product, so it will be recurring revenue. There will be a monthly fee for the paid packages (with an option to pay yearly up front for a discount).

3. Based on many, many studies, the paid package prices should end with a "9". So, the packages will be priced with that in mind (i.e., $11.99, $24.99, etc.)

4. I want to leverage our free plan to get more referrals. For example, the free members can earn more features or storage by referring a friend or posting a status update with our link in it—pretty much exactly what Dropbox (*https://www.dropbox.com/*) and AppSumo (*http://www.appsumo.com/interrupt/*) do.

Questions:

1. How generous should our free plan be?
2. What limits should we place on it?

3. We need our free plan to be something amazing so people will sign up. However, we don't want it to be so amazing that they don't ever need to upgrade.

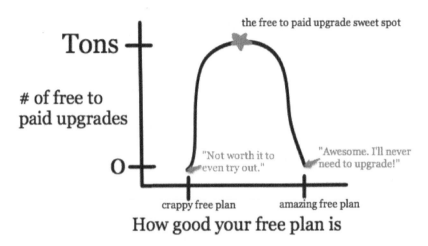

I decided to take a look at some freemium SaaS companies that I know of and analyze what I think they did well at.

I'm going to start with 37signals (*http://37signals.com/*) (the godfather of small-business SaaS). This was their pricing page before their relaunch:

I like how they have the free plan but don't promote it at all. They don't mention it on their home page and it is hidden at the bottom of their pricing page. A few years back they heavily promoted their free plan and said that 98% of all accounts were on the free plan. Check out their call to action on their home page now—they don't even mention the free plan. They do mention a 30-day free trial, though:

Some insights (and assumptions) from 37signals's pricing strategy:

- They really focus on getting paid customers.
- The number of free-to-paid upgrades is probably really low. They probably get most of their paying customers right at signup, which is why they have a 30-day free trial on paid packages and have their call-to action toward paid signup (not the free plan).
- I think a great way to launch is to have an amazing free plan and then, once you start getting bigger, focus your home page on the paid signups.

Wufoo (*http://www.wufoo.com/*) is probably my favorite SaaS business. In a presentation about SaaS they say: "Always, always display your highest-priced package to the left and your cheapest package to the right." I made this switch for Flying Cart (*http://flyingcart.com/*), and he was right about it. The Wufoo Signup & Pricing page looks like this:

Here is what I like:

- The highest-priced package is on the left—the reasoning is that customers read from left to right. The $14.95 price tag doesn't seem so bad when you've just read the $199.95 price tag.

- The free plan is perfect. Just enough to start (not super limited), but I am happy to pay once I've had a little bit of success. This is what I call investing in your customers.

- I also like how they have multiple thresholds from the free to the paid plan. Notice how the "Bona Fide" $29.95/mo plan supports five users and the free plan only allows one user. If you have five users you must be a bigger company and can afford the cost. This also gives Wufoo a chance to get paid customers right from day #1.

- I really like how they don't offer a 30-day free trial. They have a free plan so there is no need to have a free trial as well, allowing them to pull in cash as soon as possible.

Next, here is a screenshot of the Dropbox (*https://www.dropbox.com/*) pricing page at the time of this writing. They don't promote the pricing page on the home page at all.

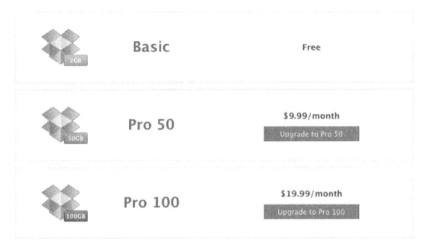

Here is what I like:

- They heavily promote their very generous free plan on their home page—they don't show any prices, just a video and a download button

- They leverage their free users to get more customers—an amazing referral program. You can earn more space by referring people.

- They up-sell customers after many months of usage and dependence on their product. I bet they have really good lifetime value on their paid customers.

- My assumption is that Dropbox has an amazing free-to-paid account upgrade ratio, which is why they focus on getting you to use the product as soon as possible.

I'm including Intuit (*http://www.intuit.com/*) here too, but I really don't like it at all:

This is exactly what I don't want:

- It's very confusing. Each pricing tier looks like it could be a different product.

- An Asterisk next to their prices? Are you kidding me? Whenever I see an asterisk I get really scared that the price is going to jump after the first month.

- The "Try It Free" is an okay call to action, but the word "Try" makes me think I'm getting roped into something.

The reason I think this works is because they have a really strong brand value. People trust Intuit and they have a solid product for business accounting.

Next up is MailChimp (*http://mailchimp.com/*):

The Forever Free Plan	Store up to 2,000 subscribers. Send up to 12,000 emails per month. No expiring trials. No contracts. No credit card required.						Sign Up Free	
Monthly Plans for frequent senders	If you send at least once a month, a monthly subscription is your best option. We'll bill your credit card every month based on the total number of subscribers managed in your account. Your monthly fee will be automatically adjusted as your list grows or shrinks. View International pricing							
Subscribers	0 - 2,000	0 - 500	501 - 1,000	1,001 - 2,500	2,501 - 5,000	5,001 - 10,000	10,001 - 25,000	25,001 - 50,000
Price	Free	$10	$15	$30	$50	$75	$150	$240
Send Limit	12,000/month	Unlimited	Unlimited	Unlimited	Unlimited	Unlimited	Unlimited	Unlimited

MailChimp is similar to Dropbox. They have an amazing free plan. One thing I like is that they put a "MailChimp" ad in the footer of the newsletter, promoting their services and allowing the end user to earn more credits with them.

Carbonmade (*http://carbonmade.com/*) has one of the most fun pricing pages:

Here is what I like:

- The top package is super cheap. $12/mo—wow. That's it, and I get it all.
- How they display free vs. paid. The paid package seems so much more fun and cool. I feel like a total loser clicking on the "Meh" package. I would rather just pay the $12 and feel better about myself. Other companies do this by highlighting their middle package with a "Best Option" headline.

Experts Exchange (*http://www.experts-exchange.com/*) is a developer-focused question-and-answer service. If you need a coding question answered, you can sign up and a real live person will email you right back. This is sometimes better than Stack Overflow or Quora, where at times no one answers your questions. Experts Exchange isn't your traditional freemium business. When you sign up, you are signing up to a paid plan (with a 30-day free trial):

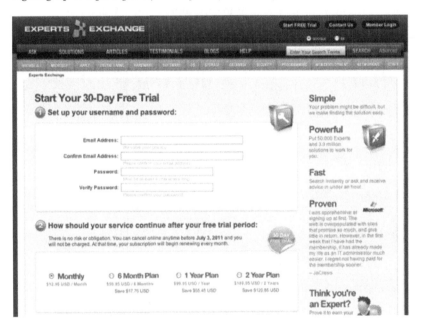

However, when you become a customer you are given the opportunity to answer questions, and the more questions you answer, the cheaper your membership becomes. This is a really interesting freemium approach. Their "Free" customers are helping Experts Exchange get paid customers.

What I like:

- The plans get cheaper if you pay for multiple months.
- They allow you to earn Free membership. It isn't given.

So what am I going to do? I'm going to take the best from each one:

1. Launch a free plan that is amazing. We aren't the first service that will be doing what we do, so we need to go the MailChimp route.

2. Allow people to earn more features and storage if they share our service (similar to Dropbox).

3. Make our paid plans feel amazing by adding a fun icon next to them (similar to Carbonmade, but it won't be as awesome).

4. Display our highest-priced paid package on the left and offer multiple barriers so we can take payment on day one for bigger companies (similar to Wufoo).

5. Learn from our data after seven months and either de-emphasize our free plan (like 37signals) or overemphasize it (like Dropbox).

Here is what my current pricing page looks like:

	Lite	Pro	Pro Plus
	Free	$9.99/month	$14.99/month
	Sign Up	FREE TRIAL	FREE TRIAL
Number of Transactions	10	Unlimited	Unlimited
Files	1	10	Unlimited
Data Transfer	250 MB	1 GB	10 GB
Maximum File Size	50 MB	500 MB	2 GB
Real Time Analytics		✓	✓
Custom Order Pages		✓	✓
Phone Support			✓
	Sign Up	FREE TRIAL	FREE TRIAL
		Buy Now	Buy Now

29

Why Churn Is So Critical to Success in SaaS

David Skok (http://www.forentrepreneurs.com/)

As a SaaS company becomes larger, the size of the subscription base becomes large enough that any kind of churn against that base becomes a large number. That loss of revenue requires more and more bookings coming from new customers just to replace the churn. As a result, growth slows substantially.

To illustrate this point, I built a very simple model and graphed the output. The model starts with MRR (monthly recurring revenue) at zero and bookings from new customers at $10k in the first month, increasing by $2k every month after that (represented by the dotted blue line in the graph).

The red and yellow lines show the lost revenue due to customers cancelling their subscriptions (churn). These show the impact of churn at a 2.5% and 5% monthly level.

Looking at this graph, we can see that churn is really not that big of a number in the early startup months. But as the company gets toward the end of its fifth year, even at a relatively low churn rate of 2.5%, you are losing $64k a month—which is extremely hard to replace with new customer bookings. And with a churn rate of 5%, that number is even worse, at $90k.

53

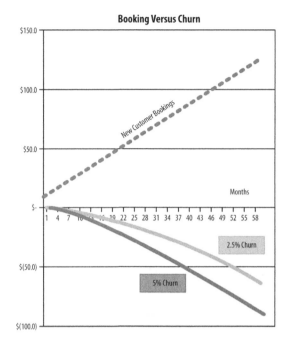

The next graph shows the impact on total MRR of each scenario, which is fairly substantial.

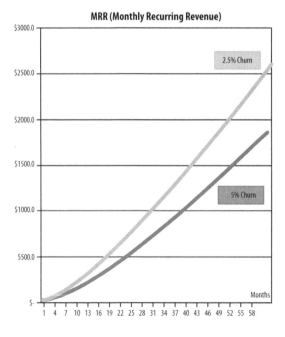

The Impact of Negative Churn

It is possible to run a SaaS (or any other kind of recurring revenue) business in such a way as to get what I call *negative churn*. This happens when the expansions/up-sells/cross-sells to your current customer base exceed the revenue that you are losing because of churn. The next graph shows what happens to your bookings if, in addition to your sales to new customers, you are seeing an expansion revenue from your current customer base of 2.5% every month (the topmost solid line).

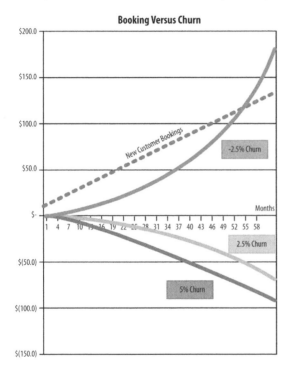

The result is quite shocking. The expansion revenue from the existing customers starts to become a huge number, and by the end of year five it is contributing close to $180k every month. Let's take a look at total MRR to see what effect this has (see the green line in the following graph).

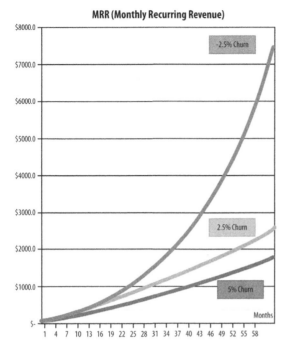

It's an amazing result. The business is nearly three times bigger than one with 2.5% churn. Clearly, getting to negative churn is one of the most powerful accelerators for growth. Since this can be hard to achieve, this does beg the question of what happens if you can't get to negative churn, but are able to get to 0% churn. See the dotted line in the next graph.

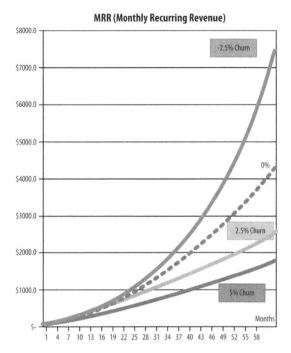

MRR (Monthly Recurring Revenue)

The 0% churn line is still achieving an MRR nearly 60% higher than the one shown in the yellow line (2.5% churn).

How Do You Achieve Negative Churn?

Getting to negative churn requires doing one or more of the following three things:

- *Expand revenue* from your current product. This is best done by having a pricing model that increases the pricing according to some usage metric that will grow over time. As an example, Dropbox charges you more as you use more storage. Email marketing companies charge you more as your email list grows, etc. For more on thinking through how to get your pricing axes designed right, you may want to read this blog post: "Multi-axis Pricing: a key tool for increasing SaaS revenue" (*http://www.forentrepreneurs.com/multi-axis-pricing-a-key-tool-for-increasing-saas-revenue/*).

- *Up-sell* customers to a more highly featured version of your product.

- *Cross-sell* customers to purchase additional products or services.

Same Sales Force for Expansion/Up-sell/Cross-sell?

While not a hard-and-fast rule, my usual recommendation is to split the sales organization into hunters that chase deals with new customers, and farmers that work on expanding the revenue from existing customers. There are two reasons for this:

- *Focus*: If I am a rep that has a choice between phoning an existing customer to increase revenue or calling a new customer, I will usually pick the existing customer, as that is easiest. That means there's a lack of focus on new customers.
- *Different skill sets*: The skill set required for expansion sales is often more about how to make the customer extremely successful with the product. This is more of a *consulting, customer service, product expert* skill set than a *sales* skill set.

How to Track the Different Factors That Make Up Bookings

Assuming that your SaaS company has a way to get expansion sales, your net bookings number will be made up of three components:

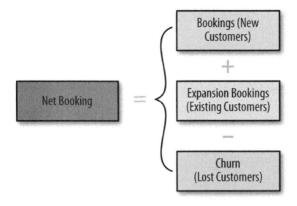

It makes sense to track each of these separately, in a graph that looks like the following:

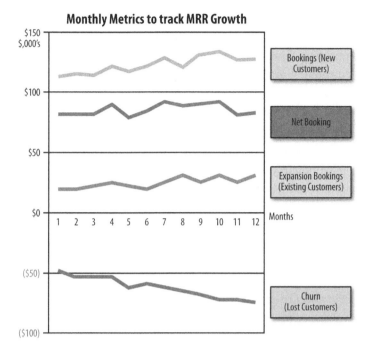

When to Focus on Negative Churn?

A lot of this blog's readers are from very early stage startups, and I don't want to give them the sense that they immediately need to focus on creating complex pricing schemes and product variations for up-sell or cross-sell. The first 12–24 months of your business's life is frequently too early to figure this out. At this stage it is more important to get broad customer adoption, and that often means simple pricing that leaves something on the table for your customers.

However, even for early-stage startups, I do recommend focusing hard on reducing churn. High churn is usually a clear indication that your product is not meeting customers' needs or expectations. And that is not a formula for long-term success.

Tactics to Help Reduce Churn

How can you reduce churn? Here are a few suggestions:

- **Call your customers**. If you are an early-stage startup with significant churn, the first place to start is to call the customers that are cancelling to find out why. I recommend that the entrepreneurs (or CEOs) themselves make these phone calls, as only they will have the ability to change the product vision or other service attributes based on the feedback. This function is far too important to delegate. Frequently what these calls will tell you is either that your product is not solving the customers' problems, or that they are having trouble implementing it. You can often solve these issues by changing the product or the way in which you support the customers during the implementation phase.

- **Measure customer engagement.** This tactic should read "measure customer happiness," but that is hard to do. So instead, I recommend measuring the customers' engagement with your product. You can do this by instrumenting the key features in the product and sending a log entry to a customer engagement database every time your customers use one of those features. By assigning a weighted value to each of these events, you can create a customer engagement score. The score is a great indicator of which customers are getting good use out of the product, and therefore are not likely to churn, and which are at risk. Now you can use your customer support folks to email/call the at-risk customers with help and advice on how to get going using the product. (I have another blog post on this topic—"SaaS CEOs: Measure Customer Engagement —Increase Conversions & Lower Churn (*http://www.forentrepreneurs.com/ customer-engagement/*)."

- **Figure out what features make your product sticky.** In the early days at HubSpot (*http://www.hubspot.com/*), the company suffered from fairly high churn. The reason for this was that a key focus of the initial product was search engine optimization (SEO), and once customers had finished search-optimizing their sites, they didn't see a need to pay for keeping them optimized. HubSpot had to work to identify what features it could add that would be sticky. The belief was that anything that became a core part of the customer's regular workflow was one way to get stickiness, and the other was to become the repository for some critical data. Once you become the system of record for that data, it is much harder to switch to another service. Ask yourself if you know what the key features that make your product sticky are, and then use measurements of customer engagement to see which customers are not using those features. Those are the customers most at risk of churning.

- **Allocate your best reps to the job of saving customers that call to cancel.** It is often possible to save a customer that is about to churn—but it requires your best sales skills to achieve good results.

- **Consider testing a longer-term contract.** The discussion so far has assumed that you have customers on a month-to-month contract. One way to lower churn is to ask customers to sign up for a longer commitment up front (usually 6 or 12 months). This has the effect of lowering churn, as they are more committed to the product, and more will get through the phase of fully implementing the product and seeing benefits. The negative is that it will dampen sales. So, the best way to proceed is to test to find the optimal level. It is also possible to encourage your sales team to sell these longer contracts without forcing them.

- **Look for other factors that correlate with churn.** For example, you might be selling to small and large customers. If so, it's likely that you will find that your smaller customers churn more than your larger customers. This might incline you to focus more of your sales and marketing efforts on your most profitable type of customers (taking both customer acquisition cost and customer lifetime value into account). But you might also find that customers from a particular vertical/lead source/etc. have a tendency to churn more. As you investigate this, you may discover either that these are a poor fit, or that your product needs some modification to better suit their needs.

Managing Churn Is Harder if You Are Selling to Small Businesses

The reason for this is that many small businesses go out of business. They are also quicker to cut costs when things are not going well.

In addition, getting to negative churn with these customers is even harder, as many small businesses have a clear limit to what they can afford to pay for any given service.

How Churn Affects Valuation

If you are presenting your SaaS company to venture capitalists, expect them to pay very close attention to your churn numbers, even if you are early stage. They will be looking at churn as a great indicator of whether or not you have good product/market fit.

Wall Street and public stock buyers have also realized the importance of churn in SaaS companies. There is a great research report out from one of the leading investment banks talking about the factors that drive public company SaaS valuations. While the top factor impacting the multiple on revenue is growth rate, the report clearly shows how both retention and up-sell are strong secondary factors. The analysis shows that an incremental 2% increase in retention leads to a 20% higher multiple, and an incremental 2% increase in up-sell leads to a 28% higher multiple.

Achieving the Network Effect: Solving the Chicken or the Egg

Brian Balfour (http://brianbalfour.com/)

One of the most defensible positions for a startup is if you can achieve the network effect. The network effect is so strong that it has kept large companies in business for a long time, despite bad products and numerous competitors. Craigslist is a perfect example. It is only recently that a new wave of startups like Airbnb, TaskRabbit, and RentJuice have started to chip away at the Craigslist stronghold; it took over 10 years.

The network effect has also defended companies like Facebook from an onslaught of competition. I remember in the early days of Facebook that almost every campus had at least a few local startups that tried to overtake it, but once Facebook established a stronghold in a campus, it was impossible to unseat it. Facebook has also been in the sights of numerous international players, yet the only areas that have seemed to hold ground are Russia and parts of Asia.

Achieving the network effect is no easy feat. It comes with a huge hurdle: the chicken or the egg problem.

Two Versions of the Chicken or the Egg

There are two versions of the chicken or the egg problem that warrant important distinctions, because each has a different solution.

TYPE #1: PLATFORMS/MARKETPLACES

Chicken or egg version #1 is when your product connects two different types of groups. Most people who call themselves platforms or marketplaces fit in this category—think eBay connecting buyers and sellers of goods or Airbnb connecting home/apt owners with vacation renters. My last company, Viximo (*http://www.viximo.com/*), was in this category: we connected social games with social networks.

In this case, the value to each group of users is dependent on the use of the other group. No renters would use Airbnb if no home/apartment owners were listing on the site, just as no home/apartment owners would use the site if no renters were coming to it.

TYPE #2: COMMUNITIES/SOCIAL NETWORKS

The second version of the chicken or the egg problem is when your product connects people of similar types to create broader value. Online communities and social networks such as LinkedIn, Facebook, and Match.com (*http://match.com*) are examples. The value to each individual user grows the more users there are in the overall community.

When a community or social network is in its infancy, there is a huge chicken or egg problem. With a small number of people on the platform, the value to each individual user is small, so how do you get more users to join?

Solving Platform and Marketplace Issues

To solve version #1 of the chicken or the egg problem, create value for one group of users that is not dependent on the other group of users. With Viximo, we internally created and licensed our own apps and games. Having a couple apps/games allowed us to offer value to our first few distribution partners without depending on signing third-party game developers. Once we had the first few distribution partners, we were then able to sign our first third-party game developers. We eventually killed the apps/games we'd built internally once we had the network going, but the point is at the beginning we manually created value for one group of customers.

Another great example is Craiglist. Craig Newmark (founder of Craigslist) curated his own set of events that he thought people would be interested in and emailed them out to friends. Eventually his distribution list grew large enough that others started submitting their own events and items and the network became self-sustaining. Users would likely not have submitted their own items if Craig had not built the initial distribution list by manually submitting items himself.

In other words, you have to be an app before you can be a platform (or marketplace).

Solving Community and Social Network Issues

In communities and social networks, the value to each individual user comes from the density of the network. Would you use Facebook if the majority of your friends weren't on it? Would you use LinkedIn if the majority of the professionals you met weren't using it? Probably not.

So how do you get network density in the earliest stages? Decrease the size of your target audience in order to make it easier to get density. The best example of this is Facebook's launch. Rather than opening to all college students at once, Facebook was restricted to just Harvard's campus. Getting network density among an audience of 6,500 (the Harvard undergrad student population) is exponentially easier than getting network density among an audience of 20 million (the total US college student population). LinkedIn successfully decreased its target audience to get network density by focusing initially on professionals solely in Silicon Valley.

A target audience for a community is most commonly decreased by geography, but there are different ways to slice it. One of my investments, GrabCAD (*http://grabcad.com/*), has focused its audience on a single profession, mechanical engineers. MySpace found its early traction by focusing its target audience on the music industry. The online dating industry has probably sliced it every way you can imagine. One can find dating sites for all different races and religions, "big and beautiful," and even those that enjoy a cougar or sugar daddy every now and then.

Don't Be Afraid of Brute Force

In today's startup environment, where the "product is everything" mantra is pervasive, many entrepreneurs get discouraged when they build it and the users don't flock naturally. Peter Thiel put it best (*http://blakemasters.com/post/22405055017/peter-thiels-cs183-startup-class-9-notes-essay*):

> *[Entrepreneurs] tend to overlook [distribution].... Even if you have an incredibly fantastic product, you still have to get it out to people. The engineering bias blinds people to this simple fact. The conventional thinking is that great products sell themselves; if you have [a] great product, it will inevitably reach consumers. But nothing is further from the truth.*

No matter which chicken or egg problem you are solving for, don't be afraid of brute force. Some companies get adoption naturally, but more often there is someone behind the scenes pulling strings. Yelp paid reviewers in the early days, while MySpace spammed the hell out of an email list from an earlier company. At Viximo we paid out guarantees to our earliest partners.

The point is, solving the chicken or the egg problem is extremely tough. Avoid the common mistakes of user acquisition (*http://brianbalfour.com/post/*

22267034213/5-essential-tips-to-finding-scalable-customer-acquisitio) and have a plan that involves brute force. *If you want to reach the network effect, don't leave it to luck —make it happen yourself.*

Reverse Network Effects: Why Scale May Be the Biggest Threat Facing Today's Social Networks

Sangeet Paul Choudary (http://platformed.info/)

Network effects are the Holy Grail for Internet startups looking for venture-scale returns. On a platform with network effects, the value to a user increases as more users use it. Facebook, Twitter, LinkedIn, YouTube, Skype, and many others benefit from this dynamic.

2012 will go down as the year when a billion people (*http://thenextweb.com/ facebook/2012/10/04/facebook-hits-1-billion-active-users/*) were connected over a single platform for the first time in history. But as online networks grow to a size never seen before, many question their sustainability and believe that they are becoming too large to be useful.

To explore the future of online networks, it's important to note how network effects correlate with value and the factors that make these network effects work in reverse.

Network Effects and Value

There is a strong correlation between scale and value in businesses with network effects. Greater scale leads to greater value for users, which in turn attracts other users and further increases scale. This rich-become-richer dynamic allows networks to scale rapidly once network effects set in.

There are three sources of value created on networks:

Connection

Networks allow users to discover and/or connect with other users. As more users join the network, there is greater value for every individual user. Skype and WhatsApp become more useful as a user's connections increase.

Match.com (*http://match.com*) and LinkedIn become more useful as more users come on board.

Content

Users discover and consume content created by other users on the network. As more users come on board, the corpus of content scales, leading to greater value for the user base. Content platforms like YouTube, Flickr, and Quora, as well as marketplaces like Airbnb and Etsy, become more useful as the number of creators and the volume of content increase.

Clout

Some networks have power users, who enjoy influence and clout on the network. Follower counts (Twitter), leaderboards (Foursquare), and reputation platforms (Yahoo! Answers) are used to separate power users from the rest. On networks like Twitter, the larger the network is, the larger the following that a power user can develop is.

Across these three drivers, a network with greater scale provides greater value in the form of:

1. More prospective *connections* for the user

2. A larger corpus of potentially relevant *content*

3. Access to a larger base of potential followers (greater *clout*), for power users

On most networks, value for users is created through more than one of these three sources. Facebook, for example, started with a value proposition centered around *connection*, but the introduction of the news feed has made *content* a central driver of value. In recent times, the addition of the subscribers feature has added *clout* for some Facebook users as well.

Why Network Effects Work in Reverse

One would expect that the bigger the network is, the more value users will derive from it. However, as networks scale the value for users may drop, for several reasons:

1. *Connection*: New users joining the online community may lower the quality of interactions and increase noise/spam through unsolicited connection requests.

2. *Content*: The network may fail to manage the abundance of content created on it and may fail to scale the curation of content created and the personalization of the content served to users.

3. *Clout*: The network may get inadvertently biased toward early users and promote them over users who join later.

Just as network effects create a rich-become-richer cycle leading to rapid growth of the network, reverse network effects can work in the opposite direction, leading to users quitting the network in droves. Friendster, MySpace, and Orkut bear testimony to the destructive power that reverse network effects wield.

REVERSE NETWORK EFFECTS: CONNECTION

Connection-first networks (dating websites like Match.com (*http://match.com*) and networking communities like LinkedIn) build value by connecting people.

These networks may suffer from reverse network effects as they scale if new users joining the network lower the value for existing users. To prevent this, an appropriate level of friction needs to be created, either at the point of access or when users try to connect with other users.

On dating sites, women often complain of online stalking as the community grows, and abandon the site. Sites like CupidCurated have tried to solve this problem by curating the men that enter the system (*http://platformed.info/online-dating-seeding-strategy/*), in a manner similar to restricted access at a singles bar.

LinkedIn creates friction by preventing users from communicating with distant connections. This ensures that users do not receive unsolicited messages. This also allows LinkedIn to offer frictionless access (OpenMail) as a premium value proposition.

ChatRoulette, in contrast, anonymously connects users over a video chat without them needing to log in. This lack of friction led to ChatRoulette's stellar growth, but it also led to reverse network effects as anonymous naked hairy men took to the network, thus increasing noise and driving genuine users away from it.

Dating sites, as well as social networks like Orkut, have imploded in a similar manner after reaching scale, owing to noise created by fake profiles.

In general, networks of connections scale well when they create appropriate barriers to access on the network.

REVERSE NETWORK EFFECTS: CONTENT

On content networks like YouTube or Flickr, a larger network is likely to have more content creators, leading to more content for the users to consume. Networks like Facebook and Twitter, in addition to being networks of connections, are also networks of content.

Most networks of content have low friction in content creation (*http://plat formed.info/product-strategy-instagram-kickstarter-itunes-aws-marketplace/*) to encourage activity from users and reach critical mass faster (*http://platformed.info/hacking-your-way-to-critical-mass/*). To ensure that the content is relevant and valuable, the network needs strong content curation and personalization of the user experience.

Reverse network effects set in if the content curation systems don't scale well. As more producers create more content, the relevance of the content served to consumers on the network shouldn't decrease.

Curation

Content networks create a curation mechanism through a combination of moderation, algorithms, and community-driven tools (voting, rating, reporting, etc.). Voting on YouTube, flagging a post on Facebook, and rating on Yelp are examples of curation tools.

Curation mechanisms often break down as the volume of content increases. When curation algorithms and moderation processes do not scale, noise on the system increases. This leads to reverse network effects and users abandoning the system.

Quora has a very strong curation mechanism in place and benefits from a tech-savvy early user base. As Quora scales, many worry that less sophisticated users entering the system may increase noise, leading to a rapid depletion of value for existing users. It remains to be seen whether its curation can scale as the network opens up to a broader user base.

Personalization

Content networks need a personalized consumption experience for users that serves them relevant content. An example is the news feed on Facebook or Quora or the recommendation system on YouTube.

Inability to maintain relevance of the consumption experience with scale may create reverse network effects.

The user experience on Facebook is centered around the news feed. However, Facebook's frictionless sharing (*http://readwrite.com/2011/11/21/why_i_shut_off_face*

books_spotify_integration) and cluttered news feeds may lead to lower relevance for users as the network scales. Several factors contribute to this:

1. When a user adds friends indiscriminately, her news feed becomes cluttered with irrelevant posts.

2. Noise is further increased when marketers and app developers get access to the news feed (*http://livepage.apple.com/*).

3. When networks like Facebook and Twitter implement monetization models like promoted posts/tweets, the signal to noise ratio suffers further (*http://plat formed.info/promoted-tweet-facebook-twitter-social-network-revenue-model/*)   as promoted content is less relevant than organic content.

Networks of content are constantly faced with the risk of reverse network effects as they scale. The poor signal-to-noise ratio in the news feed, not the size of the overall network, is Facebook's weakest link as the network scales.

REVERSE NETWORK EFFECTS: CLOUT

Networks of clout have a system of differentiating power users from the rest. Twitter, Quora, and Quibb have baked in clout through the one-sided follower model. Active users vie for greater glory while using the network.

Networks of clout tend to be biased against users joining in late. Clout is a consequence of content that the user creates, and early users get more time to create content and develop a following.

This is, ironically, aggravated by focusing on a high signal-to-noise ratio (*http://platformed.info/twitter-ecosystem-developers-reverse-network-effects/*). Twitter recommends superusers to prospective followers, as these users are likely to create better content. Hence, the platform itself helps separate the power users from the rest.

Users who join later find it more difficult to develop a following and may stop using the network. These networks need a mechanism to ensure new users have equal access and exposure to the community to develop network clout. 500px (*http://500px.com/*), for example, differentiates Top creations from Upcoming creations to expose recent activity (often from undiscovered users) to the community.

In Conclusion

Reverse network effects often cause a large and thriving network to implode. As a network scales, its ability to maintain a high signal-to-noise ratio is the leading indicator of its usefulness. Networks can, in fact, scale very well and prevent reverse network effects from setting in if they have:

1. An appropriate level of friction in network access and usage, that prevents abuse
2. A strong curation system that scales well with the size of the network
3. A highly relevant and personalized user experience
4. A democratic model for users to build influence

Networks that have excelled in the above have scaled well. In a world where networks are reaching unprecedented scale, a keen focus on maintaining a high signal-to-noise ratio will enable them to remain valuable and effective as they grow.

12

Business Model Canvas for Puppies (Part I)

Tristan Kromer (http://grasshopperherder.com/)

As some of you may know, TaskRabbit launched a new business model on April 1, 2012: Puppies-as-a-Service *(http://www.taskrabbit.com/blog/kobe/taskrabbit-pivots-business-model-to-become-tech-worlds-first-on-demand-puppy-delivery-service/).*

Although they chose not to continue down that path, I think it's a fabulous idea and it'll make a great example to use with our new Business Model Canvas *(http://grasshopperherder.com/business-model-canvas-for-user-experience/).*

Note

For those not familiar with US traditions, April 1st is also known as April Fools' Day *(http://en.wikipedia.org/wiki/April_Fools%27_Day)*, and it generally involves a lot of silliness.

(Update: Truth is stranger than fiction, and there are no new ideas—Suzanne McElwee points out that there *is* a pet rental service in New York *(http://www.flexpetz.com/).*)

Puppies-as-a-Service

In her post, Leah Busque *(http://twitter.com/labusque)*, founder and CEO of TaskRabbit *(http://taskrabbit.com/)*, laid out an impressive vision to change the world:

> *Puppies are highly social and adorable animals, a leading source of uncontrollable joy and delight, with a cuddle presence on all seven continents.*

I couldn't agree more. While I'd love to have a dog, it's a lot of effort, and I don't have room in my tiny San Francisco box apartment. If I could just rent a puppy for rainy days I'd probably be much less of a jerk and the world would be a better place.

But how can I make this vision come true? Let me start by laying it out with the Business Model Canvas.

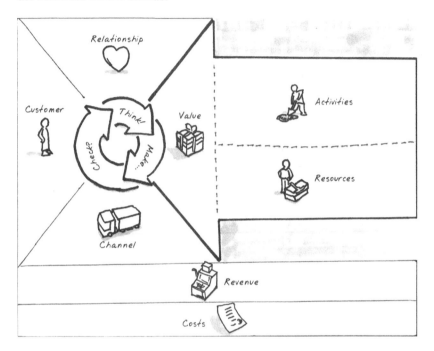

Note

The Business Model Canvas I use here is my own variation that I've even adjusted since some valid criticism by Erich von Hauske (*http://grasshopperherder.com/business-model-canvas-for-user-experience/#comments*). But this example will still work with the original Business Model Canvas by Alexander Osterwalder (*http://www.business modelgeneration.com/canvas*), so use whatever you're comfortable with.

Find a Wall

The first thing I need to do is prep my workspace.

I'm 6'4" and I like UX, so I'm going to do what any UX person would do and break out the masking tape and sticky notes so I can work in a highly visible way with an information radiator (*http://www.atlassian.com/wallboards/information-radiators.jsp*). My goal is that any new employee working to make the awesomeness of puppies available to everyone will be able to walk into my office and understand the business model at a glance.

So, I've picked a nice big chunk of wall and sketched the Business Model Canvas with masking tape:

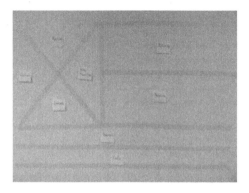

Note

I work directly on the wall with sticky notes, but since I'm photography-challenged the following illustrations are digitally manufactured.

Now I've got the skeleton up and I'm ready to put my grand vision down.

Looking at my canvas from left to right, I'm reminded that I need to start with the...

Customer

Obviously everyone in the world will want to rent a puppy, but that's not going to help me get my first customer. I need to focus on a *customer persona*. Specifically, I want to know, "Who will camp out overnight to be the first person in line to rent a puppy?"

The first person in line is an early adopter and evangelist. Mine looks like this:

	Behaviors
Zeek	*Pushes face against pet store glass* *kicks kittens* *chills out with heroin* *treis to pet tray rats* *loitters at dog parks* *groans uncontrollably*
Facts and Demographics *lives in SOMA, SF* *28 years old* *$78,000 per year* *radiologist* *single*	*Needs and Goals* *feel warm and fuzzy* *stop dealing with poop* *better stress outlet* *than heroin* *doesn't want to deal* *with poop* *find a gimmick to pick* *up girls*

This is a persona in the quick and dirty LUXr (*http://luxr.co/*) format, which I learned from Janice Fraser (*http://twitter.com/clevergirl*) and Kate Rutter (*http://twitter.com/katerutter*). It takes about 15 minutes to do.

If you haven't seen this before and you'd like a complete breakdown on how (and why) to make one, you can tweet me at @*TriKro*.

A few things to note:

- First, Zeek has a name! That will serve as verbal shorthand so that when I'm talking with my team I can talk about Zeek and not just "a user," where we all mean different things by "user."

- Second, Zeek has a face. The picture will serve as a mnemonic so everyone in my team can remember who he is.

- Third, Zeek is not a great guy. He does heroin to unwind and kicks kittens.

You may not think this is a great early adopter for Puppies-as-a-Service (PaaS), but I think the world will be a better place if Zeek gets in touch with his inner cuddle monster and gives up heroin in favor of a puppy time-out. So I'm sticking with him for my early adopter.

After all, the customer persona is a hypothesis about our customer, not an immutable vision beyond questioning.

Next, I need to understand why Zeek might rent a Puppy-as-a-Service. So I need the...

Value Proposition

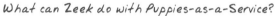

I've gone straight back to my LUXr training here and done 6-ups Uses using the prompt, "What can Zeek do with Puppies-as-a-Service?" This took about five minutes and I have six ideas about what value Zeek might get out of PaaS.

Note

If you need a more detailed post on 6-ups, tweet @ me.

After doing a quick consensus vote with my team (ego, id, and super-ego), I've decided to focus on just three critical issues for Zeek.

My two big ones are pretty similar: "Be happy" and "Stop being angry." Although they're slightly different flavors in terms of emotive resonance, they're a bit too broad, so I'm going to eliminate those.

A more concrete value proposition is that Zeek really needs to get off heroin, and that's at the top of my priorities. After all, I'm in this puppy business to help people and make the world a better place!

If I don't have respect and sympathy for my customer, I deserve to fail.

However, since Zeek is an addict, he doesn't *want* to kick heroin. That means although I think Zeek has a serious problem, so far as Zeek is concerned, that problem doesn't exist (*http://grasshopperherder.com/problems-dont-exist/*). Zeek does, however, have a real desire to get laid. So that'll be Use #1.

When Zeek knows he has a problem, it's a much easier value proposition to communicate and a cheaper marketing campaign to run.

Next, I'm going to include "No poop!" because Zeek just can't deal with it. (I concur.)

Finally, I'm going to keep "Stop hating kittens" because Zeek's cat-kicking habit is going to put off a lot of the ladies that Zeek wants to attract with his rented puppy.

Now I've finally got something to start filling in my Business Model Canvas. We'll put the visual mnemonic from the *persona* and the three *uses* onto sticky notes and put them in their rightful places:

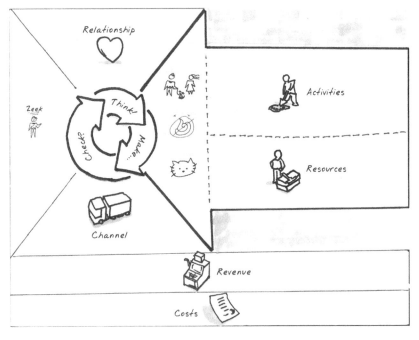

Next I should really think about how I'm going to get my first feedback from the customer, so I need to fill in...

Relationship

What if puppy-nappers (that is to say, people who steal puppies, not puppies who are inclined to snoozing) steal the pup? What if a puppy springs a leak? How will Zeek get support for his puppy?

self serve   pet stores

customer   support
forums   desk

The first thing to do is a 30-second brain dump using my favorite UX tool, the sticky note! Now I've got four ideas about how I could start with my customer relationship and provide customer support.

Osterwalder notes that I can give the customer a self-service relationship, which would greatly reduce my long-term costs. That's my preference for this business model, but I don't need to sketch out that whole vision here.

The Think-Make-Check (or Build-Measure-Learn (*http://grasshopperherder.com/ build-measure-learn-vs-learn-measure-build/*), if you prefer) cycle (along with the left-to-right nature of reading) reminds me that the customer relationship is value that the customer provides to my business.

I desperately need feedback from the customer.

While I'm absolutely certain that everyone in the world is going to want to rent a puppy and that I'll be bigger than Facebook, I should remain skeptical. I need to believe in my vision but question my strategy and tactics at every step.

Feedback from the customer will allow me to understand if my value proposition has hit the mark or if my customer persona is really accurate, so I'm going to scrap the self-service option for the moment. Customer forums seem like a whole lot to build right now and pet stores will be expensive (and distance me from the customer), so I'm going to have a direct phone number to a support desk for instant puppy support.

Channel

Next up, how am I going to get my puppies to Zeek? Another quick 30-second brain dump is in order.

dog walkers   pedicabs   kennels

direct sales   pet stores   breeders

Now I've got six possibilities, with a clear winner: pet stores!

Why pet stores? From my customer persona I can see that Zeek "pushes face against pet store glass."

So a pet store is probably a great sales channel for me. When I see Zeek (or someone who is close enough) with his nose up against the glass, I can try and rent him a puppy.

Unfortunately, some quick customer development with the pet store reveals that pet store owners think that puppy rentals will cannibalize their puppy sales. So this is out of the question. Fortunately, Leah's original TaskRabbit post (*http://www.taskrabbit.com/blog/kobe/taskrabbit-pivots-business-model-to-become-tech-worlds-first-on-demand-puppy-delivery-service/*) provides some key inspiration here:

> *TaskRabbit's new fleet of pedicabs... have been retrofitted as puppy delivery vehicles.*

Great! I'm going to use my fleet of pedicabs to loiter outside pet stores and directly rent my puppies to Zeek. That way when the store owner comes out with a baseball bat, the superior speed of the pedicab will allow me and my sales force to beat a hasty retreat.

Now with the primary product/market fit quadrant filled out, my canvas looks like this:

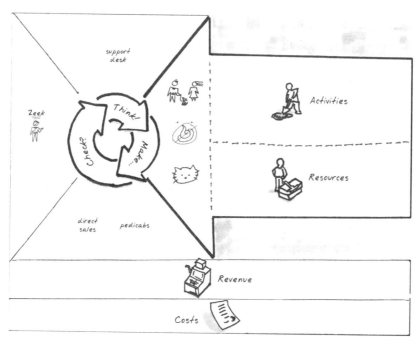

Minimum Viable Product

I'm not done with the canvas, but I've already got a pretty good idea of what to build for my MVP. The three uses in my value proposition will drive the bulk of what I need to build.

Clearly, I'm going to have to get a puppy to Zeek so he can pick up girls outside somewhere. That's one feature, and I'm only going to need one puppy to start with. With a little luck, I can borrow one to get going. Worst-case scenario, I'll head to the pound.

Feature #2 is going to have to be some sort of poop management service. I can probably concierge-test this and run after Zeek with a pooper-scooper if it's an issue.

My last use isn't going to generate any more features, because my guess/hypothesis is that when Zeek gets to the park with his rent-a-pup he's not going to have to worry about stray cats in need of a swift kick. Cats don't really hang out in the park, and my hope is that Zeek will also be distracted by all the new lady attention. So that's a bonus.

That's not all, though. A Minimum Viable Product without a channel to reach the customer is a Maximum Waste of Time.

In addition, I'll need the relationship to provide support, and I need to complete the Think-Make-Check (or Build-Measure-Learn) cycle, so I'll also rent one pedicab to do my first direct sales. I'll keep my mobile phone number on the puppy collar for the support desk so that Zeek can call and the pedicab can rush me to an "emergency cleanup."

The End?

There's a lot more to do, but after that rigorous 30 minutes of work (in BMC time, not writing time) I'm ready to take a break. When you're ready... read on to part two of the Business Model Canvas for Puppies-as-a-Service (*http://grasshopperherd er.com/business-model-canvas-for-puppies-part-ii/*).

PART III

Customer Discovery and Validation

13

All Customers Are Not Created Equal

Cindy Alvarez (http://www.cindyalvarez.com/)

Customer development and Lean Startup techniques have been so loudly touted by, well, *startups* that many people in non-startup or non-technology companies think these tools don't apply to them.

"The rules are different when you're talking to large enterprise customers," they say. "This doesn't work when you're dealing with customers who are already using your products and have certain expectations," they say.

Yes and no. *Yes*, the techniques I write about *will* work on your customers. *No*, you can't blindly apply them in the same way to all types of customers.

While I've worked in technology startups throughout my career, I've actually spent much of that time working with large, traditional, non-technology corporations. I've launched a few new products to new audiences—but I've also managed product redesigns and new features while working with outspoken and change-fearing existing customers.

There are some pretty big differences between these segments: consumers, non-technology SMBs, technology startups, large enterprise customers, and existing customers.

Part I

I'll talk about the first three customer segments first.

CONSUMERS

- **"Cold contact" methods are much less effective.** Consumers tend to be more suspicious that you're trying to sell them something or scam them; they can also be fearful that a cold email means their privacy has been violated somehow.

- **More likely to be polite than honest.** Talking to a person in a consumer context is seen as more of a social engagement than a business one—and most people have been trained to be pleasant and avoid conflict in social situations. Any question that can be answered with "yes" will be. "How" and "why" questions will allow consumers to be more honest without feeling uncomfortable.

- **Cost is more likely to be a big decision-making factor.** In this context, your idea isn't "validated" unless you've seen concrete purchasing intent. You can easily get consumers to identify their problem, give you details, and loooooove your solution... and then not pay you $5 for it.

- **Time is undervalued.** Most people are terrible at estimating how much time they spend on a certain task, how much time they waste, how long they spend on various activities. In a work environment, we are more likely to have deadlines, be paid hourly, fill out timesheets—and any of these activities make people at least somewhat more aware of their time usage.

- **Don't forget about "external stakeholders"!** Just because a consumer doesn't need to seek approval from the boss or finance department doesn't mean there aren't additional people who can and will veto your product. Family members may refuse to use a new product; friends may express disapproval of changes.

SMALL AND MID-SIZED NON-TECHNOLOGY BUSINESSES

- **Be specific.** Asking about specific tactical activities and outcomes is more likely to engage SMB folks than aspirational/"vision" concepts.

- **Less motivated by "feeling smart."** Consumers, tech nerds, and people within larger companies are often happy to talk about a subject just because they care about it/are a subject matter expert. I've found this to be less the case with SMB folks. Offer them value, like answering questions, sharing data, sharing curated content, or making introductions for them.

- **"If it ain't broke, don't fix it" mindset.** If consumers are more likely to say "yes" (even if they don't really mean it), SMB people are more likely to say "no." There are fewer people to absorb the impact of a learning curve or clean up a failed experiment.

TECHNOLOGY STARTUPS

- **Harder to keep focused on the *problem*, not the solution.** We can't help it. We spend our days building and designing, so we naturally slip into talking about solutions. You'll need to actively refocus the conversation, maybe many times, on the what/when/why questions.

- **Easiest to reach via "cold contact" methods.** As long as you're brief, non-spammy, and respectful, you'll get a high response rate from emails, Twitter, and follow-ups from finding people on social media/topical forums.

- **Overly optimistic/aspirational.** We set really high goals for ourselves, which often means we'll tell you about all the things we want to do, intend to do, aspire to do... but never actually get around to. Like the consumer segment, if we can answer "yes" to a question, we will.

- **Like sounding smart *and* getting information.** You can get an initial conversation with a technology startup person just because we love talking and thinking about stuff. But you can build an ongoing relationship by following up with a summary of your learnings, providing intel on what other companies are doing (anonymized, of course), or offering sneak previews of what's coming next.

Part II

So how can you apply customer development techniques to large enterprise customers and existing customers? They're still *people*, so fundamentally they also have problems and pain points and constraints. But there are some things to keep in mind if you want to maximize how productive your conversations are.

LARGE ENTERPRISE CUSTOMERS

- **Expect anything they see to look "good."** This doesn't mean that you need to show a working app—trust me, big company folks are plenty accustomed to being sold products by PowerPoint deck—but it does mean that you should spend a few hours or days turning your Balsamiq wireframes into visuals that are simple, specific, and polished-looking. Don't use lorem ipsum; take the time to write the actual text that a customer might see. Don't use clip art. Correct your typos. If you don't, you'll immediately take a credibility hit.

- **Need a memorable narrative.** These folks are *constantly* being pitched. All the features and benefits and overblown language like "best-of-breed" and "cutting-edge" blend together into a haze. What they'll remember is a story: "Let's say you have an employee, Jill, and here's what Jill does each day when she...."
- **Are accustomed to hearing "yes."** Sales people tend to say "yes" to everything in order to close a deal; this means that saying "no" may end the conversation abruptly. (This doesn't mean you have to agree; it does mean you have to be very creative in how you proceed when the customer is asking for something that you have no intention of providing.)
- **Are often pleasantly surprised by being asked "why."** All enterprise customers have been burned by hearing "yes" and then finding out that that "yes" has a lot of exceptions or an additional cost. Having someone who actually listens, and asks thoughtful questions, may shock them into revealing a lot more about how their business works.
- **Are offended by being told what to do.** A multimillion-dollar widget-making company does not want to hear from you that they're making widgets wrong. If you try to sound credible by flaunting your widget-making expertise, that is unlikely to go well. Be humble: acknowledge that they're the expert, and you're the one trying to understand. (Note: this is *always* good advice.)
- **Have a lot of stakeholders.** The end user is probably not the buyer. The decision maker is probably not the implementer. You will need to talk to a lot more people in order to validate your assumptions. You will also need to approach them in different ways (the way marketers perform due diligence or assess your credibility is usually very different from how the IT department does it).

EXISTING CUSTOMERS

- **Are really easy to get in touch with.** There's a perception that customers "don't want to be bothered," but I don't know where this comes from. This has never been my experience! As long as you're clear that you're not trying to sell something, current customers are usually eager to talk to you. Remember, they have already invested a lot of effort in learning your product—it's in their best interest for you to thrive as a company.

- **Their top priority is their current product/service.** Have you ever been to a concert where the artist kept playing all the songs from his new album instead of the greatest hits that you wanted to sing along with? *Start* by answering the customers' existing questions, and make sure you learn as much as possible about how they're using your current product or service. Once you've covered that, they will be far more receptive to answering questions about potential new use cases or products.

- **Hate change.** Hold off on the mockups for as long as possible. You want your customers to recognize that they have a problem first, before you threaten them with something new and different.

- **Are biased by what they're already using.** They have strong opinions on the solutions they want, and are highly motivated to push those solutions instead of talking about the problems. It will require a lot of conscious effort to keep directing the conversation back to the why/how questions.

- **Need reassurance that you're not going to deprioritize or drop their current product.** If they think that answering your questions might cause you to stop working on the current product (remember, the one they have already invested effort in learning), it's going to be a short and pointless conversation. You can cut this off before it starts by immediately reassuring them that their current product is safe, and that this is early/exploratory research.

I hope this is useful in encouraging you to extend customer development to some new audiences.

14

You Shouldn't Use a Survey If...

Cindy Alvarez

Surveys are an incredibly useful market and customer research tool. But you use them too often. (Not, you know, you personally. But "you" in a global companies and organizations kind of sense.)

You shouldn't use a survey if:

You aren't sure which type of people you should ask to take your survey.

There are almost zero contexts where you'll get useful data out of having "anyone" take your survey. (And thinking, "I'll just get thousands of responses, and then filter by some criteria later" is both a copout and unlikely.) Do you want to hear from existing customers? People from a certain region? People who share a common activity? People with a specific job title?

Your "type of people" can be subjective, too—in a recent survey I conducted, I wanted to hear from "smart people that we'd want to hire if we had the chance." So I distributed the survey through coworkers' personal networks, letting them make that subjective determination.

You know which type of people you want to take your survey but have no idea how to find them.

Surveys are not an "if you build it, they will come" exercise. Don't waste your time on a survey if you don't have a ready bank of people to send it to or a distribution strategy. It's a waste of time and social capital to send out a survey and get only four or five responses.

You're better off conducting freeform interviews first so you can increase the "learning density" you get from each person. For the long term, you'll need to invest time in figuring out how to find more people. This usually means "find where these people already are, and put yourself there"—participate in forums, join clubs, build up your network.

All of the questions you want to ask require a freeform response.
This is a sign that you don't really know what the questions are yet; that you aren't really sure what the problem is yet.

If you have an existing product or customer base, look at usage patterns and past feedback first. Then start with freeform interviews, so you can tease out information in a back-and-forth context. The survey format is bad for this type of learning. People don't like to write a lot, and even if they do, their first response is usually not where all the "meat" is.

You don't have a clear plan of action for how you're going to use the results.
If you're thinking, "We might learn something" or "It would be nice to know...," then save yourself the time (and save the time of the people who would fill out your survey). Data without action is meaningless.

Is this information going to help you make a better decision on a specific feature or project? Will it help you choose better wording or smarter defaults in your application? Will it validate a specific hypothesis so that you can continue or pivot?

You can't prioritize your list of questions down to fewer than 10.
This is another sign that you "aren't really sure what the problem is yet." Of course, you're bound to have more than 10 things that you'd like to know—you probably have hundreds of things you'd like to learn—but you can't possibly act on more than 10 at a time anyway.

I often see long surveys where the first three or four questions are asking about age, gender, zip code, income level. Those are lazy questions. If you need to segment by demographic, that should be part of your distribution plan, or you should "buy an audience" from a market research firm.

You aren't willing to write a draft, have another set of eyes review it, and then revise.
The first survey draft you write will suffer from at least one of these flaws:
- Unclear language ("Wait, what are they asking?")
- Biased language ("How much do you like feature X?")
- Stilted language (technically makes sense but just sounds awkward)
- Stupid questions (if you ask, "Do you want X?" of *course* they will say "yes"; that doesn't reveal anything about actual intent)
- Too many freeform questions (there should be no more than one freeform question for every three click-to-answer questions)
- Mistakenly using single-choice instead of multiple-choice, or vice versa

- Doesn't actually ask the question that you wanted answered
- Inadvertent rudeness (use of words with negative connotations, or a phrasing that sounds brusque or judgmental)

It is very difficult to catch these on your own. I've been writing surveys for years, and I still always have at least one other person read each one and comment on anything that is weird or confusing, and I still always have to change at least one thing.

15

A Perfect Use for Personas

Laura Klein (http://usersknow.blogspot.com/)

I just read Dave McClure's post about changes to menus and its not-always-flattering Hacker News thread (*https://news.ycombinator.com/item?id=4978719*), and I found myself both violently agreeing and disagreeing with both. I kept thinking something along the lines of, "That would be great! Except when it would be incredibly annoying!"

That's when I realized what was missing for me: personas.

First off, apologies to Dave, who certainly doesn't need me to defend or improve on his ideas. This is just meant to be an explanation of the process I went through as a designer and researcher to understand my weird, ambivalent reaction to his product suggestions. Here are the problems that Dave listed in his post that he was solving for:

- Too many items, not enough pictures, simpler and more obvious recommendations
- Not online, no order history, no reviews, no friends, no loyalty program, no A/B testing
- Have to wait forever for waiter to order, reorder, and pay
- Nothing to do while I'm waiting

Then he presented reasonable solutions to these problems. All of the suggestions seemed geared toward making restaurants quicker, more efficient, and lower touch. Interestingly, both the Hacker News complaints and my own seemed to be from the point of view of people who do not have these problems. They were saying things like, "This would make restaurants awful!" but what they really meant was, "I, as a potential user, don't identify with that particular problem you're trying to solve, so your solution does not really apply to me."

In other words, Dave's suggested solutions might be great for people who have these problems but might not appeal at all to people who don't have these problems.

So, then I started to think about the types of people who would have those types of problems. I put together a few rudimentary personas of people who likely would benefit from things like recommendations, entertainment while waiting, a more efficient order process, and a faster way to pay.

As a note, these personas are behavioral, not demographic. This means that you might sometimes fit into one of them, and at other times you wouldn't. It depends more on what you do than who you are.

The Business Person

Imagine that you're on a business trip to someplace you've never been. You're quite busy, and it's likely that you'll have to eat a few meals on your own, possibly on the way to or from a meeting or the airport. You're not a fan of fast food, so you'd rather be able to find something you like at an interesting local place than at a big national chain.

In this instance you might *love* having things like recommendations from people you trusted, pictures on the menu of unfamiliar dishes, and a quick, efficient ordering and payment system that guaranteed you wouldn't hang around for 20 minutes waiting for a bill. You might also really enjoy some entertainment so that you'd have something to do that wasn't stare creepily at the other patrons.

The Barfly

Now imagine that you're at an incredibly crowded nightspot. You are desperate for a bourbon, but you don't want to queue up five deep at the bar to try to get someone's attention. You manage to get a table, but now you have to decide whether to leave it to flag down one of the few waitresses or just wait it out.

In this instance you would almost certainly be excited to be able to order and pay directly from your table using some sort of tablet. You'd also be able to quickly order your second, third, and (dare I say it) fourth rounds without having to go through the whole process again or count on the waitstaff knowing exactly when to ask if you want a refill.

The Group Luncher

Last one for now, I promise. You're out to lunch with eight of your coworkers. You need to get back to the office in 45 minutes for another stupid meeting. You don't want to spend 10 of those minutes just waiting for a waiter to make it to your table and take your orders. Also, you really don't want to be the one in charge of figuring out how to split the bill, especially since three of your coworkers always get booze, one of them never eats more than a salad, and two of them order the most expensive thing on the menu.

In this instance, you'd be thrilled to be able to just sit down, punch in your order (and your credit card details!), get your food delivered to you quickly, and get to spend more time chatting with that cute new person in accounting rather than negotiating who forgot to figure in tax to the amount they owe on the bill.

And the Rest...

There are probably a half dozen other hypothetical persona groups, all of which would obviously need to be validated (or invalidated) with various forms of user research and quantitative testing.

The persona groups that aren't on this list are also important. Many of these types of innovations might make things worse for the types of folks who are enjoying the experience of being in a restaurant as an event. For example, a romantic dinner for two at a high-end restaurant is not improved by shaving 30 minutes off the wait between courses. Other people might enjoy the personal exchange with the waiter or a consultation from a sommelier more than reading about items on a tablet.

That's okay. These products aren't necessarily going to be for every type of restaurant all at once. There's no need to worry that suddenly Manresa is going to be putting pictures on the menu like Denny's.

The reason I bring this up is that it often helps me to evaluate product ideas through the eyes of the people I expect to use the product. When I find myself saying things like, "Driving sucks! I'm going to fix driving!" I have to step back and realize that driving (like eating in restaurants) is an almost universal activity that has a constellation of problems, many of which are not shared by all types of drivers (or eaters). If you think your startup has a brand-new product that's going to solve all the driving problems for stock car drivers, commuters, and truck drivers, I think you're probably wrong.

Instead of arguing back and forth whether or not these problems exist, it's very easy to identify particular types of people for whom these problems *might* exist and then do some simple qualitative research to see if you're right. After all, we know at least one person (Dave) has these problems that he wants solved. Presumably Dave (or the companies he invests in) is doing the sort of research necessary to make sure that there are enough people like Dave to make a profitable market. That market might not include you, but there are lots of wildly successful products you don't like.

So. Long story short: personas, yay!

Postscript

For those of you who notice these things, you're right, I didn't include the personas for the other side of the equation: the restaurant owners. Whenever your customers (the people who give you money) and your users (the people who actually use your product) are different, you're in a much more complicated space from a user experience point of view. I'm assuming that if we can make a specific type of end user happy enough it will make the types of restaurant owners who cater to those users interested in purchasing the product.

That's just another hypothesis, and all hypotheses need to be validated, not assumed to be facts.

16

Fucking Ship It Already: Just Not to Everyone at Once

Laura Klein

There is a pretty common fear that people have. They're concerned that if they ship something that isn't ready, they'll get hammered and lose all their customers. Startups who have spent many painstaking months acquiring a small group of loyal customers are hesitant to lose those customers by shipping something bad.

I get it. It's scary. Sorry, cupcake. Do it anyway.

First, your early adopters tend to be much more forgiving of a few misfires. They're used to it. They're early adopters. Yours is likely not the first product they've adopted early. If you're feeling uncomfortable, go to the Wayback Machine (*http://archive.org/web/web.php*) and look at some first versions of products you use every day. When your eyes stop bleeding, come back and finish this post. I'll wait.

Still nervous? That's okay. The lucky thing is that you don't have to ship your ridiculous first draft of a feature to absolutely everybody at once. Let's look at a few strategies you can use to reduce the risk.

The Interactive Mockup

A prototype is the lowest-risk way you can get your big change, new feature, or possible pivot in front of real users without ruining your existing product. And you'd be surprised at how often it helps you find easy-to-fix problems before you ever write a line of "real code."

If you don't want to build an entire interactive prototype, trying showing mock-ups, sketches, or wireframes of what you're considering. The trick is that you have to show it to your real, current users.

Get on a screen share with some users and let them poke around the prototype. Whatever you do, never tell them why you made the changes or what the feature is supposed to be for or how awesome it is. You want the experience to be as close as possible to what it would be if you just released the feature into the wild and let the users discover it for themselves.

If your product involves any sort of user-generated content, taking the time to include some of the testers' own content can be extremely helpful. For example, if it's a marketplace where you can buy and sell handmade stuff, having the users' own items can make a mockup seem more familiar and orient the users more quickly.

Of course, if there's sensitive financial data or anything private, make sure to get the users' permission *before* you include that info in their interactive prototypes. Otherwise, it's just creepy.

The Opt In

Another method that works well is the *opt in*. While early adopters tend to be somewhat forgiving of changes or new features, people who opt in to those changes are even more so.

Allowing people to opt in to new features means that you have a whole group of people who are not only accepting of change, but actively seeking it out. That's great for getting very early feedback while avoiding the occasional freak-out from the small percentage of people who just enjoy screaming, "Things were better before!"

Here's a fun thing you can learn from your opt in group: If people who explicitly ask to see your new feature hate your new feature, your new feature probably sucks.

The Opt Out

Of course, you don't only want to test your new features or changes with people who are excited about change. You also want to test them with people who hate change, since they're the ones who are going to scream loudest.

Once you're pretty sure that your feature doesn't suck, you can share it with more people. Just make sure to let them go back to the old way, and then measure the number of people who actually do switch back.

Is it a very vocal 1% that is voting with their opt out? You're probably okay. Is half of your user base switching back in disgust? You may not have nailed that whole "making it not suck" thing.

The n% Rollout

Even with an opt out, if you've got a big enough user base, you can still limit the percentage of users who see the change. In fact, you really should be split-testing this thing 50/50, but if you want to start with just 10% to make sure that you don't have any major surprises, that's a totally reasonable thing to do.

When you roll a new feature out to a small percentage of your users, just make sure that you know what sorts of things you're looking for. This is a great strategy for seeing if your servers are going to keel over, for example.

It's also nice for seeing if that small, randomly selected cohort behaves any differently from the group that doesn't have the new feature. Is that cohort more likely to make a purchase? Are they more likely to set fire to their computers and swear never to use your terrible product ever again? These are both good things to know.

Do remember, however, that people on the Internet talk about things. Kind of a lot. If you have any way at all for your users to be in contact with one another, people will find out that their friends are seeing something different. This can work for or against you. Just figure out who's whining the loudest about being jealous of the other group, and you'll know whether to continue the rollout. What you want to hear is, "Why don't I have New New New New New Thing, yet?" and not "Just be thankful that they haven't forced the hideous abomination on you. Then you will have to set your computer on fire."

The New User Rollout

Of course, if you're absolutely terrified of your current user base (and you'd be surprised at how many startups seem to be), you can always release the change only to new users.

This is nice, because you get two completely fresh cohorts where the only difference is whether or not they've seen the change. It's a great way to do A/B testing.

On the other hand, if it's something that's supposed to improve things for retained users or users with lots of data, it can take a really long time to get enough information from this. After all, you need those new cohorts to turn into retained users before seeing any actual results, and that can take months.

Also, whether or not new users love your changes doesn't always predict whether your old users will complain. Your power users may have invested a lot of time and energy into setting up your product just the way they want it, and making major changes that are better for new folks doesn't always make them very happy.

In the end, you need to make the decision whether you'll have enough happy new users to offset the possibly angry old ones. But you'll probably need to make that decision about a million more times in the life of your startup, so get used to it.

So, are you ready to fucking ship it, already? Yes. Yes, you are. Just don't ship it to everybody all at once.

17

Stop Validating Your Product

Laura Klein

I talk to a lot of very small companies that are trying to do customer development, and the conversations are often the same. The entrepreneur explains that the company is working on a fabulous product, and they want to figure out a) if anybody wants to buy the product and b) if they need to change anything about the product so that more people will buy it.

The entrepreneurs always ask questions like, "How will I know if I have talked to enough people?" and "How do I know if the people who like it are just early adopters?" and "How do I know if I should change the product in response to feedback or if I should just keep trying to find the right market?" The ones who have already been out in the field trying to conduct these interviews all have a sort of glazed, terrified look.

These are all really important questions. I'm going to give you a way to avoid having to ask most of them:

Stop trying to validate your product.

Now, I fully expect a bunch of people to stop reading here and totally miss the point of this post, but for those of you who stick it out, I promise this will make sense in a minute.

The trick is, it is far, far easier to conduct customer development before you have settled on a product or even an idea for a problem.

Why is that? Well, think about products as solutions to problems. Sometimes that "problem" is "I'm sort of bored while I'm waiting for the train," and the unexpected solution is flinging virtual birds at virtual pigs. But often, the problem is something more concrete, and it's frequently shared by a large group of similar people.

So, instead of focusing on validating a solution, try one of the following techniques.

Validate a Problem

Let go of your preconceptions about *how* you are going to solve a problem for people and concentrate on first figuring out whether lots of people have a particular problem and what they're currently doing to solve it.

For example, let's say that you've posited that people have a really hard time finding and making appointments with trustworthy auto mechanics. The mistake you will probably make is to jump right into solving that problem and then going out into the world with some half-baked idea for Yelp meets OpenTable meets AAA and trying to find out whether it solves this problem that you're not technically sure exists yet.

Instead of doing that, *first validate the problem*. Get on the phone with lots of different types of people and ask them how they found their mechanics. Talk to them about all of their mechanic-based issues. Find out what causes them the most pain.

Also, this is a good time to narrow down your market. Start with the market "people who have cars and will talk to you," but quickly start noticing patterns. Do all the busy people have similar problems? What about people who live in cities vs. suburbs? How about people who are new to an area? Try people with special kinds of cars. I'll bet that they all have very different problems, any of which you might want to solve.

Once you've spent time talking to people in various markets with various problems, you'll come up with all sorts of ideas of how to solve those problems. The great thing is that then you can validate your product idea with people who you already know have a solvable problem.

This is a great way to do things if you have a particular problem yourself, and you want to find out if there are other people like you who have that same problem. By talking to lots of people with the same problem, you're going to come up with a much better solution than you would if you just solved things for yourself.

Solve a Problem for a Particular Market

A slightly different approach is to pick your market first. Let's say you have a special affinity for auto mechanics or busy moms or accountants at mid-sized companies.

The trick here is that you're not going to change your market. You're going to figure out some massive problem that is being experienced by a large portion of the market, and you're going to solve it for them.

Your first step is going to be some ethnographic research. You need to really get into the heads of your target market and see what makes them similar and what's driving them nuts. You're not going into the research with an idea of the problem you want to solve for them. You're going to let their needs drive your product decisions.

This is a great method if you happen to have some specific connection with a group or industry. Let's say you collect porcelain owl figurines. You might desperately want to solve a problem for other porcelain owl aficionados, but you should be open to what problem you want to solve for them. For example, it might be how to get large numbers of high-quality porcelain owls. Or it might be ways to contact therapists that deal with severe hoarding issues. Let the user research guide you!

The Easiest Kind of Customer Development

Hopefully you're noticing a pattern here. The easiest kind of customer development is the kind that you do *before* you have a very solid product idea.

If you figure out your problems and your market before you come up with an idea or a solution or a product, then when you do build something, you've already done a huge amount of the work in figuring out if anybody's going to use it.

This is really about controlling which variables you're testing. It's hard to simultaneously find a problem, a market, and the problems with a real product all at once.

However, once you've validated your market and your problem, you can create something that solves that specific problem for that particular market. The beauty of this is that if you build a product for a problem you know exists in a market you know needs it and still nobody uses it, you can be pretty certain that the problem is your product.

18

Using Surveys to Validate Key Startup Decisions

Brent Chudoba (http://www.forentrepreneurs.com/surveys/)
with introduction by David Skok

Introduction

By now pretty much every entrepreneur knows the basics of the Lean Startup (*http://theleanstartup.com/*) methodology. Start by searching for product/market fit. Get out of the building and talk to customers. Run a series of experiments to validate your ideas. Above all else, validate your thinking as early as possible: don't spend millions of dollars building something before you have tested the ideas and concepts with customers.

Where this tends to fall down in practice is that many entrepreneurs find it hard to reach real customers. Getting feedback from cofounders, friends, small focus groups, user testing sessions, and even existing customers can be very helpful to qualitatively understand how others view your offering. But many times the sample group that you can reach is too small and biased toward people who will be polite to you, or who have self-identified as liking your product.

What if you could ask 1,000 potential customers about your product, new feature, or idea? Would that help you make better decisions, create content or collateral, or gain important insights?

Many survey firms, including SurveyMonkey (*http://www.surveymonkey.com/*) (discussed here), offer the ability reach a large, specifically targeted audience that they have worked to identify. The following article describes how you might go about designing a survey, and interpreting the results, to gain actionable insights for your startup.

Background

My name is Brent Chudoba (*http://www.brentchudoba.com/me.html*); I'm a VP at SurveyMonkey and General Manager of the SurveyMonkey Audience (*http://*

fr.surveymonkey.com/mp/audience/) business, which provides on-demand respondents for our customers who need a targeted audience. My background, pre-SurveyMonkey, was in investing: I worked for the investment firm Spectrum Equity (*http://www.spectrumequity.com/*), which acquired SurveyMonkey in a leveraged buyout in 2009. As an investor, quantifying a market opportunity was key to validating a business through diligence. Whether I realized it then or not, I've always been a researcher, only now I have a much better grasp of which tools are available to help people conduct more efficient and effective research. A big part of my investment work was gathering company and industry data to form an investment thesis on the companies in my universe. As an operator, I'm still collecting data and trying to make good decisions as I help grow a business.

So How Do You Get Quality Feedback?

You have two groups of potential survey respondents available to you: current and prospective customers.

LEARNING ABOUT YOUR OWN CUSTOMERS

If you want to talk to your own customers, and understand product satisfaction, feature requests, or anything else, a survey can be a great tool. You most likely have email addresses for your customers, or can provide a feedback link on your site, or even embed a survey in-product. However, your respondents are likely to be either your biggest advocates, who want to help you, or your least-satisfied customers, who may want to complain. Surveying existing customers is no doubt a valuable exercise and can create preliminary benchmarks, but the focus of this article is on surveying non-customers, or people you may not immediately be able to access.

LEARNING ABOUT POTENTIAL CUSTOMERS

I always find it hard to generalize feedback programs without diving directly into a use case. I hope the following will help give you some ideas and inspiration for the topics that are most important to you when it comes to gathering feedback.

I have a friend who runs a startup called Modify Watches (*https://www.modifywatches.com/*). It's been around for two years, is starting to grow nicely, and is primed to add more resources and start spending money to grow. The company sells affordable watches that have interchangeable faces and bands, giving consumers hundreds of customization options. Modify Watches has a unique approach on accessories—you wear a different combination of pants and shirts most days, so why not also switch up your watch face and band whenever you want, to match your style or mood? The company has an ecommerce model with online as the primary sales channel. Modify could really benefit from talking to potential customers to understand its market opportunity, target customers, pricing tolerance, and feature needs. Modify knows a lot of information about its business anecdotally and through customer data, but what about the potential customers that are harder to reach?

Since Modify is a startup focused on finding ways to gain new customers and is testing out different pricing, advertising, and business model concepts, I asked my friend, "Why don't you talk to a representative sample of US adults to see if they would buy your product, and what their pricing tolerance is on something like watches?"

My friend, the founder, was very interested. Apparently, Modify's biggest problem (not dissimilar to most startups) is getting its product in the hands of more people. He told me, flat out, "Modify has a great product, people love it, people evangelize it, but there aren't enough people with the product on their wrists." To change this Modify had to decide how best to put resources to work on marketing campaigns, PR, and partnership efforts to help jump-start growth and awareness.

The risk, from his perspective, is in having the confidence to expend resources and/or raise more capital to accelerate growth while relying on a relatively limited set of customer data and questions around business model approach, ideal customers, and price point.

So what's a resource-efficient way to find data and insights around key business questions, in order to gain the confidence to push forward on growth and awareness efforts, while still staying nimble enough to pivot if needed?

Talk to potential customers. Determine the key business questions where feedback from a large audience would help you make better decisions. Using a survey or even a series of recurring surveys to monitor trends can help you find answers quickly, and help give you the confidence to sprint forward and grow your customer base.

The next section covers how you might run such a project and gives some examples of how to test some common topics faced by startups, using Modify as a specific example.

Using a Survey and a Targeted Audience to Make Smart Decisions

How do you get started? Work backward. First, think of what you are going to do with the data once you have it. This will help you determine what exactly you need to ask, and how to ensure the data is usable. Starting by just typing out questions can actually prolong the process. I also recommend keeping your goals narrow and focused. You can always run more survey projects, so don't overthink the first project and try to address too many topics at once, which leads to longer surveys and more survey creation and QA time. You are also going to learn a lot every time you run a project, which will make each subsequent project more successful.

Before you create your survey, you need to think about two things: your objectives and your target audience.

CREATE CLEAR OBJECTIVES

The following were the key objectives for Modify:

1. Understand if its core offering is priced appropriately.
   a. Determine from the data (output of answer options) whether people think the current pricing is too high, too low, or about right.
   b. Understand brand recognition (unaided and aided) in the market to get a sense of how the company should position itself in marketing/PR (and be able to cut this data based on watch/accessory budgets and demographics).
2. Find out which types of customers are most likely to purchase its product.
   a. Where are the demographic sweet spots in terms of pricing and interest?
3. Get custom market stats it can use to build a TAM (total addressable market), sanity check its market understanding, and build customized data for presentations, potentially for fundraising.
   a. How frequently do people buy watches?
   b. About how much do people spend on watches?
   c. How likely are people to purchase a watch online?
4. Understand key info around its new watch subscription (*http://www.modify watches.com/watch-of-the-month.php*) offering to validate whether this is a business initiative it should focus on.
   a. Are people interested in a subscription offering that allows them to get new watches on a regular or semi-regular basis?
   b. How much should they charge?
   c. How frequently do people want new watches?

DETERMINE YOUR TARGET AUDIENCE—WHO DO YOU WANT TO SURVEY?

Modify is asking questions related to watches. Pretty much everyone in the world has one or wears one—particularly those who can afford Internet connectivity.

> *Sample size*: 1,000 people should be enough to give us a sample size with high confidence.
> *Targeting*: US, gender balanced. We want the sample to look pretty similar to the US population. Everyone is a potential watch buyer that Modify wants to hear from.

Create a Great Survey—Turning Key Objectives into Great Questions

The following is a sample survey illustrating how Modify can achieve its feedback objectives by eliciting actionable data to help inform the business decisions it's considering. The survey questions are shown without the multiple-choice options for answers.

A live version of the full survey can be found here (*https://www.surveymon key.com/s/R3Z8TZW*). A PDF version of the survey can be found here (*http://www.slideshare.net/SurveyMonkeyAudience/modify-watch-survey-0712*).

MODIFY SURVEY QUESTIONS:

WATCH BASICS

1. Do you wear a watch on a daily or frequent basis?

2. Approximately how many watches do you own?

3. How often do you purchase watches?

WATCH PRICING AND PURCHASING

4. On average, how much do you spend when purchasing a new watch?

5. Have you ever purchased a watch online?

6. How did you purchase your last watch?

7. When you think of watch brands, which brands come to mind?

AIDED BRAND AWARENESS

8. Which of the following watch brands are you familiar with? (Select all that apply.) [randomize]

- Casio, Modify, Rolex, Omega, Cartier, Tag Heuer, Movado, Diesel, Timex, Starck, Fossil, None of the above, Other (please specify)

MODIFY WATCHES

Modify Watches is a cool new watch company seeking opinions and feedback. Our company sells great, interchangeable watches and prices watch straps and faces separately, in order to give customers ultimate choice. All of our straps and watch faces are interchangeable, so any band you buy can be mixed-and-matched with any face. The bands are silicone, so swapping in new bands is easy, and the watches are made from high quality, water-resistant materials.

9) Based on the information above, how likely would you be to purchase a Modify Watch?

10) About how much would you be willing to pay for a Modify Watch face and band?

MODIFY PRICING

11) Modify prices its watches based on the price of a watch face ($25) and the price of a band ($15). The bands and faces are interchangeable, so various combinations can be created for customers who purchase multiple bands and/or faces. Do you think that Modify watch face and band pricing is expensive or inexpensive?

12) Modify has recently created a subscription offering where customers can sign up for a subscription to receive new watches periodically. Customers also receive a discount on each watch as part of the subscription package. How likely would you be to sign up for a subscription offering to receive new watches periodically at discounted prices?

INTERESTED IN SUBSCRIPTION

13) If you were to sign up for a watch subscription package, how frequently would you want to receive new watches?

14) If you were to sign up for a watch subscription package, who would you like to choose the watches you receive?

- I would like Modify Watches to choose new watches for me
- I would like to choose new watches myself
- I don't know
- Other (please specify)

15) How much of a discount off of the base pricing for watch faces ($25) and bands ($15) would you require to sign up for a watch subscription package?

Uncovering Critical Insights

After launching the survey, results came in immediately. After just a couple of days, Modify was ready to begin analyzing its data, finding the key insights it needed to act on to help grow its business.

Since Modify used sound survey creation principles, the results and data were actionable and a key step in the process could begin. The topic we at SurveyMonkey ask a lot of customers or potential customers (and even ourselves) before, during, and after running projects is, "Now that you have answers and data, what are you going to do with them?"

So, how is Modify going to use this data to help grow its business and make better decisions?

ACTIONABLE INSIGHTS FOR MODIFY

Objective: Understand pricing

Modify wanted to understand how much consumers were willing to pay for its watches. Two key questions it asked can unlock the answer to this critical topic. And, since the survey also asked respondents whether they would be interested in Modify watches after providing a description and an image, the company can focus on the reactions of likely customers by filtering out those who were not at all interested.

Question: On average, how much do you spend when purchasing a new watch?

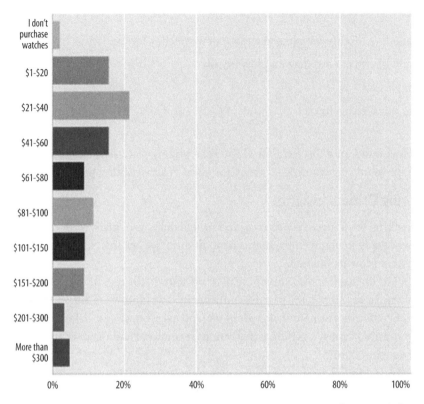

Responses were mixed, but encouragingly, more than 80% said they spend $20+ when purchasing a watch and the weighted average price people spend was around $70 per watch, which makes sense given typical watch pricing. So, without yet exposing its current pricing, Modify has an unbiased view of what watch buyers are willing to pay for a new watch. Given its current pricing of around $40 per watch, this shows that Modify isn't overpriced for the typical watch buyer and may have room to increase pricing over time as it keeps a low entry point to gain market share and awareness.

Question: Modify prices its watches based on the price of a watch face ($25) and the price of a band ($15). The bands and faces are interchangeable, so various combinations can be created for customers who purchase multiple bands and/or faces. Do you think that Modify watch face and band pricing is expensive or inexpensive?

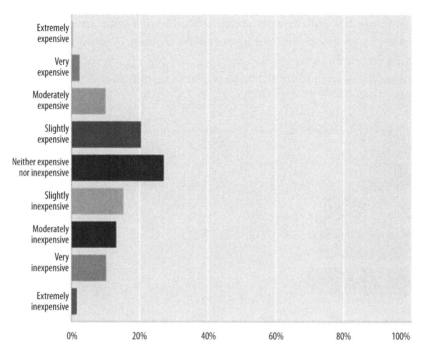

After exposing some information about its product and pricing to those respondents who had indicated at least some interest in the Modify offering, Modify could see that potential customers felt that its pricing was already in the sweet spot of what customers were willing to pay. Around 30% of respondents felt the offering was priced appropriately, and more than 60% felt it was appropriately priced or only slightly expensive or inexpensive. This is a major insight, since it let Modify know that it isn't way off on pricing and that any campaigns and marketing efforts targeted to its target customers should be well received if executed well.

Pricing is right. Modify isn't planning any major price changes, and spending time and resources on price testing isn't a major concern that should limit Modify's ability to grow the business.

Objective: Identify demographics of Modify's target customers

Modify had an initial sense of its target market demographics, largely based on knowledge of where its product has been well received so far, but this was highly anecdotal. By looking at the age and gender breakdowns of survey respondents who identified that they were "Extremely likely" or "Very likely" to purchase a Modify Watch, the company could see if its assumptions and intuition were correct. Of course, Modify could also look at geography, income, and a variety of other demographic attributes individually or in combination to build out a comprehensive analysis of key target groups, but getting an initial indication by looking at age and gender cross sections was the focus.

Question: Based on the information above, how likely would you be to purchase a Modify Watch?

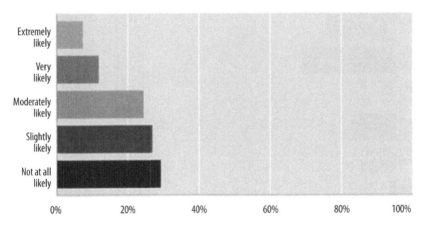

Roughly 70% of people are at least slightly likely to purchase a Modify Watch! Not bad for a startup watch brand. Roughly 20% of customers indicated high likeliness to purchase a Modify Watch (the sum of the "Extremely likely" and "Very likely" respondents). Drilling down into those answers and seeing which demographic groups expressed high likeliness to purchase will help pinpoint the types of customers who will be more likely to convert and become buyers.

Key demographic insights. The survey data allowed Modify to draw the following conclusions about its potential customer base:

- Women are nearly 30% more likely to purchase than men.
- People under the age of 30 are about 30% more likely to purchase than people 30 and above.
- The categories that showed the strongest likelihood to purchase, in order, were:

  - Females under 18
  - Males under 18
  - Males 18–29

- Females >60
- Males 30–44

Modify was under the impression that people of both genders aged 18–29 and females aged 29–60 would be great targets. This was mostly accurate, but the 60+ female group was a surprise, as was the strength in the <18 category. Creating offerings for and targeting campaigns toward teenagers, young males, and older females is going to be a recipe for success for Modify.

So how did Modify identify this actionable data for its business plans? By applying filters and crosstabs in its survey analysis and comparing the results against those of the overall population who answered the survey. An example of the filters and crosstabs applied are shown below.

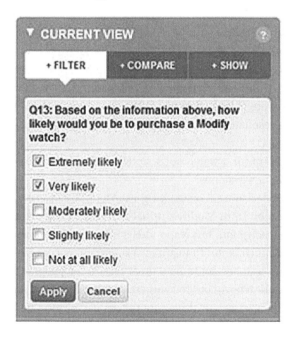

Objective: Understand if a subscription option is viable

Question: How likely would you be to sign up for a subscription offering to receive new watches periodically at discounted prices?

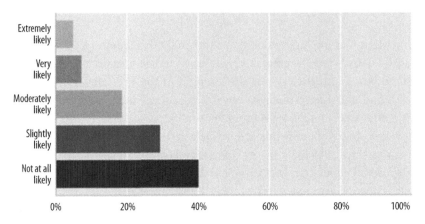

Around 60% of people indicated they would be at least slightly likely to sign up for a Modify Watch subscription. It's always difficult to judge what people will actually do versus what they say they will do, but this gives a strong indication that a subscription offering is in fact viable. Another great comparison point is that roughly 70% of people said they were at least slightly likely to purchase a Modify Watch, so a subscription offering resonates with a majority of those willing to purchase the product.

Question: If you were to sign up for a watch subscription package, how frequently would you want to receive new watches?

This was a key question in the decision set on creating a subscription offering, and an answer that skewed quite a bit from Modify's initial thinking. Modify had initially planned for a monthly subscription, but respondents indicated that a frequency of 3–9 months might be a much better fit to attract a subscription commitment. Modify believes that gifting watches could be a great reason for people to purchase a more frequent subscription term, but focusing marketing on gifts, and perhaps extending the term out to every two or three months instead of monthly, may be a big win to gain more subscribers and to retain them for longer.

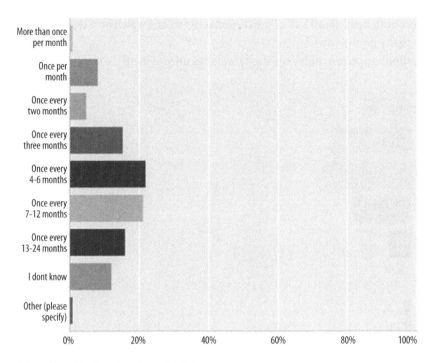

Objective: Understand market sizing

How big is the market?

We know that watches are popular. You are sure to see them on the wrists of most people, but what percentage of the population owns a watch, how many do they own on average, and how many are willing to purchase watches online? The answers to these questions are certain to go into any pitch deck Modify has for investors, and may underpin its market sizing as it builds a financial model to go seize the opportunity.

Question: Do you wear a watch on a daily or frequent basis?

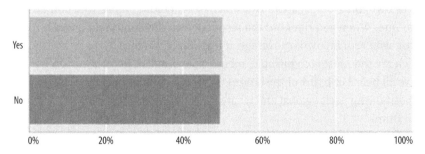

A near dead heat: about half of the respondents wear a watch on a regular basis. But how many do they own?

Question: Approximately how many watches do you own?

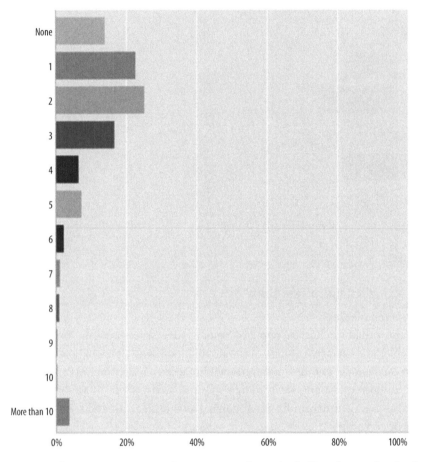

People own, on average, about two watches—including those who don't regularly wear one. When you filter out the respondents who don't wear a watch regularly, those who remain own on average at least three watches.

Which are the most recognizable, memorable brands?

We've all heard of many of the largest major watch manufacturers, but who is Modify positioning itself against and what smaller brands are gaining share that it can learn from?

Question: When you think of watch brands, which brands come to mind?

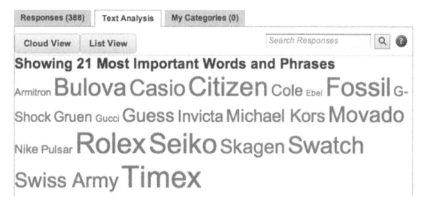

This is a great unaided brand awareness question. Many of the strong brand names show up, with Timex and Rolex leading the way, but lots of interesting companies showed up too, and Modify now has a great baseline to test awareness and see how the landscape shifts over time, and a great way to monitor if any core competitors start to gain market share.

Looking at these three key market questions, we find that watches are relevant to at least half of the population, the majority of whom own at least two watches. From other survey questions, we found that they spend about $70 per watch. So, in the US alone, using those metrics we have more than $20 billion in watches on people's wrists or in their dresser drawers and jewelry cases. If Modify can gain more awareness, there is quite a bit of discretionary money being spent on watches that it may be able to win.

Putting Results into Action

Now that the results are in and have been analyzed and buttoned up, what is Modify going to do to make full use of this great project?

PRICING

Keep it the same. Data indicates that Modify Watches are priced appropriately for its core offering. If anything, Modify has room to increase pricing, but it should keep pricing as affordable as possible as it gains brand awareness and share in its key demographic target areas. Lowering pricing could result in trivializing the brand/product, since potential consumers indicated that pricing was generally about right for the product offering.

BRAND RECOGNITION

As expected, the popular brands are well known. But the landscape seems wide open. This question and set of answers were more important to set a benchmark for future projects than to understand the landscape. However, given the open-ended format of the question, several smaller competitors surfaced, which can be helpful references for Modify to check out pricing and positioning.

DEMOGRAPHICS

Those most likely to purchase a Modify Watch are spread across a wide range, but noticeable clusters emerge that should be the target of new marketing campaigns and product efforts. Target groups for future campaigns and product design initiatives should include or consider:

- *Teenage males and females*: Social media campaigns could be more effective than expected; pop culture watch face designs could resonate.

- *Young males (18–29)*: media formats with high exposure to young males (e.g., men's magazines, gaming sites) could be fruitful; sports or demo-focused watch faces could resonate.

- *Older females (60+)*: TV or other media avenues with a highly female or older demographic could be beneficial; certain colors or designs on faces/bands could resonate.

SUBSCRIPTION VIABILITY

Thumbs up for Modify. Respondents in general, and those who were likely to purchase, seemed to embrace the idea of a subscription. While the cadence of Modify's initial subscription offering (monthly) may be too frequent, moving to a two- to three-month subscription and offering a slight discount off base pricing is likely to be a success, and worth the work involved in pushing out the offering and working through all the billing and marketing projects required.

MARKET SIZING

It's big. No surprises there. Rough stats can peg the watch market at $20bn in watches sitting at home and on wrists. And more importantly, watches are relevant to more than half of Americans, who either own at least one or wear one on a frequent basis. It's not a revelation, but it is hard data that makes creating a pitch deck or advertisement that much easier.

Conclusion

I hope this in-depth case study and discussion on feedback can serve as a helpful template or reference point for any feedback work you may do. There are lots of fantastic web tools that can be used to create, collect, and analyze survey data, and also many ways to find the appropriate respondents to help get you the opinions and feedback you need to accelerate your own decision making and business growth.

The SurveyMonkey survey tool was used to create the survey presented here and analyze the results, and SurveyMonkey Audience was used as the data source.

PART IV

Marketing: Demand Generation and Optimization

19

Very Basic Startup Marketing

Rob Go (http://robgo.org/)

Recently, I was spending some time with an MIT senior who is very involved with the startup community and has spent some time working at venture-funded companies. We were chatting a bit about marketing for early-stage companies. How important is it? Who does it well? Does it even matter? Etc.

She asked a pretty simple question: "What is marketing for a startup, really?"

I was a bit struck by the simplicity of the question. But I think marketing is one of those disciplines that is a bit of a black box to startup founders who come from more of an engineering background. I've heard founders think about marketing both as something that doesn't really matter (since all that matters is the product), and something that matters a lot and requires hiring a fancy CMO or VP of Marketing.

I disagree with both of these paths, but that's for another post. In a nutshell, here is the basic way I think about marketing for startups.

Marketing as a Funnel

First, I think of marketing as a funnel. It can be a very basic funnel, but you can drill down to much more specific subcomponents of the funnel. At the highest level, I see it as: Awareness –> Conversion –> Raving Fans. Let's look at a couple examples of each.

AWARENESS: HOW PEOPLE FIRST HEAR ABOUT YOUR COMPANY

- For starters, this usually means a referral from an existing user, PR, or ways that the product talks about itself (e.g., "posted by Instagram" on Facebook).

- A big part of awareness to me is crisp positioning. Potential users need to "get it" right away. You'll spend 30 minutes reading about each great feature of a new Apple product. But you'll only spend 10 seconds trying to understand a new no-name product that someone tells you about.

- The product impacts awareness, which seems strange given that awareness happens before trial.

- The challenge for startups is how to create broad awareness with limited resources. When Gillette launches a new razor, it spends millions to make sure that in short time, every male knows about it. As a startup, you have to focus on cheap awareness channels and get the most value out of your efforts/dollars. This usually means focusing on a narrow user segment that has a particularly strong need for your product, and expanding from there.

CONVERSION: GETTING PEOPLE WHO ARE AWARE TO TAKE ACTION

- Most of the stuff on startup marketing is about this part—getting people to hit your web page, try your product, come back and engage, and ultimately pay. There are tons of great resources on this on the Web. David Skok's blog (*http://www.forentrepreneurs.com/*), for example, is one of the best for SaaS marketing.

- But, I think optimizing conversion can be a red herring for early-stage companies early on. Some of our fascination with conversion stems from the desire to analyze and measure stuff. But without enough traffic, testing conversion is meaningless. It's fun to optimize conversion because it's concrete and rewarding. But be mindful about whether this effort is a big rock or a small rock (*http://robgo.org/2010/03/08/the-most-important-lesson-ive-learned/*).

RAVING FANS: GETTING CUSTOMERS TO LOVE YOU AND BE EVANGELISTS

- The best marketing comes from customer success. That's why I think it's incredibly important that the functions of product and marketing not be thought of as two silos. The job is not done when you've gotten someone to pay. It is done when you have delighted a customer to the point that they can't help but tell others about you.

- You want to make it really easy for customers to evangelize for you. Referral links need to work really well, and incentives should feel like a win-win. Again, the value proposition needs to be very crisp, and easy. That's why it's often best for startups to deliver simple services with discrete value propositions even at the expense of being fully featured.

- This is why "Swiss Army knife" products rarely work. You hopefully create a raving fan by being an amazing scalpel for a particular problem. Then, that person will tell everyone else who needs a scalpel that you are a great solution. Then, people who've heard the same recommendation 3–5 times will finally give you a try. That's much harder to achieve if you are trying to be all things for all people.

Marketing as Understanding

So, that's marketing as a funnel. Next, I think of marketing as understanding your customers. And I mean really understanding them. It's not a box to check—let's do 10 customer interviews and we're done. It a continuous process that goes very deep. That's why most early-stage companies find success when the founders are solving problems that stem from authentic experiences.

A big part of understanding your customers is understanding customer segmentation. For an early-stage company, the most important goal is creating raving fans out of some market segment. And when you are starting, narrowly defining your target segment is okay. VCs may beat you up about "how big that market is," but you have a much better chance of success by winning a narrow segment first and broadening rather than taking a shotgun to the entire market. That's why I always cringe when I see companies talk about their customers as "everyone that is computer literate, aged 25–60, with incomes over $50k." That is not segmentation.

Marketing as a Cycle

Third, I think of marketing as a cycle that evolves. It's not a machine that you build and then set and forget, nor is it a black box of unfocused activities. Very early on, you might focus quite broadly on driving awareness in a bunch of customer segments to see what sticks. You may later choose to go very, very narrow with your marketing once you've got a hunch that a particular segment is promising. You might also lean in on one or two tactics that really work to drive low-cost customers to your service. But over time, that channel may change, dry up, or get expensive, so you need to always be experimenting with new channels and tactics. You need to have the instrumentation to keep a pulse on your marketing machine and know what's going on. But you have to continuously experiment and be creative at the same time.

It's also both a macro and a micro cycle. Even at the level of individual marketing campaigns, the cycle of hypothesis, testing, measurement, and iteration happens. And for Internet-based businesses, this is happening faster and faster. This is why, often, classically trained marketers at large consumer products companies struggle greatly when they start competing in Internet businesses. The cycles of iteration are so much faster, and your resources so much more constrained.

So, that's it from a high level:

1. Marketing is a funnel of awareness –> conversion –> raving fans.

2. Marketing is about understanding your customers deeply.

3. Marketing is a cycle that constantly evolves.

20

The Ultimate Guide to Startup Marketing

Renee Warren (http://blog.kissmetrics.com/ultimate-guide-startup-marketing/)

Starting a business is exhilarating. Unfortunately, the "build it and they will come" theory doesn't hold much weight, and those overnight success stories you hear about are often the result of (behind the scenes) years of hard work. Simply put, startup marketing is often a unique challenge because of limited resources, whether it's time, money, or talent.

You have to be sure every effort, no matter how small, is well planned and flawlessly executed. And to make it even more difficult, the traditional marketing strategies don't always work.

Startup marketing is a whole different science. How so? The secret is properly combining the right channels: *content marketing and PR.*

So, starting from the beginning, here's the complete Startup Marketing Manual.

Foundation

Before you start laying bricks, you need a solid foundation. A successful startup marketing strategy follows that same principle. Before you jump into marketing your startup, make sure you have the following bases covered.

1. CHOOSING A MARKET

It's easy for startup founders to believe the whole world will love their products. After all, founders eat, sleep, and breathe their products. The reality is that only a small portion of the population is interested in your product.

If you try to market your startup to everyone, you waste both time and money. The key is to identify a niche target market and go after market share aggressively.

How do you choose a market? There are four main factors to consider:

1. *Market size*: Are you targeting a regional demographic? Males? Children? Know exactly how many potential customers are in your target market.
2. *Market wealth*: Does this market have the money to spend on your product?
3. *Market competition*: Is the market saturated? As in, are there many competitors?
4. *Value proposition*: Is your value proposition unique enough to cut through the noise?

2. DEFINING KEYWORDS

With a clearly defined market, you can begin building a keyword list. You'll use the keyword list primarily for blogging, social media, and your main marketing site. Essentially, you want to build a list of words or phrases that are highly relevant to your brand. Ask yourself this: what would someone type into Google to find your startup's website?

Start with a core keyword list. This is a list of three to five keywords that completely summarize what your startup does. For example, Onboardly (*http://onboard ly.com/*)'s core keyword list is: *customer acquisition, content marketing*, and *startup PR*. Your core keyword list should be based on your value proposition. What is it that you're offering customers?

Note

Your core keywords make excellent blog categories.

Now you'll want to expand your core keyword list to include secondary keywords. Secondary keywords are more specific. Take the core keyword "content marketing," for example. Secondary keywords might include: *corporate blogging, blogging best practices, email marketing how to*, etc.

Use free tools to find the keywords already sending traffic to your website. Then run your core keywords through Google's Keyword Tool (*https://adwords.google.com/ o/KeywordTool*) and Übersuggest (*http://ubersuggest.org/*). The best keywords found through those tools will be identified by *low competition* and *high traffic*. In other words, a lot of people are searching for them, but few results are displayed.

3. DEFINING SUCCESS

Success is different for every startup. Maybe success is 500 new signups per month for Startup A, while Startup B thinks success is $50,000 in revenue per month. Whatever your idea of success may be, define it early and define it rigidly. *Write it down or send it to the entire team.* Just make sure everyone you're working with knows your definition of success and is prepared to work toward it.

Be sure to stay consistent. It doesn't matter if you're defining success by sign-ups, revenue, profit, or anything else you can think of. What does matter is that it's tied to real growth (no vanity successes (*http://blog.kissmetrics.com/throw-away-vanity-metrics/*)) and that it's measured the same way each month. For example, don't define success as 500 new signups one month and then $50,000 in revenue the next. Pick one definition and commit to it.

4. SETTING CORE METRICS

Just as you shouldn't indulge vanity success, you shouldn't indulge vanity metrics. Eric Ries (*http://techcrunch.com/2011/09/24/founder-stories-eric-ries-vanity-metrics/*) refers to working with vanity metrics as playing in "success theater." While vanity metrics are appealing, if only to your ego, they are useless. They are not tied to real growth, meaning you won't know if your startup is a roaring success or a total flop until it's far too late.

Be sure your core metrics are accurately measurable and specific. For example, let's assume you've defined success as 500 new signups per month. You might measure the conversion rate of three calls to sign up. The idea is to have a few highly valuable metrics based on actions taken throughout the customer acquisition fun-nel (e.g., signups, newsletter subscriptions, ebook downloads). Don't try to measure everything. Focus on the key indicators of success.

Note

Record baseline metrics right away so you can easily determine your growth.

5. ESTIMATING A CONVERSION RATE

The next step is to assign conversion rates and values. Consider newsletter signups, for example. A hundred new newsletter signups per month could be incredible growth if your conversion rate is 20% (that is, if 20% of your newsletter subscribers become paying customers). If your conversion rate is closer to 1%, those 100 newsletter signups might be insignificant.

Estimate (based on historical data) your lead conversion rate. Now do the same to estimate the lifetime value of a customer. If you know how many of your leads convert and how much those conversions generate for your startup, you can assign values to goal completions like newsletter signups. Getting $2,500 per month from your newsletter is a lot more indicative of success than 100 new newsletter signups.

6. SETTING A BUDGET

At the end of the day, it all comes down to the money. How much can you afford to spend on your startup marketing strategy? Remember that while inbound marketing leads cost 61% less (*http://blog.hubspot.com/blog/tabid/6307/bid/31555/ Inbound-Leads-Cost-61-Less-Than-Outbound-New-Data.aspx*) than outbound marketing leads, they are not free. Set a budget early in the game and accept that limitation.

> *57% of startup marketing managers are not basing their marketing budgets on any ROI analysis. (http://www.iab.net/media/file/2012-BRITE-NYAMA-Marketing-ROI-Study.pdf)*

More importantly, carefully plan how you intend to divide that budget. Maybe your blog has been your most powerful tool to date and you want to invest 40% of the budget on it. Or maybe you want to spend 35% of the budget to develop a new ebook or online course. Just be sure you have the logistics settled before you start spending (or you might just lose your hat).

Social Media

Social media is one of the most popular (*http://blog.hubspot.com/blog/tabid/ 6307/bid/32985/20-Revealing-Stats-Charts-and-Graphs-Every-Marketer-Should-*

Know.aspx) ways to promote your content and reach influencers. Since a great content promotion plan brings potential customers to your website and influencing the influencer can generate thousands of new leads, social media is invaluable to startups. Of course, there are a few tricks to get the most out of it.

1. CHOOSING THE RIGHT SOCIAL MEDIA NETWORKS

Startups tend to choose the social media networks they engage with without much strategy. The two most common mistakes are trying to master every network and trying to master certain networks just because the competition is doing it. If all of your competitors are on Facebook, Twitter, and LinkedIn, you should be too, right? Maybe, but maybe not.

Facebook, Twitter, LinkedIn, Tumblr, Reddit, Pinterest, and now Instagram are some of the most popular social networks today. All of them can be great content-promotion and community-building tools, but they all have unique characteristics. Facebook, for example, is typically powered by your existing customers, who enjoy visual posts like pictures and videos. Twitter, on the other hand, is often powered by potential customers who respond well to links (e.g., blog links).

Each social network "works" differently—as in, how the community takes, interprets, and digests your sharing and content varies. Reddit is often referred to as a very guarded network and detests spammers. Unlike Twitter, here you can't just schedule various messages every day. The content you share on Reddit has to be specific and unique to the categories you choose. Reddit, like other networks, requires a slower approach. You can't just jump on, run some ads, and expect people to upvote all your content. Be mindful of the network and community you are trying to reach, as it may not be in the social space you first thought.

Note

Consider the demographic of the social network itself. Take Tumblr, for example. Tumblr caters to a young, laid-back audience that loves sharing inspiring quotes and funny pictures. If you're targeting this audience, don't spend your time on LinkedIn.

2. DEFINING THE BEST TIMES TO POST

The idea that there is a perfect time to post a tweet or Facebook update is a myth. If you're targeting teenagers, mornings and nights might be the best times to post during the school year. During the summer? That's a whole other story. There simply is no universal "perfect time to post." There are, however, some best practices (according to Dan Zarella (*http://danzarrella.com/*)).

Facebook:

- Saturdays are best.
- 12 p.m. EST is the best time to share.
- 0.5 posts per day is the best frequency.

Twitter:

- 5 p.m. EST is the best time to get a retweet.
- One to four link tweets per hour is the best frequency.
- Tuesdays, Wednesdays, Thursdays, Saturdays, and Sundays are best.
- 6 a.m. EST, 12 p.m. EST, and 6 p.m. EST are the best times to tweet in terms of clicks.

3. USING A KEYWORD LIST

Now it's time to put that keyword list you created earlier to good use. When it comes to social media, you'll use your keyword list to maximize your engagement efforts. If you're marketing an online shopping club for families like MarilynJean (*http://www.marilynjean.com/index.php*), you'll want to ensure you're having family and shopping focused discussions on social media.

The easiest way to do this is to use a social networking management tool like HootSuite (*http://hootsuite.com/*). That way you can set up search streams of your core keywords. Using MarilynJean as an example, one of its streams might be for the keyword "online shopping club." It'll be able to monitor all of the conversations happening around that keyword and join in. More importantly, MarilynJean will solidify a reputation in the space.

Note
Use your keyword list to help target any online ads you may be running.

4. CREATING AND USING AN INFLUENCER LIST

As mentioned earlier, one of the best marketing techniques online is to influence the influencer. It will take a long time for your startup to develop a highly influential relationship with thousands of people. Instead, focus on connecting with the people who already have that influence.

> 78% of social media users (http://www.marketingprofs.com/charts/2012/7850/brands-posts-rival-friends-in-social-media-influence) said posts by brands "influenced their purchase behavior moderately or highly."

For example, MarilynJean might look to connect with a famous celebrity mother via Twitter. If that mom loves what the company is doing for families and tweets about it to thousands (if not millions) of loyal followers, MarilynJean will see a huge surge in both followers and traffic.

Note

Journalists and community leaders are great influencers as well. Don't limit yourself to celebrities, who can be very tricky to connect with.

Build your influencer list with a bit of market research. Start by finding popular blogs in the space. Who writes for those blogs? Who owns them? Search for your core keywords on Twitter. Who appears in the results? Who are they following?

Remember that a high follower count is not always a good indication of influence. Look for how engaged the people's followers are and their follower to following ratio.

5. SETTING UP A BLOG

Setting up a blog can be quite simple. It's a matter of downloading the software, uploading it to your server, and following the setup instructions. WordPress (http://wordpress.com/), for example, is free and offers many amazing plug-ins. One example is Yoast SEO (http://wordpress.org/extend/plugins/wordpress-seo/), a plug-in that will help Google and other search engines locate and rank your content. (Other great plug-ins include Akismet, Calendar, and featured posts.). Start by installing Yoast, then set up the basics like blog categories and tags.

Once the backend of your blog is ready to go, think about the curb appeal. How does your design look? Ask a professional designer to help you design your blog or give it a small revamp. Then invite 10 friends to check out the design and offer feedback. You'll get a feel for the aesthetic appeal. Remember, design is important as it relates to the user experience, but it shouldn't be all-consuming. Your blog is about publishing really great content, at the right time, to the right people. Your design should simply enhance that experience.

Be sure your design is also functional. Ask yourself these questions:

- If I stand back and squint my eyes, does my call to action still pop?
- Do I have search functionality?
- Do I have social media information and sharing functions (e.g., Twitter feed, Facebook plug-in)?
- Do I have a blog subscription and RSS feed option?
- Do I have featured images on my blog's home page?
- Do I have social sharing buttons on each blog post?

Note

While WordPress is not the only blogging platform, it is one of the most widely used.

Startup PR

PR remains a mystery in many startup circles.

When's the right time to tell people about your startup? Is there value in getting early coverage on industry blogs? What message is going to resonate with writers? How can you maximize the press coverage you do get and translate it into sales? Should you hire a PR firm to help you out?

The good news is it doesn't need to be such a mystery. Fundamentally, it all boils down to this:

- What to say
- When to say it
- Who to say it to

1. CRAFT MEANINGFUL POSITIONING STATEMENTS

Much like a great elevator pitch should lie in the mind of any entrepreneur, a series of engaging positioning statements is vital. And while constructing two sentences may seem easy, crafting effective statements is quite the challenge.

Start by identifying what the product is and how it will affect others. Think of the product as a solution created to solve a worldwide problem. This is an important measure to remember when marketing and selling the product. Don't think of it as selling a product. Think of it as solving a problem. Lastly, who will care about your product?

- What is your product?
- How will it affect others?
- Who will care?

Positioning statements combine these three key factors into two sentences that are used to market the product and pitch it to the media. To ensure success, it is important not only that these statements articulate what the product is capable of, but that they clearly describe its value proposition as well.

2. DEFINE YOUR STARTUP SENSITIVITIES

> *"Keep your friends close and your enemies closer."*
>
> —Sun Tzu

By identifying competitors' strengths and weaknesses, one can better understand how to market one's product as better. Why is your solution to the universal problem your product solves better than those before it?

Be creative. Use spreadsheets, visual imagery, or lists. Harness all of the information available on the product and its competitors, and study it. Look at each product closely and determine its strengths and weaknesses. If there are others who have an edge, then look at an angle where they are lacking.

Creating "the next social network for penguins" might be your ultimate passion, but be conscious of the fact that you've got a remarkably short span of time to engage writers when pitching them. Focus on the one (or two) strongest aspects of your value proposition (what your customers love about you most) and lean heavily on those hooks to gauge media interest.

3. IDENTIFYING THE RIGHT WRITERS FOR A MEDIA LIST

"Build your network before you need them."

—Jeremiah Owyang (https://twitter.com/jowyang), Partner and Industry Analyst at Altimeter Group

The importance of identifying who will care about the product is not only relevant in terms of crafting positioning statements, but in identifying the right writers for a media list as well. Any media outlet employs a number of qualified writers capable of telling the story, but you should be careful to pitch only writers who will be the best fit for your product. Though time-consuming, this simple step should never be overlooked.

Determine key media outlets of interest, then search for stories with similar themes or relevance to your own. Look at the writers who've covered those stories.

Always pitch the right writer for your story. For example, if your product is exclusively for iPhone, don't pitch a journalist who only reports on Android products.

Once you have identified the writers to connect with, utilize social media to engage with them. Build relationships and ask nothing of them. Set up private Twitter lists of the writers of interest, and actively respond to them and retweet their posts. Make friends with them!

Relationships with writers are not always easy to build, but the effort you put in to achieve them can mean great story coverage and the opportunity to be covered again in the future. Even if you are not in a position to leverage journalists or writers, you should still be connecting and making those relationships. In due time, they will always benefit you and your startup.

4. CREATING A PRESS KIT

The key to a successful media launch is rooted deep within a killer media kit. Begin by identifying the items needed:

- Media advisory
- Logos and screenshots
- Founder bios and photos

A media advisory should include all major points that are important to the product, the company, and its success. It should include how the product is changing the world and why it is important. More importantly, it should be written for and directed toward people who will care. The "pitch" should be included in the headline and/or the first paragraph of the release. This is an excellent opportunity to use your positioning statements from earlier.

Include brief and necessary background information on the company and its founders—enough to offer a taste of the team behind the product. By offering quick stats at the end of the media advisory, you give writers a brief snapshot of the company. Include the following:

- Company name
- Website
- Twitter handle(s)
- CEO and cofounders
- Launch date (if applicable)
- Fees (if applicable)

Be conscious of time restrictions or sensitivities. Is there an embargo present or a set launch date and time?

Remember, most writers will merely skim a media advisory. By ensuring that your media advisory is tight and effective, you'll increase the chances of story coverage.

Always offer the media options to use as supplementary visuals to accompany the story. Include the company logo(s) and relevant screenshots of the product. Anything that offers a glimpse of features and capabilities is appreciated.

Provide a brief biography of each founder, and their respective photos. Who are the driving forces behind the company, and how have their beliefs shaped it to become the success it is now? Include any tidbits of information that writers could use.

An important takeaway is that your press kit can be your ultimate weapon in securing great coverage. We recommend using a personalized Dropbox (*https://www.dropbox.com/*) folder or Google Drive (*https://www.google.com/intl/en_US/drive/start/index.html?authuser=0*) for each journalist you approach so that you can easily share by inviting them to the folder. You'll also be able to see when they join or view the folder, confirming interest—and hopefully that a story is about to be written.

5. REACHING OUT TO JOURNALISTS

Engagement with journalists prior to reaching out is key. When interacting with writers beforehand, you should request to send information on a story that may interest them. As previously mentioned, by building a relationship first, you ensure that this request doesn't come off as insincere. Writers may still decline, but by continuing to build on the relationship created, you could potentially convince them to accept in the future.

Content Creation

With a blog set up and your PR in full swing, it's time to kick content creation into high gear. Managing a blog and other forms of content can seem daunting, especially to not-so-great writers. Fortunately, four little steps will give startups the information they need to get serious.

1. CREATING A TOPIC LIST

You've got a good-looking blog designed and a great content promotion strategy, but something's missing. Oh right! The content.

Before you dive right in and start writing, create a topic list. The perfect topic list is based on your core keywords for SEO purposes. Using your core keywords on your blog builds your startup's credibility with search engines. Start by brainstorming 10 topic ideas around each of your core keywords. Where possible, use your keywords in the titles, but not where it feels unnatural.

With between 30 and 50 topics, you can start thinking about writing. But first, put all of these ideas into a calendar. When will each be published? Who will write them? Are any of them in progress? A blog calendar helps you track your topics from conception to completion. Gantt charts are often shrugged off, but for the purpose of properly managing an editorial schedule, they are extremely helpful. Check out the multitude of templates and spreadsheets available for free online, like a 90-day calendar (*https://drive.google.com/templates?q=calendar&pli=1*), a Google Doc template, or these free guides (*http://www.bobangus.com/free-editorial-calendar-template/*) from Bob Angus.

Note

Be sure to add descriptions to your topic ideas. You might not remember your main points when you go to write the post three months from now.

2. KNOWING WHAT TYPES OF CONTENT TO PUBLISH

> *"Information products have the best margins. If you can get them into a subscription, then you'll have monthly reoccurring revenue."*
>
> —Dan Martell (https://twitter.com/danmartell), Founder of Clarity

There are four main types of content to be published (excluding blog content). Like social networks, each one has unique advantages and disadvantages. Consider your options carefully, always keeping your target market in mind. And remember: *don't try to do a little bit of everything right away.*

The content options are:

- *Ebook/guide*: Information products are huge. Offer a free ebook in exchange for a name and email address. Just like that, you have a new lead. You know they're interested in your product because they were interested in the ebook, and now you have their contact information. Now, follow up. Ask their opinion of the ebook and open the door for conversation.

- *Webinar*: Hearing your voice and engaging with you live gives your customers (and potential customers) a sense of ease. Webinars (*http://www.gotomeeting.co.uk/fec/webinar*) capitalize on this! Cross-promote your webinar on your blog. Also, have someone on your team live tweet during the webinar using a custom #hashtag. At the end of the webinar, after providing real value to the attendees, post your contact information. It's a simple, interactive way to generate new leads.

- *Newsletter*: Email marketing is far from dead, despite what you might have read. Make subscribing to your newsletter quick and easy. Don't go overboard with your email blasts, though, because if you overuse the connection, you'll lose it. For the same reason, you'll want to ensure every newsletter offers real value and is not just an excuse to push a new product. Try offering a discount, a promotion, industry news, or a contest—whatever!

- *Video*: If a picture is worth a thousand words, imagine how much a video is worth. Keep it simple by having an explainer video created or by shooting an introduction video. Put the video on your startup's home page and/or blog. You might be camera-shy, but statistics show that most people would rather watch than read.

3. GUEST BLOGGING

Guest blogging is vital for startups. First of all, guest posting on a popular blog is a great way to build your reputation in the space. Second, having someone influential guest blog on your startup's blog is an easy way to drive traffic.

Start by looking for outgoing guest blogging opportunities (*http://blog.kissmet rics.com/guest-blogging-for-kissmetrics/*) on the top blogs that are writing for your target market. Most blogs will accept guest posts openly, so look for a writers' page or contributors' page. If you're having trouble, track down the blog owner or editor on social media. Ask to email him a first draft of your blog post idea. Just make sure it's high quality and 100% original.

Once you've built a reputation, it will be easier to find influencers willing to contribute to your startup's blog. Create a writers' page of your own or reach out to select influencers individually via social media or email. When the guest post is published, be sure to ping the contributor so she can promote the post to her whole network.

4. CAPTURING EMAILS

Email subscription has been mentioned a few times already. Capturing emails can be divided into three categories: email submits, newsletter subscriptions, and blog subscriptions. Email submits could come from ebook downloads or similar offers. Newsletter subscriptions are just that: people interested in reading regular updates and content from your startup. Blog subscriptions are straightforward as well.

Email submits and newsletter subscriptions are best managed by tools like MailChimp (*http://mailchimp.com/*), which allows you to easily send well-designed custom emails to leads. Blog subscriptions, on the other hand, are best managed by tools like Feedburner (*http://feedburner.google.com/*), which allows you to automatically notify leads when you published new blog content.

Test and Iterate

By now, your marketing strategy is in full motion. Of course, no one gets it perfect on the first try, and there's always room for improvement. That's where testing and iteration come into play. Remember back to the core metrics and definition of success from earlier. Keep those two things in mind here.

1. SETTING UP ANALYTICS TOOLS

The key to measuring success is a great analytics tool. If you need a no-frills solution, check out Google Analytics *(http://www.google.com/analytics/)*. It'll give you the basics and, over time, you will learn to master the somewhat complicated behind-the-scenes mechanics of it. If you want something more user-friendly and advanced, tools like KISSmetrics *(https://www.kissmetrics.com/)* are always available.

Your experience setting up your analytics tool will be different depending on the solution you choose. However, all analytics tools will have you insert a snippet of code on your web pages, which allows them to track visits and events. Be sure to look for analytics tools that are committed to preserving fast load times, like Measurely *(http://measurely.com/)*. Some codes leave visitors waiting for the website to load, which can increase the bounce rate dramatically.

2. MEASURING AGAINST BENCHMARKS

> *"If you can't measure it, you can't manage it."*
>
> —Peter Drucker, Management Consultant

Earlier, you recorded your baseline metrics, which you'll use as benchmarks going forward. Ideally, you're measuring week-over-week and month-over-month growth. If you make the mistake of waiting for solely month-over-month data, you could be too late. Each week, compare your core metrics to the week before. Some give and take is normal. Each month, do the same. Here, you should look for consistent growth.

When you see significant growth or decline, be sure to attribute it to some event(s): for example, a tweet that went viral or a newsletter that was a huge disaster.

Isolate what you did differently and either replicate it or avoid it going forward. Don't just measure your data—act on it!

3. BRAINSTORMING CREATIVE NEW IDEAS

While tweaking what you're already doing is great, coming up with brand new ideas is even better. It's not enough to only iterate and optimize what you've been doing. The most successful startups are always trying creative new things. Maybe a social contest, a funny video, a new online course, a clever PR angle—the list is endless.

Many of your new and innovative ideas can easily fail, but the few that succeed will be well worth it. Never get complacent! As a startup, the name of the game is agility, flexibility, and thinking forward.

Best Practices

What are the industry experts saying? What are the top startups doing? Here are three startup marketing best practices.

1. SELL THE SOLUTION

Too many startups focus on the problem instead of the solution. It makes sense, of course. Founders design a solution for the problem, which makes the problem a founder's first love. Unfortunately, it's the solution that appeals to potential customers. Realistically, there are hundreds of products that could solve the problem of, for example, low productivity. What makes your solution the perfect choice?

2. HAVE A COMPELLING STORY

Storytelling is a powerful sales tool. Just ask Seth Godin (*http://www.sethgodin.com/sg/*)! If you have a compelling story, use it. How did you come up with your solution? Did you struggle in the beginning? Are you still struggling? Use your story to differentiate yourself from the competition. Startup marketing is all about the customer and establishing an authentic relationship. Having a relatable story to tell is a fast track to success.

3. USE ALL YOUR RESOURCES

Your team is arguably one of your biggest marketing tools. Their passion for what your startup is doing is called *evangelism*. Use it to your advantage. Send them out into the world excited to tell your startup's story to anyone they meet. But don't stop there. Ride the buzz from a trending topic by writing a blog post on it or creating a video about it. Run a contest around a major holiday to drum up some hype. Be sure you're not overlooking any marketing resources, big or small.

Conclusion

Startup marketing is a complex science. Some great ideas have failed due to a lack of media attention and customer awareness. Others have gone under thanks to a poor strategy. Still, other great ideas have spiraled to billion-dollar fame! Well, founders everywhere can stop searching for that elusive secret to startup marketing success. It's simply the sweet spot between content marketing and PR.

21

What the Highest-Converting Websites Do Differently

Zach Bulygo
and Sean Work (http://blog.kissmetrics.com/)

Did you know that companies that take on a structured approach toward conversion optimization are twice as likely to see a large increase in sales (*http://econsultan cy.com/fr/reports/conversion-rate-optimization-report*)?

Given this, you'd think more companies would test and run experiments. Yet 61% of companies do less than five tests per month (*http://www.slideshare.net/ Emerce/emerce-performance-bryan-eisenberg*).

My gut tells me the reason for this is that *most* companies are too caught up in the "business as usual syndrome," and they rarely take a second to stop and think about really focusing on conversion optimization.

In this post we're going to go over what the highest-converting websites do differently. But before we get into the details, we want to highlight a few points to get you thinking:

- You have 0–8 seconds (*http://www.interactivemarketinginc.com/landing-pages.html*) to make a compelling headline and landing page. After 8 seconds, the majority of visitors leave.

- Approximately 96% of visitors (*http://blog.hubspot.com/blog/tabid/6307/bid/ 31097/12-Critical-Elements-Every-Homepage-Must-Have-Infographic.aspx*) that come to your website are not ready to buy.

- The more landing pages (*http://blog.hubspot.com/blog/tabid/6307/bid/15424/ The-Key-to-More-Leads-Create-More-Targeted-Conversion-Opportunities-Data.aspx*) you have, the more leads you are likely to get.

- Product videos can increase purchases of the product by 144% (*http://www.inter netretailer.com/2011/03/07/product-videos-raise-purchase-likelihood-stacks-and-stacks*).

- A 1-second delay in your site speed can result in a 7% reduction in conversions (*http://blog.kissmetrics.com/loading-time/?wide=1*).

- A/B testing (*http://econsultancy.com/fr/reports/conversion-rate-optimization-report*) is becoming the preferred testing method and has brought a lot of companies the most success.

Got that? Okay, let's get into what the best do differently....

1. They Make Their Unique Value Proposition(s) Clear

Visitors should clearly see on your home page or landing page why they should do business with you and the benefit of it.

A great example of this is MailChimp (*http://mailchimp.com/*):

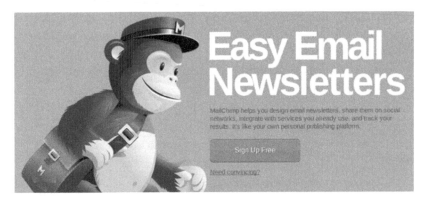

There are plenty of email service providers out there, so for a company like MailChimp it's quite difficult to differentiate yourself from the pack. MailChimp made itself different by focusing on making email campaigns *easy*.

If you think about it, who's usually tasked with sending out the email newsletter? It's usually someone whose specialty is not marketing, who's not technical, and who has a never-ending "to-do" list. Making it easy is really important!

And looking at the home page, MailChimp makes this very clear:

Not to mention, if you have ever used the service, everything from campaign creation to sending out your emails is really simple and clear.

Another example is Helzberg Diamonds (*http://www.helzberg.com/*). They are a little more subtle about their USP, but they definitely address why you should buy from them.

For example, they state free shipping on orders over $149:

Scroll down the page a little bit, and you'll see some reassurances:

Welcome to Helzberg

Since 1915, Helzberg Diamonds has been committed to providing our customers with unparalleled customer service, industry expertise and custom jewelry that makes that special someone say, "I Am Loved."

👍 Like   12266 likes. Sign Up to see what your friends like.

Quality & Expertise

(AGS) Our AGS membership & GIA certification ensures you'll get the best service, education and quality. *Learn more* ▸

Shipping & Returns

Our FREE shipping and 60-day FREE return and exchange policy means no-risk shopping. *Learn more* ▸

Certainly having 12,266 fans on Facebook doesn't hurt their conversion rate, either.

What are the reasons customers should buy from you? Do you offer a money-back guarantee? Free shipping? Identify your selling points and make them clear.

2. They Test Their Calls to Action

HubSpot (*http://www.hubspot.com/*) featured a company on its blog that increased its conversions by 105.9% (*http://blog.hubspot.com/blog/tabid/6307/bid/31104/Extreme-Homepage-Makeover-How-to-Increase-Your-Conversion-Rate-106.aspx*) by having a clear call to action that leads to a whitepaper. In this whitepaper, the company informs the visitor about the company and what it offers.

The company also made a more effective headline and used meaningful graphics to help guide the user. Just these three changes led to more than doubling the conversion rate.

Mozilla increased downloads (*http://blog.mozilla.org/metrics/2008/11/21/ changing-the-firefox-download-button/*) of its popular Firefox browser by having a stronger call to action. "Download Now – Free" performed better than "Try Firefox 3". The new call to action made it clear that Firefox was free and invited the viewer to download the program.

ProFlowers (*http://www.proflowers.com/*) is a site known for high conversion rates, with some estimates being around 40%. The site makes it really easy for customers who are in a hurry to buy flowers—they can start by simply picking the day they need the flowers by:

ProFlowers eliminates any initial questions that the prospect may have. The prospect knows right away the answer to the question, "Can you get this to me by xxx?" The site helps to overcome any obstacles to a purchase. See if you can do something like ProFlowers has done—answer one of your most popular questions in a clear, above-the-fold headline. If a potential obstacle to prospects purchasing from you is "I don't feel comfortable purchasing from a small company like yours," some ideas to help overcome this fear could be:

- Include a behind-the-scenes video of your company and how your operations work.
- Include a banner at the top of the page with customer testimonials, each one showing for a few seconds.
- Give your unique value proposition right at the top. Tell how long you've been in business, how many orders you've shipped, your customer satisfaction rate, etc.

HOW DO YOU FIND OUT WHAT QUESTIONS YOUR CUSTOMERS HAVE?

You should always be asking your customers questions to get their feedback. Understanding your customers' pain points, points of confusion, and what they are really looking for can help you design a site with a higher conversion rate. KISSinsights (*https://qualaroo.com/*) is a tool that allows you to do just that:

3. They Test Their Headlines

The headline can make or break your website, and possibly a sale. As mentioned earlier, the first impression is formed quickly, and the headline is a big part of that impression. It's important to test and see what resonates most with your visitors. There is no magic formula, but there are some good guidelines that you can follow.

37signals (*http://37signals.com/*) improved conversions of its Highrise product by 30% (*http://37signals.com/svn/posts/1525-writing-decisions-headline-tests-on-the-highrise-signup-page*) by having the headline "30-day Free Trial on All Accounts." Its worst-performing headline was "Start a Highrise Account."

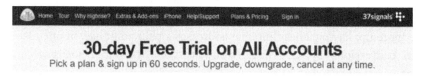

The key lesson from this is that it's important to have a clear headline with a unique value proposition. "Start a Highrise Account" doesn't tell of any benefit. It doesn't give a reason why prospects should sign up *now*. Consider adding "free trial" in your headline, or try "Save xx% and start [enter the benefit of your product here]." The important thing is to test to see what works.

CityCliq (*http://www.citycliq.com/*) improved its conversions (*http://visualwebsi teoptimizer.com/split-testing-blog/using-ab-split-testing-to-refine-your-startups-positioning-90-increase-in-conversion-rate/*) by making a clear headline that tells the users what they'll get. First, the tested headlines:

- Businesses grow faster online!

- Online advertising that works!
- Get found faster!
- Create a webpage for your business.

The winner:

This is the best headline because it's clear and avoids any language that you may find in your spam folder. Be creative with your headlines and inform the visitor of what you do or the benefits of your product.

One more tip: having a headline that addresses a pain point has, in one case, increased conversions by 32% (*http://www.abtests.com/test/99001/homepage-for-carelogger*).

4. They Tend To Have Short Forms

Conversion expert Tim Ash recommends keeping forms to only the essentials (*http://blog.milestoneinternet.com/website-promotion/ppc_landing_page/*). How many times have you been ready to sign up for something, only to see 25+ fields that you have to fill in? I have many times, and I'll often just leave the site. It's important to respect the users' time. If you've gotten the users as far as wanting to sign up, it's pivotal that you don't let them drop off because your form is too long.

Take a look at Dropbox (*https://www.dropbox.com/*)'s signup form:

Create an account (or sign in)

First name

Last name

Email

Password

☐ I agree to Dropbox Terms

Create account

Dropbox is only asking for what it needs. No username, no security questions, no birth date, no verification code, no re-enter password field, nothing unneeded.

ProFlowers doesn't even force you to sign up before you order. If you're a first-time buyer, the buying process is not interrupted at all. You don't have to create a new account; you have the option to do that *after* you make your purchase. ProFlowers is removing any obstacles to ordering.

Building more concise forms is important (*http://www.imagescape.com/clients-like-you/contact-form/*).

TEST THE NUMBER OF FORM FIELDS

Most conversion experts will agree that simplifying forms and making them clearer should be the direction you aim for when you're ready to start iterating.

Sometimes, having more fields can improve your form conversion rate. However, in general, fewer fields tend to produce better conversions (it depends on what your form is for). The point is, don't look for rules of thumb; test and find out for yourself!

OTHER TECHNIQUES TO TRY

- Implementing a "Chat Now" button increased free signup form fills by 31% (*http://visualwebsiteoptimizer.com/split-testing-blog/live-chat-increases-signups/*).
- Cars.com recently boosted its conversion rate by 2.7% (*http://www.internetretailer.com/2012/03/15/carscom-boosts-its-conversion-rate-security-seal*) by having a security seal on its site.
- Including discount information in the title (e.g., 15% off) increased add-to-cart conversions by 148.3% (*http://www.abtests.com/test/263001/product-for-the-corkscrew-wine-merchants*).
- Benefit, social proof, and credibility indicators led to a 144.1% improvement (*http://www.abtests.com/test/257001/landing-for-writework*) on landing pages.
- Putting people on your home page can have a huge impact on conversions (*http://37signals.com/svn/posts/2991-behind-the-scenes-ab-testing-part-3-final*).
- Including a pain point in a headline increased conversions by 31% (*http://dmix.ca/2010/05/how-we-increased-our-conversion-rate-by-72/*).
- Changing your call-to-action button from green to red (*http://dmix.ca/2010/05/how-we-increased-our-conversion-rate-by-72/*) has been shown to increase conversions by as much as 34%.
- Try moving around your Buy Now button. AppSumo did this (*http://okdork.com/2010/08/27/how-we-doubled-appsumo-coms-conversion-rate-in-2-days/*) (among other things) and doubled its conversion rate.
- Changing a button from "See Plans and Pricing" to "Get Started Today" increased conversions by 252% (*http://blog.kajabi.com/post/42443814885/a-dead-simple-change-that-increased-our-conversion-rate*).
- Turning CAPTCHA off (*http://www.seomoz.org/blog/captchas-affect-on-conversion-rates*) led to no conversions lost and very little spam mail in a case study.
- Showing testimonials can drive validation (*http://www.quora.com/What-are-some-top-strategies-for-conversion-optimization/answer/Andy-Johns?srid=hiM*).
- Using natural language on forms has been shown to increase conversions by 25–40% (*http://searchengineland.com/using-natural-language-to-improve-conversion-rates-41632*).

- Having a nice mobile site can double conversions (*http://www.internetretail er.com/2012/03/06/touch-mobile-improves-conversion-and-sales*).

- Segmenting your users can increase conversion rates (*http://www.conversion-rate-experts.com/voices-case-study/*) by giving more relevant content to the user.

- Putting your call-to-action button in the content area can really improve conversions (*http://www.blastam.com/blog/index.php/2009/06/google-website-optimizer-increases-conversion-591/*).

The important thing is to test and experiment.

22

Understanding the Customer Buying Cycle and Triggers

David Skok

The Customer Buying Cycle

A simple way to look at the buying cycle is to break it into three stages:

- *Awareness*: when a customer first becomes aware of your product. This could also refer to the point when a customer first becomes aware of a need that he wants to fulfill.
- *Consideration*: when a customer starts evaluating solutions to her need.
- *Purchase*: when a customer decides to buy.

How the Buying Cycle Impacts the Sales Approach Needed

Imagine that you wander into a clothing store while walking around a neighborhood. You don't have a particular idea of anything you want to buy. You are approached by a hungry salesperson who is convinced he can get you to buy something. You are annoyed by too much attention, and feel that this person is ruining the peaceful browsing experience that you hoped to have.

Now imagine that you have gone into the same store, but in this situation, you have an urgent need to purchase a black sweater and you don't have much time to spend. You want a salesperson to help you immediately, so you don't waste your time looking for the item. However, you can't seem to get the attention of any of the salespeople. You are highly irritated by the lack of attention.

WHAT'S THE DIFFERENCE?

The difference between these two examples is where you are in the buying cycle. In the first situation, you are early in the Awareness stage, and in the second example, you are right at the end of the buying cycle.

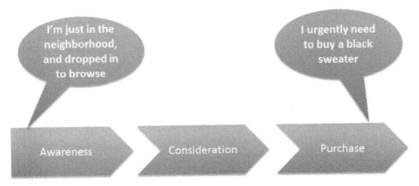

Depending on where you are in your buying cycle, your expectations for how the salespeople in the shop should treat you are different. If you are early in the cycle, you want to be largely left alone to browse around and get educated. If you are later in the cycle, you want highly responsive help to complete the purchase. Using the wrong sales approach leads to buyer frustration.

HOW DO YOU ADAPT MARKETING TO A BUYER'S STAGE IN THE CYCLE?

In the online world, we need to provide different paths through the website that are appropriate for each stage. It turns out that visitors will self-identify where they are in the buying cycle by the paths they take, provided you give them the option.

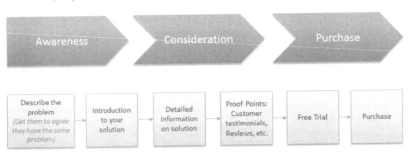

WHAT DO YOU DO WITH VISITORS THAT ARE NOT READY TO BUY? (LEAD NURTURING)

Since visitors who are early in the buying cycle are not likely to buy on their first visit to your website, you need to know how to best handle them in case they do turn into buyers later. This is a path that I am surprised to see is often not given the right level of attention, which results in leads leaking from the funnel and lost marketing investment.

The key is to do a great job of staying in touch with these visitors over a period of time, and building a trusted relationship (this is known as *lead nurturing*). Then, if they do hit an event that *triggers* a buying cycle, your product is likely to be at the top of their shopping list.

To allow you to do this, you need their email addresses. Since website visitors are initially reluctant to provide this information, you need to entice them with something of value to them. (For tips on how to do this, see my blog entries "When Selling Is the Worst Way to Win Customers" (*http://www.forentrepreneurs.com/build-trusted-relationships/*) and "Optimizing Your Customer Acquisition Funnel" (*http://www.forentrepreneurs.com/sales-funnel/*)).

Once you have their email addresses, you can nurture them through the buying cycle using customer success stories, a blog, newsletters, webinars, etc.

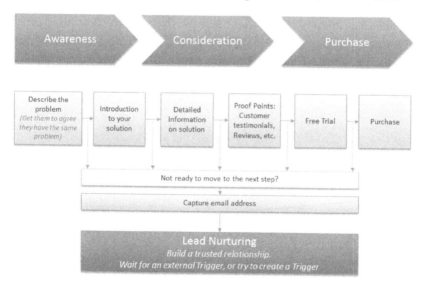

Lead nurturing is best done with marketing automation software like that provided by HubSpot, Marketo, Eloqua, etc. Those products allow you to segment your customers to make the messages you send most directly relevant to them, and therefore most likely to be read. They also allow you to track who is advancing in the buying process by observing whether they come back to visit pages, such as the pricing page, that indicate buying intent. You can then apply more expensive sales resources to those leads, knowing that they are qualified enough to warrant the additional cost.

Effective lead nurturing is all about accelerating leads through the consideration process. Customer success stories, product comparisons, etc. all help to provide the data and info that prospects look for in their own research. If you provide it for them, you make it easy for them to consume that info and move to the next step in the process.

HOW ONLINE LEAD SOURCES RELATE TO THE CUSTOMER BUYING CYCLE

Different lead sources produce buyers at different stages of the customer buying cycle:

- People that are later in the buying cycle are most likely to be using tools like Google and review sites to search for vendors and products to solve a problem. Those leads are highly valued because there is a high level of buyer intent. They are usually in the Consideration or Purchase stages of the buying cycle.

- Many other lead sources (e.g., social referrals, Twitter, Facebook ads, banner ads, PR stories, educational presentations at conferences, etc.) produce buyers that are earlier in the cycle, and frequently just becoming aware that there is a potentially interesting product now available.

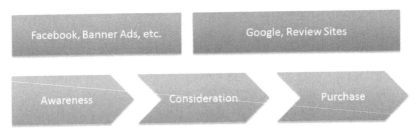

Market maturity also plays an important role in the stage that your leads will be in. For early-stage markets where there is still a lot of education required, most leads will be very early in their buying cycles.

Understanding Buying Triggers

A *trigger* is an event that causes a buyer to have a clear need, which usually converts into a sense of purpose and urgency in their buying process. As an example in your own personal life, you might have had a vague interest in getting a new camera. This might have caused you to browse the Web, reading various reviews. But an upcoming safari trip could act as the trigger that gets you shopping with clear intent to purchase.

Other examples of triggers:

- Your hard disk fails, and you realize you need a better backup system.
- You have a burglary, and you realize you want a far better video security system.
- Your company grows beyond a certain size, and your old manual HR systems can no longer cope..

The specific trigger that gets a buyer going will not only differ from startup to startup, but also depending on the person's role in the organization. Having a very clear understanding of these triggers helps you:

- Recognize who to target.
- Improve your messaging to those target prospects.
- Do a better job of qualifying who is really ready to buy.
- Help a customer recognize when a trigger has happened.

WORKING WITH TRIGGERS TO IMPROVE MARKETING

Let's look at this in four steps:

1. Identify the different buyer personas that buy your product.
2. Identify the trigger or triggers that typically get them into a serious buying mode.
3. Create messaging and content for each persona and trigger combination.
4. Look to see if you can create the trigger event, or help potential buyers recognize that one has occurred.

I will use one of my portfolio companies, CloudBees (*http://www.cloud bees.com/*), as an example of how this might work. CloudBees provides a PaaS (Platform-as a-Service) that can be used by application developers to drastically cut time-to-market for development of new applications. Let's work through the four steps.

1 & 2. Identify the Personas that buy, and their specific triggers

In the CloudBees case, there are four types of buyers:

- The business unit owners who want to solve a problem by developing a new application
- The developers
- The IT organizations that are responsible for providing the development infrastructure
- The systems integrators who are used to outsource projects for development

Taking just the business unit owners as an example, what might get them interested in CloudBees is the general notion that they can get applications built far faster than using the old internal IT processes. However, they are unlikely to try to transition an existing development project onto a PaaS, as they have already built the IT infrastructure required for it. That means that the trigger needed to actively start these people looking to purchase is a new project.

To better understand what the most common types of new projects are, Cloud-Bees talked to its customers. It found out that the top new application type that business owners want is mobile applications for smartphones and tablets. That made it even clearer how to build the messaging.

3. Build trigger-specific messaging and content

Understanding the trigger helps you to create messaging for the target persona on the front page of the website—i.e., below your standard intro video, etc., you could place messaging for each persona. In this case, that might read: "Business owner looking to get a mobile application built in a fraction of the usual time?" This would lead to a landing page that contains content specially tailored for that use case. The content should be designed to help move that persona through the buying cycle.

4. Look to see if you can create the trigger, or help a customer realize a trigger has happened

If you are nurturing a bunch of leads that came to your website early in their buying cycles, your goal with lead nurturing is usually to wait until some *external* event occurs that triggers them into active buying mode. However, the more you understand about these triggers, the higher the chance is that you can actually help create the trigger.

One example of this is HubSpot's Marketing Grader (*http://marketing.grad er.com/*) tool. This free tool provides customers with a clear indication of where they have gaps in their marketing versus best practices. They also use a score, which is a powerful trigger to get a customer to act to try to improve that score.

If we look at the CloudBees case, we might help create the trigger by using our blog and newsletter to talk about how mobile applications for customers have helped boost sales for other companies, then discuss how quickly and cheaply they can be built. With some luck, this could plant the idea in the customers' minds that they need to build new mobile applications. That is the trigger needed to have them seriously engage with CloudBees. The power of this message could be increased by leveraging highly respected analyst groups such as Gartner, Forrester, etc., quoting them on the need to interact with customers via mobile apps.

Encountering a Customer Too Late in the Buying Cycle

Many of you have seen the situation where you encounter buyers late in the buying cycle. They have already shaped their feature list around some other vendor's product, and you are now forced to react.

If you're selling a simple product, where the features and price can be easily assessed to be superior, this isn't too much of a problem.

But if you're selling a more sophisticated product where the customers need to understand how your unique features can uniquely change their business and give them greater return on investment (ROI), you're likely to be at a disadvantage to the company that helped shape the buyers' pictures of what they need.

So, in more complex sales cycles, the ideal situation is to make sure you get to know customers earlier in the process and become the player that helps shape and define their shopping list/request for proposal (RFP). That means finding customers earlier in their buying cycles, and building relationships with them over time.

Conclusions

This article discusses two concepts that are important to online marketers: the customer buying cycle and triggers. Your own customer buying cycle may be more sophisticated than just the simple three steps that I have outlined here. To take full advantage of this information, you might want to:

- Figure out where most of your top-of-funnel website visitors and leads are in their buying cycles.
- Make sure you have appropriate paths for them to follow to answer their questions, and move them forward in the cycle.
- Recognize that a large portion of them won't be ready to buy when they first encounter you. Instead, capture their email addresses, and develop a rich lead-nurturing system to help move them through the buying cycle.
- Develop rich content to support their personas and stages in the buying cycle.
- Understand the different buying personas and what triggers them to make a purchase.
- Look to see if you can't help create the trigger event that moves different personas into the buying phase. Alternatively, create messaging that helps them recognize when a trigger event has occurred.

23

Building It Is Not Enough: Five Practical Tips on User Acquisition

Brian Balfour

Stories about the growth of "hot" startups such as Facebook, Instagram, Airbnb, and others have created a belief that if you build the right product, customer acquisition will be easy. Don't be fooled. These stories are the exception, not the rule, and don't tell the entire story of the immense effort it took to grow their customer bases. Finding scalable acquisition channels is a time-consuming and strategic effort.

If You Build It, They May Not Come

You probably have a product road map and a development process. But do you have a process and plan for discovering your scalable customer acquisition channels? For software development, we have well-documented processes such as Agile, Waterfall, and Kanban. For finding product market fit, we have an increasingly defined process in customer development and the Lean Startup methodology.

Finding scalable customer acquisition channels is as much of a process as software development or finding product market fit. Here are five mistakes to avoid in finding your initial customer acquisition channels.

1. DO NOT TEST A LOT OF CHANNELS AT ONCE

This is the ol' throw stuff against the wall and see what sticks strategy. Unfortunately, this rarely works. Consider this: with Facebook ads you typically need to change your creative every 24–48 hours across 10–20 different segmentation combinations, with 4–10 ads per combination. That is in addition to all of the landing page testing you'll need to do for those combinations. It is easily a full-time role. Think you will have time to focus on another channel at the same time?

Inbound marketing takes an incredible amount of time for content development. SEO requires testing thousands of page combinations, time to build influential links, and plenty of on-page optimization. My point is, properly testing any single customer acquisition channel is extremely time-consuming and requires focus.

It is easy to think that the fastest way to find a channel is to test a lot at once. But with limited resources, it is the exact opposite. Let's look at it a different way. If you had very limited engineering resources, would you have them try to build four different products at once to find one that works? I hope not. You would end up with four partially built products with little information on which one is going to work.

Instead, you would likely evaluate each product idea, strategically choose one, focus, iterate on it for at least a couple of months, and only then decide whether to keep moving forward or move on. Finding scalable customer acquisition channels requires a similar amount of strategic decisions, focus, and iteration.

The quickest way to find your first scalable channel with limited resources is to focus on one at a time and iterate based on feedback (metrics), just like you would with building product. At Boundless (*https://www.boundless.com/*), we have been lucky to have enough resources to test two channels at once. But even with close to $10m in funding, we won't go beyond testing and optimizing two channels for a while. Don't underestimate what it takes to properly test and optimize a single customer acquisition channel.

2. DIVERSITY OF CHANNELS IS NOT IMPORTANT IN THE EARLY STAGE

Entire companies are typically built on the back of one or two channels. Look how far Zynga has gotten with basically two channels: Facebook ads and viral mechanics. Only now is the company starting to diversify with the launch of its new platform. Facebook itself relied completely on viral growth until it had reached millions of users. Only then did it start optimizing for SEO. Airbnb grew its initial user base almost completely on the back of Craigslist.

For reasons discussed in the previous section, diversity of channels actually increases the risk that you will never find a scalable channel at all. Remember this —momentum of growth trumps diversity of channels. Once you find a channel that is working at a small scale, don't be tempted to add another channel to the mix. Instead, focus on optimizing, scaling, and milking your initial channel for all it's worth.

Your goal in the early stages is to grow as fast as possible with limited resources. Finding further growth in a channel that is already working is typically easier than finding a completely new acquisition channel. When you start to reach the max potential (where the growth curve starts to flatten), only then should you add another channel to the mix.

3. PAYING FOR USERS IS OKAY

Magical stories of instant viral growth have formed a negative stigma around paying for users, especially in the early days of a product. Entrepreneurs almost feel guilty if they pay for users. This leads to startup pitches that often include a slide that says "We've grown to X# of users without paying for a single one."

Every, and I mean every, acquisition channel costs money. It is just a question of whether the cost is direct or indirect. Channels such as PPC obviously have a direct cost. However, channels such as SEO and viral are commonly seen as "free" channels. They aren't. Properly optimizing SEO and viral mechanics takes significant engineering and other employees' time. That time is costing you money. The cost is indirect, but you are still paying for users.

Those "free" channels are certainly valuable in the long term. But they often come with short-term disadvantages. For example, SEO typically takes months of effort before you gain meaningful traffic. In the early stages, speed of learning is the most valuable thing. Do you really want to wait a few months to learn the same thing you could learn in less time with another channel?

Viral growth deserves its own mention here. It is the treasure that most entrepreneurs are seeking. They want to be the next Pinterest or Instagram. Keep in mind that a lot of products aren't suited for viral growth. I think a lot of entrepreneurs overestimate whether or not their products are a fit for pure viral growth. If your business isn't suited for viral growth, that doesn't mean you have a bad business. You just need to find a different customer acquisition strategy.

4. YOU ONLY NEED THREE TOOLS TO TEST YOUR CUSTOMER ACQUISITION CHANNELS

The "measure everything" mantra has led to a belief that an array of tools is needed to find a scalable channel. Between analytics, A/B testing, ad platforms, feedback, support, and a host of other tools, it is easy to get lost. If you wanted to learn to play basketball, would you go out and spend $1,000 on the latest gear first? Or would you just grab a ball, find a hoop, and start playing? Hopefully you answered the latter.

To test any customer acquisition channel, all you typically need is Google Analytics, Excel, and some basic SQL skills. Those three things will take you surprisingly far for any channel before you need anything else. Don't get caught up with the tools, just get testing.

5. AVOID THE BUTTON COLOR A/B TESTING RABBIT HOLE

The rise of A/B testing and other analytics tools has led to fairy-tale stories of changing a button color, or moving the call to action from the left to the right, and suddenly having game-changing improvements. Once again, these stories are the exception, not the rule. It typically takes 10 A/B tests to find one that produces any improvement at all. And when you do have a positive improvement, it is typically incremental instead of game-changing.

Being metrics-focused is important. But knowing how to properly influence them is even more critical.

In the early stage, you should not be focused on incremental improvements. Your initial cost per acquisition for any new channel is likely to be a long way from your target. That means you need to try and make big improvements to understand the viability of the channel. To see big improvements, focus on messaging, targeting, and activation methods. Save your color experiments for when you are ready to optimize and scale a channel, not when you are testing the viability of a channel.

24

Introduction to A/B Testing for Landing Pages

Lance Kidwell (http://muddylemon.com/)

Everyone loves the story about how a scrappy upstart changed the color of a button on its landing page and suddenly increased its conversion rate by 200%. Stories like that make for great headlines. They also often spawn copycats naïvely trying to replicate that anomaly in completely different contexts.

Do you remember when Dustin Curtis ran an experiment (*http://dustincur tis.com/you_should_follow_me_on_twitter.html*) trying different ways of wording a link to his Twitter account? He noted that writing "You should follow me on Twitter" had a greater conversion rate than just "I'm on Twitter." In response, blogs and websites all over the world began demanding I follow them on Twitter in increasingly imperative tones. Did that trick actually increase the Twitter followings of anyone? I have no idea, and neither do the majority of the people who tried it. It really seems like a "tip" that you can easily port to another context and have similar results. However, there is no way to predict what results any change will have—either positively or negatively.

Incremental changes that lead to huge jumps in performance are rare. To be more specific, incremental changes that lead to *statistically valid* jumps in performance are rare. Most websites do not get anywhere near enough traffic for the data collected in such an experiment to mean anything. It is easy to claim that no two snowflakes are identical when you've only looked at a few. It will take a couple of blizzards before you can really say so with confidence.

Even sites that do have significant traffic have difficulty conducting valid experiments. If you don't come from a math or statistics background, one of the first things you'll notice about the literature around optimization and testing is how fussy everything is. If you are going to run successful experiments, you have to acquire a fussy sensibility.

Figure 24-1. Cat and laser (image courtesy Drregor (http://www.flickr.com/photos/drregor/4098936015/) on Flickr)

By knowing what kinds of mistakes and weaknesses have caused other experiments to fail, you can develop a sixth sense for the traps and how to avoid them. Below I've listed several common traps that can obscure your real results and leave you spinning like a cat chasing a red laser dot across the floor.

Improperly Segmenting Traffic

To run a valid experiment you have to isolate the variable(s) that you are measuring. Differences in the time of day, the referral source, browser characteristics, bandwidth, and other variables can skew your results in unpredictable ways.

To counter that noise it is important to first "test the null hypothesis *(http://en.wikipedia.org/wiki/Null_hypothesis)*." To test the null hypothesis you construct an experiment that divides your web traffic into segments but provides the same experience to each visitor in either segment. The null hypothesis states that if you don't change anything, then nothing will be different.

If you divide your traffic and see significant differences in your metrics, you have rejected the null hypothesis. As the Wikipedia article *(http://en.wikipedia.org/wiki/Null_hypothesis)* and an astute commenter on Hacker News *(https://news.ycombinator.com/item?id=3829373)* point out, you will never "prove" the null hypothesis. You can either reject it or fail to reject it.

Figure 24-2. Null hypothesis (image courtesy Kevin Forbes (http://robotandghost.com/comics/ simulated-comic-product/scp-2009/))

It is important to understand that the null hypothesis can never be proven. A set of data can only reject a null hypothesis or fail to reject it. For example, if comparison of two groups (e.g., treatment, no treatment) reveals no statistically significant difference between the two, it does not mean that there is no difference in reality. It only means that there is not enough evidence to reject the null hypothesis (in other words, the experiment fails to reject the null hypothesis).

If you have rejected the null hypothesis, you may suppose that you have either somehow upended the laws of causality or screwed something up. No offense, but my money is on you being a screwup. Finding the leak is a matter of combing through the observations to look for unusual results and combing through your code to see if there is a logical failing or hidden dependency that is favoring one result over another.

If your logic is sound yet there are still unexplained differences between the control and treatment, you may want to look at the outliers and see if there is a common thread.

For a web application, browser differences are common culprits. From rendering issues to JavaScript execution quirks, the mix of browsers accessing your site are a mass of conditions that you have to control. Services like *browser-shots.org (http://browsershots.org/)* are essential tools for spotting obvious visual differences and errors. You should use your own traffic analysis to see what browsers are worth optimizing for.

Another hotspot is bandwidth issues. The speed of a page load is a more significant variable than most people assume. Google and Amazon have both published reports that show how even sub-second delays can result in outsized lost conversions. The best way to address this issue is to make your site run as fast as possible.

Use caching, content delivery networks, asynchronous scripts, and the other tools available to mitigate this factor. You may still wish to collect page load speed results to measure the impact and possibly control for time-bound anomalies like a slow-loading third-party script or slow and unreliable user connections.

Misunderstanding Randomness

"That's so random" is one of the more annoying clichés in recent circulation. In popular parlance, the word "random" often means something between "unexpected" and "unusual." For our purposes we will stick with the more rigorous definition, "selected without aim or reason." Randomness is hard to understand but easy to fake. Our brains are very good at picking up short patterns. Recognizing long patterns, however, is an understandable failing. Our stone-age brains tap out a few digits into any jumbled-up looking string.

For a small experiment, fake randomness is likely impossible to detect simply because its effects are less significant than margin of error. In the same way, a ship with a broken compass can get across a harbor without getting off track, but could end up in the wrong hemisphere if it sets out for a transoceanic journey.

Pseudorandomness often occurs when the random assignment algorithm uses a value like the visitor's ID to seed the decision. If you assign a visitor to a treatment based on an algorithm like $treatment = $visitor_id mod 2$, you are introducing outside information that will synchronize the treatments in an unpredictable way. What you are then testing is not a random group A vs. a random group B, but a selected group A against the resultant group B. The selection criterion may seem meaningless, but it will invariably warp your results.

Solving the randomness problem, as you can see, is very difficult. Fortunately, there are plenty of mathematicians, computer scientists, and careful coders out there who have built tools to deal with it for you. It's well out of the scope of this article to describe specific implementations, but I can say that the one you wrote sucks. Randomness, like encryption, is best left to a well-supported library.

Mixing Experiment Factors

It is hard enough to test one variation—mixing multiple factors and trying to divine actionable intelligence is a task that requires an enormous amount of data and a mastery of math and statistics that is rarely seen outside research universities or the Googleplex.

That's not to say you can't test widely varying treatments against each other. But the comparison you can make is between the treatments as a whole, not specific elements.

For example, let's say you are selling widgets online. You have a landing page that has produced mediocre results. You and your team sit down and brainstorm to come up with a list of changes that you could try. Perhaps rewording the headline? Changing the button text? What about adding a picture near the form? What if we removed the last question on the form? Why not Zoidberg?

Having produced such a prodigious list, it is tempting to get in there and really mix things up. If you have a list of 100 things to change, hearing that you only have enough traffic to call for one experiment a month is depressing. "If we're clever," you may think, "and really careful, we could make a matrix of all the variations mixing a headline from column A to the button color of Column D...." Before you know it, you're sifting through piles of data with no clear direction. At worst, you'll find a real winner but have no idea what it is about that treatment that is responsible for the improvement or if the improvement is just a fluke. To solve this problem, insist on writing a hypothesis for each experiment.

Data Dredging

When you design an experiment, you have to make a hypothesis. Throwing everything against the wall and hoping to figure out what makes some parts stick after the fact is a recipe for disaster.

I was in a meeting once where a well-meaning team member was pointing out a peak in a chart. He had discovered that visitors from a particular source who checked a certain option on the form and were also in the 45–65 age range had significantly higher conversion rates than other segments. He proposed a plan to auto-check that particular option for people coming from that source and to segment the incoming traffic to favor older visitors.

What that product manager was doing is data dredging (*http://en.wikipedia.org/wiki/Data_dredging*). Another form of this mistake can be seen in the people obsessed with looking for patterns in the stock market or the lottery and then attempting to implement a strategy that would have worked had they been using it in the past. It's an enticing mistake. It seems perfectly logical that if a pattern appeared in the past it likely will repeat in the future.

To picture the problem with data dredging in a more concrete fashion, imagine you own an ice cream store. One day you ask your employees to write the color of the shirt of each customer that comes in that day on that person's receipt. At the end of the day you compile the numbers and find that people wearing red shirts buy nearly twice the amount of ice cream compared to people wearing other colors.

In hopes of capitalizing on this discovery, you research locations and find that people in St. Louis wear red shirts much more than people in other cities (at least in the summer during baseball season, which as an ice cream maven is the only season you're concerned with). Can you guess how much moving all of your operations to St. Louis will help your profits?

You can't guess, because it is outrageously unlikely that the color of the shirts your customers are wearing has anything to do with your sales figures. To use a cliché, you've confused correlation with causation. Even if the correlation is a very high number, it doesn't mean anything unless it's repeatable and falsifiable.

Comparing the Results of Different and Unrelated Experiments

A similar mistake is comparing the results of independent experiments with each other. Often this takes the form of comparing the results of a recent experiment with one that ran earlier but not consecutively. Another form of this mistake is comparing the results of experiments that have run for different lengths of time or on different traffic sources. The worst, but surprisingly common, variant is when you compare the results of your experiment with the results of someone else's—like the published results of another site's A/B tests.

The only valid comparison is between the control and the treatment(s). Also, that comparison is only valid for metrics that are measuring the same thing. The bounce rate of a squeeze page with one prominent CTA button might be shockingly better than a treatment that asks for an email address in a form on the landing page. That difference in bounce rate tells you something, but if the difference washes out in lead quality, revenue per lead, or other metrics that translate more directly into dollars, it's not telling you anything useful.

Inconsistent or Unimportant Metrics

One thing the Web does not lack is things to measure. Never has it been so easy to collect and compare so many attributes of your customers and their actions. But not every metric is equally important.

How to evaluate metrics:

- Is the metric measurable? Is it a discrete value that doesn't need subjective interpretation?
- Is the metric dependent on something not being measured?
- Is it meaningful? Does it correlate directly with something you want to improve?
- Can you improve it by doing anything on your site? If you can't do anything about it, why bother measuring it?

You should have core metrics that directly represent your business goals. For many commercial ventures, this would be a *revenue per X* number. In other contexts it might be email newsletter signups, social sharing, or some other action.

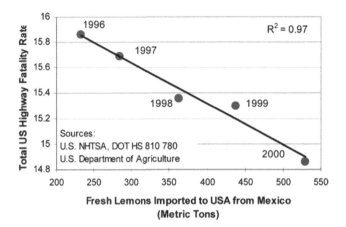

**Fresh Lemons Imported to USA from Mexico
(Metric Tons)**

By focusing your attention on the same metrics for each experiment, you will have a context to your learning. Also, you will avoid being led down the rabbit hole of paying attention to misleading or irrelevant measurements.

An example of a misleading measurement is an abnormally high or low result on one metric that isn't reflected or explained in related metrics. Noise and outliers are expected. Not every anomalous result is significant. You can tell which are significant by testing again (or letting the current test continue) and seeing if the spike continues to grow or regresses back to the mean.

Another class of misleading measurement is the "vanity metric." A vanity metric is a number that seems significant but has little to no effect on results coming out of the conversion funnel.

Unique visitors and page hits are the most common examples. Those are often the biggest numbers you have, but they are easy to pump and hard to keep. Your site might get a runaway link on Reddit (*http://www.reddit.com/*) or a writeup on TechCrunch (*http://techcrunch.com/*) that will result in a massive influx of visitors. However, they're not likely your target market and are notoriously adverse to clicking ads or buying things.

Changing the mix of traffic to each treatment is dangerous. If you are running an experiment split between treatments A and B at a 60/40 split and decide to even it out to 50/50, your old data is worthless. You are including people who should have been As in your B group, and thus invalidating the earlier data. You can change the mix, but you have to keep the proportions the same.

Naïve Analysis of Results

In a later article in this series I will describe concepts like the G-Test, the Z-Test, statistical significance, confidence, and other implementation details. For the purposes of this article I'll summarize it like this: numbers don't lie, but you can misinterpret the hell out of them.

The best way to combat misinterpreting your data is to figure out what numbers are important and design easy-to-understand reports that display that data. Automation of these reports is essential. When you have a set of consistent numbers, you can then apply standard analytical tools to understand your experiments. Don't make the mistake of pulling numbers in an ad hoc fashion. As a human you have millions of years of evolution encouraging you to see patterns in everything.

Define what success means to your business and what numbers represent that. If a number you are using—perhaps the unique visitors per product page—varies more widely than the other numbers you are measuring, that is a sign that your metric is not tightly correlated with your conversion funnel. The granularity of your metrics needs to match the unit you use to make decisions. That might be visitors, sessions, events, or another metric.

When designing your reports, you have to make sure you are comparing the same metrics. If you compare page views with conversion events and find a strong correlation, you have discovered nothing useful. You can't just force your current visitors to view more pages. Even if you change your site in a way that encourages more page views, you don't have any results to suggest that increased page views are causative or an effect of some other unrelated visitor attribute.

Substituting Testing for Creativity and Common Sense

Once you begin to see actionable results from your testing, you'll probably notice your approach to business problems shifting. You'll find yourself speculating less and proposing experiments more. You'll be quicker to dismiss fuzzy thinking and untestable conjectures.

However, you would be remiss to skip the other parts of customer development and marketing. Talking to your users will give you insights unavailable on any chart or graph. Writing clear and compelling copy is an art that pays real dividends. Attractive and persuasive design can put you far ahead of your competitors.

Testing and experimentation are powerful tools that are remaking online and offline business. You must remember that they are tools for refinement and decision making. What you are testing is still the behavior of people. That behavior is erratic and irrational. No amount of testing will make up for being insensitive to your customers, providing bad service or shoddy products, and other marks of a failing business.

Make It Easy on Your Developers

No matter how you design your experiments, the process of deploying and removing the treatments must be simple and safe. If your process is not simple, you will be constantly chasing bugs due to bad deployments. If deploying an experiment requires pushing a lot of code to production, you are going to get constant push back from the developers and sysadmins and will be in a real tight spot when a bug takes down the site.

If the process of setting up an experiment is easy and painless, you will create more experiments and find the data they produce more reliable.

25

You Built It But They Didn't Come: Eight Tricks for Marketing Your Mobile App

John Koetsier (http://venturebeat.com/author/johnkoetsier/)

If a tree falls in the forest, does anyone hear it? And if your app joins the 50 bajillion other apps already on the market, will anyone notice?

I've had the privilege of building apps with hundreds of thousands of downloads, but sadly, the default answer is a big, bold *no*. In fact, a recent study revealed that 60% of apps don't make money (*http://venturebeat.com/2012/05/04/ios-developers-lose-money/*). You, however, want to be in the 40% that do. Don't leave it up to luck—take action.

In a roughly descending order of importance, here are some ways to beat the odds.

Build a Great App

I know it's shocking, but great apps are going to sell better than crappy apps. So make sure you're working on something great!

That could be a totally new type of app, or it could be a completely reimagined approach to a common app type. What it cannot be is yet another boring matching-jewels game: there are 5,000 of them already.

Having a great app isn't just about a great idea. It's also about great execution: design, user experience, even details like a great icon. Perhaps shockingly, having a stunning icon is hugely important. It's often the first thing users see, and they will base their impressions of your professionalism, design, and hipness on that tiny little square of pixels.

Get Great Reviews

Users are going to decide whether or not to risk the time cost and dollar cost of downloading your app based on the reviews they see. It can be cruel and brutal, but your app's life is dependent on users who may not see important features, sometimes make stupendously stupid assumptions about what a $0.99 app should offer, and can even, in a few cases, be malicious.

So do whatever it takes to get good reviews. Test, retest, and re-retest. Make sure your app is solid. Send promo codes to friends and family, people who are likely to give you a bit of a break and maybe rate your product just a little bit higher. Make sure everyone in your company, if you work for a company, downloads the app, rates it, and reviews it.

Do what you need to do to get 4+ stars and great comments, because the next two marketing methods are *100% dependent on this step.*

Build in Social

If there's anything that the explosion of social has taught us, it's that people like to share—and that the best way for your company to grow is to crowdsource marketing by giving your passionate users a bigger voice.

If your app is a game, do a leaderboard. Use Game Center on iOS, and equivalent functionality on Android when it arrives (*http://www.androidauthority.com/ rumor-google-game-center-android-84778/*). Let people tweet and share, boasting about their high scores.

If it's a utility, find social equivalents: sharing notes with colleagues, tweeting app activity, publishing accomplishments, highlighting insights.

The best social, of course, is baked right in. Think Draw Something (*http:// omgpop.com/drawsomething*)—it has the network effects of a fax machine: one is useless, but each one added to the network makes all the others more valuable.

A final note: an app with one star and withering reviews is not going to become successful through social channels. It may very well be highlighted in social networks, but not for the reasons you want, and not with the results you're looking for.

Pitch, Pitch, Pitch (and Then Pitch Some More)

Get comfortable with selling. To make your app move, you need to sell yourself, your vision, your angle, and most importantly, your app. You want to get noticed by the app blogs and the top tech blogs, and you need reviews.

To get them, you're going to need to pitch. It helps when you have a good story (rinse and repeat, see the first tip), but that is not going to be enough. You need to confidently and competently pitch editors, journalists, bloggers, and ordinary people on the shining merits and sheer awesomeness of your wonderful app.

If you can't get excited about it, why should anyone else?

SEO Your App Description

Discovery in the crowded App Store or Google Play is a function of popularity (which you don't have on day one) and placement (if you happen to get lucky enough to know the second cousin twice removed of an App Store editor, who places you in the Featured Apps category) and search (yeah, that's where you sit).

Search on the App Store is just like search on the Web: more and better data equals higher ranking. So write your description with care. Look at what your competitors are saying... especially those who are ranking well. Craft your description with appropriate keyword density for the search terms that you think your potential customers will use. And tweak it from time to time to shake it up.

Unfortunately, multivariate testing is not really a viable option here.

Be Free, Freemium, Cheap...

Unless you're Disney or Zynga, no one knows you and no one cares. Taking a risk on your app is just that: a risk. And most people don't like risks.

So reduce the riskiness by being free or cheap. Use a freemium monetization model to drive initial downloads, if that works for your app. Do a lite version that rocks, but leaves users wanting just a bit more. Give away lots of promo codes initially. Have sales. Try different price points.

If All Else Fails, Advertise

It was Jon Bond, an ad exec, who said (*http://www.fastcompany.com/1702130/future-advertising*) that "In the future, marketing will be like sex. Only the losers will have to pay for it." Well guess what, sometimes we're losers, and yes, we have to pay for it.

Advertise for downloads on AdMob and other networks, but note that costs per download can be in excess of $1, and just like in the Google AdWords world, there are scammers looking to suck up your cash and leave you with no real users.

Or, cross-promote your app with other apps using services like Playhaven (*http://www.playhaven.com/*) or Applifier (*http://www.applifier.com/mobile/*) so that you and other developers can share users and build an audience.

If All Else *Really* Fails, Buy Users to Get in the Top App Lists

If you are really desperate, you can enter gray-hat or even black-hat territory and simply buy downloads so that you rise in the top app lists, which hopefully will generate real customers and real revenues. (Just to be clear, I don't recommend this... but it does happen.)

To do so, pay a company like GTekna $10,000 or so (*http://www.business week.com/articles/2012-03-15/anarchy-in-the-app-store*) and let the magic happen. You'll get on the leaderboard and have a shot at hundreds of thousands of downloads, just from the visibility. Whether you can stay there or not depends on how good your app is, and how well you've done all the other steps.

Marketing your app is just as hard, if not harder, as building your app. It's a long, tough slog, and not everyone can do it.

PART V

Sales, Marketing, and PR Management

26

At Times Not Losing Is as Important as Winning

Steve Blank (http://steveblank.com/)

Customer Validation

E.piphany was an 11-month-old startup with 31 people and on fire. We had closed four $100,000 deals for our customer relationship management software.

Joe Dinucci, our VP of Sales, was hot on the trail of our next big order. He had just demoed our product to his friend, the CFO of Autodesk. After seeing the demo, the CFO walked Joe over to the office of Autodesk's VP of Sales, and said to her, "I think this product might solve your sales reporting problem."

After a demo, she agreed it would.

Joe came back to our company excited. If we won the Autodesk account, it could be worth half a million dollars or more.

They Have a Problem and Know It

At the time Autodesk's sales organization was frustrated with its IT department. It took weeks or months for Sales to get financial, sales results, and customer reports from IT. Autodesk's VP of Sales fit the profile of a earlyvangelist: she understood she had a pressing problem (couldn't get the timely data needed to forecast sales), she was searching for a solution (beating up the Autodesk CIO on a weekly basis to solve her problem), she had a timetable for a solution (now), and her company had committed budget dollars to solve this problem (they'll spend anything to stop missing forecasts.)

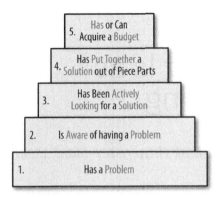

A Match Made in Heaven

For the next several weeks, the entire E.piphany engineering department worked with Autodesk's sales operation team to build a prototype using real Autodesk data. Joe made a compelling ROI (return on investment) presentation to the VP of Sales and the CFO. E.piphany and Autodesk seemed like a match made in heaven, and it looked like we had a $500,000 deal that could close in weeks.

Not quite.

The CIO

The CFO casually mentioned that as the IT team would install and maintain the system, they would have to recommend and sign off on an E.piphany purchase. As the CIO worked for the CFO, Joe paid what he thought was a courtesy call to Autodesk's CIO.

The CIO didn't say much in the presentation (warning, warning), and he passed Joe on to his manager of data warehouse development. What Joe didn't know was that months ago, this IT group had been tasked to solve the Sales department's reporting problems and was struggling with the complexity and difficulty of extracting data from SAP.

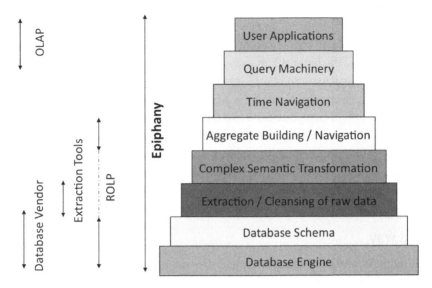

Joe was aware of the tense history between Autodesk's Sales and IT departments, but given how happy the VP of Sales was with E.piphany's prototypes, plus Joe's personal relationship with the CFO, he didn't see this as a serious obstacle. Joe believed the IT people had nothing but technical piece parts to compete with E.piphany's complete solution. Given that E.piphany had a vastly superior solution, Joe believed there was no logical way they could recommend to the CIO to deploy anything else but E.piphany.

Wrong.

The IT Revolt

Unbeknownst to Joe, a revolt was brewing in Autodesk's IT organization. "Sales keeps asking for all these reports, and now they are telling us what application to buy? If we deploy E.piphany's entire solution, we'll all be out of jobs. But if we recommend software tools from another startup, we could say we're solving the needs of the Sales VP and still keep our jobs."

Late in the afternoon, Joe got a call from a friend in Autodesk's IT department warning that they were about to give the order to another startup. And the CIO would approve the recommendation and pass this to his boss, the CFO, the next day.

We're Going to Lose

Joe arrived in my office, his face making it clear he brought bad news. E.piphany was now about to lose the half-million-dollar Autodesk sale. Joe looked at his shoes while he muttered his frustrations with internal Autodesk politics.

We had a long discussion about the consequences if we lost. It was one thing for a startup to lose to a large company like Oracle or IBM. But to lose the sale to another startup with an inferior product would have been psychologically devastating to our little startup. E.piphany's product development team had spent weeks inside the account, and they believed the deal was all but won. The competitor would trumpet the sales win far and wide and use the momentum to get more sales.

We couldn't afford to lose this sale. What could we do?

The Third Way

It struck me that there might be more than two outcomes. Sales had defined the problem as a win or lose situation. But what if we added a third choice? What if we formally, publicly and noisily *withdrew from the account*? The worst case was that we could tell our engineering team that we should have won but the game was rigged. While we certainly wouldn't win the business, withdrawing would solve the more emotionally explosive issue of losing. (And in the back of my mind, I believed this third way had a chance of giving us the winning hand.)

At first Joe hated the idea. Like every great sales guy, he was eternally optimistic about the outcome. However, I wasn't in the mood to put the company's future at risk based on the testosterone levels of our sales guy. Withdrawing by claiming that Autodesk's IT staff had already decided that it was "any solution but ours" was making the best of a deteriorating sales situation.

Joe called his friend the CFO, waiting until after 5 p.m., when he was sure he wasn't in his office, and left him a message: "Thanks for introducing us to the VP of Sales and your technical staff. We really appreciate the opportunity to work with you. Unfortunately it looks like this deal isn't going to happen. You have a bunch of smart guys working for you, but they are determined to make sure that the status quo won't change. We have limited resources and can't continue to give demos and hold meetings when the outcome is predetermined. My guess is we'll be back in six to nine months when the VP of Sales is still unhappy. I'm going to call her and let her know that we can't put in the system that she wanted, but I thought I'd check in with you first. Thanks again for the opportunity."

The "Take-Away" Gambit

This is known as the "take-away" gambit. I believed that by pulling the deal away, we created at least a 50% chance that the CFO would do what I knew he didn't want to do—go to his CIO and help him make the "right" decision. I understood that a potential downside to this maneuver was encountering an uncooperative IT organization when we tried to install the product, but by then Autodesk's check would be in the bank, and I had a plan to win them over.

Joe was concerned that we had just lost the account, but he made the call and left the message.

Two hours later Joe got a call back from the CFO, who said, "Wait, wait! Don't pull out. Why don't you come up and meet with me tomorrow morning. I've chatted with my staff and we're now ready for a contract proposal."

Autodesk became our third paying customer. Over the next year they paid us over $1m for our software.

After a full-court charm offensive, the IT person who had wanted anyone but us became our biggest advocate. She keynoted our first user conference.

Lessons Learned

- In complex B-to-B sales, multiple "yes" votes are required to get an order.
- A single "no" can kill the deal.
- Understanding the saboteurs in a complex sale is as important as understanding the recommenders and influencers.
- We needed a selling strategy that took all of this into account.
- In a startup, not losing is sometimes more important than winning.

27

Nine Ways to Make Your Startup Grow Virally

Vinicius Vacanti

If you want your startup to become the next big thing, *it's not good enough to just build a great product. Unless you can afford to buy users, you'll have to grow virally.*

The difference between getting one of your new users to convince one friend to sign up and that person getting *two* new friends to sign up is huge. Assuming you start with 1,000 new users, after nine months, *it's the difference between having 9,000 users and 511,000 users!*

Let's look at nine ways you can get your startup to grow virally, and some examples of each.

GET YOUR USERS TO SPREAD THE WORD

1. **Get users to tell others about your app simply by using it**. This is probably the best item on this list, and one of the hardest to achieve. It's generally true of communication and content-creation apps.

   - **Tumblr**. People create their tumblrs and link to them from their email signatures and Facebook and Twitter profiles. When visitors come, at the top of each tumblr page is a pitch for the visitor to "Join Tumblr."
   - **About.me**. Users can create beautiful landing pages for themselves, and as with Tumblr, they link to their about.me pages on their social media profiles. But, as you'll see below, there's a reason why Tumblr has grown much faster than about.me.

2. **Get users to push content they create on your app to Facebook, Twitter, etc.** This is a recent and huge phenomenon. However, users won't push *any* content they create, just content that they are proud of or think their friends will find interesting.

   - **Instagram**. This is probably the best example of a site taking advantage of this trend, by enabling its users to take beautiful pictures that they then share on Facebook, Twitter, etc.
   - **Foursquare**. People want to tell their friends where they are, especially when they're at high-profile locations like sporting events and music concerts.
   - **Tumblr**. When people create a new post, they share it on Facebook/Twitter.

3. **Get users to generate content that you optimize for search engines**. While this isn't traditionally thought of as a viral growth strategy, it's very important. Millions of potential new users are searching on Google, and if your users create content that addresses these search needs, you'll be able to pitch those searchers to join your service.

- **Wikipedia**. This is probably the best example of this tactic. Wikipedia users create massive amounts of really strong content that Google searchers access every day.
- **Yelp**. Yelp did an amazing job of turning local business reviews into great business listing pages that Google often places at the top of its search results.
- **Quora and StackOverflow**. Users of these services answer questions that are then presented in Google search results for the millions of people asking those same questions.

4. **Make it in your users' best interests to invite their friends**. If your strategy is to ask users to invite their friends "just because," they won't.

- **Twitter**. Giving every user a follower number encouraged people to tell others to "follow them on Twitter," including many users that hadn't yet signed up for Twitter. Twitter also became a way to retain fans, to push content to them at a later date. The same dynamic applies to Facebook pages.
- **Kickstarter**. When people create their Kickstarter projects, they email all of their friends and family members to contribute to the project.
- **Groupon and Gilt**. Since both of these services have a high enough user value, they can afford to give their users a referral credit for telling their friends about the services.
- **Dropbox**. This service gives users extra memory for their dropboxes in exchange for inviting friends.

5. **Get celebrities to use your app**. Celebrities have huge followings. Early Facebook didn't take advantage of this as it was all about just your friends, but with fan pages, it has tapped into this strategy.

- **Twitter**. Twitter has done an amazing job of courting celebrities to use their service with some of the most high profile celebrities having millions of followers.

- **MySpace**. While they have done many things wrong since, they created THE page where bands resided online and, with bands, came their legions of fans.

6. **Get content created on your app to be newsworthy.** If the content created on your app becomes interesting for journalists to cover, you can tap into something more valuable than traditional PR.

    - **Twitter**. Celebrities are constantly tweeting things they shouldn't, and journalists have a field day every time it happens.
    - **Kickstarter**. Successful projects on Kickstarter like the Robocop statue in Detroit transcend the service and are covered by journalists and bloggers.
    - **Groupon/Living Social**. Whether it's Amazon, Whole Foods, or GAP, these deals will get covered by journalists.

INCREASING CONVERSION

7. **Adjust your product to become more mainstream.** It won't help much to have all your users constantly telling everyone about your service if most people aren't interested. If you want to reach millions of users, millions of people have to potentially want your product. For instance, about.me has very strong viral potential (as described above), but not everyone wants their own about.me page (at least not yet), and so its conversion rate suffers.

    - **Instagram**. This could have been a niche product, but by making it so easy that even an absolute beginner could take a beautiful picture, it went from niche to mainstream.
    - **Tumblr**. Blogging platforms have been around for a while, but Tumblr makes it so easy to blog that it has been able to convert many non-bloggers.

8. **Get your users to use your app every day.** The more your users visit your app, the more likely they are to invite their friends, create content, etc. A great example of this struggle is Plancast (*http://techcrunch.com/2012/01/22/post-*

mortem-for-plancast/), a product that created content, but not content that was created every day.

- **Groupon and Gilt**. Because there's new content every day, these services email their users every day.

9. **Optimize your signup and referral funnels**. If you are getting one extra user a month and you optimize your landing page and referral funnels, you'll cross over into viral territory. It's not uncommon to see conversion rates double after a few optimization experiments. (At Yipit (*http://yipit.com/*), we use Google Website Optimizer (*http://support.google.com/analytics/bin/answer.py? hl=en&topic=1745146&answer=2661700*).)

Conclusion

Building a great product is only half the battle. Take the time to think through how you can build in as many viral growth opportunities as possible. It's worth the effort to go from linear to exponential growth.

28

Our PR Stinks: Here's What Your Startup Can Learn from It

Susanna Gebauer (http://bit.ly/onstartups-PR)

At exploreB2B (*https://exploreb2b.com/*), we were convinced from the very beginning that strong PR would be the answer to our market entry prayers. This is the story of how our reality turned into something of the opposite effect.

The Familiar Doubt

Many friends, fellow founders, and business professionals told us along the way that creating a B2B interactive business platform would be a difficult project. (Hey, we knew that.)

People later told us that the most difficult aspect would be market entry. (Again, no surprise there.) The consensus among those critical of our venture was consistent, and usually along the lines of, "Don't you want to do something more glamorous than a B2B platform? Maybe something B2C?" (Actually, we believe our concept (*https://exploreb2b.com/*) is glamorous and, quite frankly, exactly what we believe the B2B market calls for.)

Any way we thought about it, the task at hand was going to be tough. The start was the most challenging, with an idea and an empty platform. But we were not the first facing this issue; surely there would be ways to maneuver our way into our key markets?

We knew some companies who'd successfully bought profiles or created fake ones, but we decided that if we really believed in our concept, we would need real people behind genuine profiles and articles. And that we would need press coverage.

How Did We Solve the First Problem of Filling the Platform?

We first talked face-to-face with various professionals we knew to get them interested and excited enough to participate in the platform, even though it was new. It was hard, but we did it. Twice. Once on the German site, and again when we went international with the English platform.

We were ready to move on to the next stage.

Growth

How do you go about growing something like a self-publishing platform for B2B professionals? How do you create public awareness? Would press coverage do the trick? High-profile technology publications, with all of their reach, would be a nice start... wouldn't they?

Indeed, we tried various forms of press outreach. After making a bad choice with a PR company for the German market, we chose the PR company for our international venture with care. After months of consideration, research, and negotiation, we made a deal with high hopes that we would see the benefits of this lucrative investment. While it would be wrong to say we gained *nothing* from this several-month contract, it would be an exaggeration to say that it was worth the time, energy, and money we put into it.

Maybe we chose the wrong firm or worked with people not experienced enough with an international startup market. Regardless of the reason, we only barely inched along.

Eventually, we were forced to go out on our own to create brand awareness and ignite public interest.

The Big Guys

This time, we aimed for the big guys and landed one on our own. Coverage on GigaOM (*http://gigaom.com/2012/04/10/lets-make-a-deal-exploreb2b-social-network-goes-global/*) inspired positive feedback surrounding our concept and functionality. But as it turns out, getting highly coveted coverage is not enough. What happens is this: you get a spike of traffic, a couple of hundred or even thousands of visits for a day, but only a fraction of the traffic persists.

PR can work if you manage to stay continually on the radar of journalists. We did not succeed in getting enough "coverable" news out over and over again and thus faced the problem of limited exposure.

After these efforts, what did we learn?

Our PR Still Stank

Without a celebrity investor or seven-figure financial round each month, we were forced to do what startups do best: build something from nothing, by using what we had.

Looking back, this hardship turned out to be a great thing for our business development. Without being able to rely on press coverage, we were forced to learn and engage in a marketing strategy—to find other ways to generate traffic and convert our target audience.

Essentially, our lukewarm PR made us better entrepreneurs.

How, Exactly, Did We Manage to Grow?

As a social publishing and content marketing platform, we decided to do exactly what we had been advising our target group to do: run a content-based social media campaign. The steps were as follows:

1. **Research our target group.** This involved getting to know the habits and motivations of our target group within each social media and online channel. It also required us to understand the conversations that were talking place about issues relevant to our service, and to know what our industry influencers were saying. Specific to our success were analyzing Twitter and LinkedIn.

2. **Connect with influencers.** Connecting with influencers allowed us to learn the language of our industry and lay the foundation for future interaction. When we later began to produce content, we could guest post on these influencers' blogs/websites and involve them in a series of interviews. In both cases, we found ways to expose ourselves to their followers.

3. **Create content of utility.** We knew that our content had to be informative and engaging. Yet, the content that really made a difference for us was that which offered our platform and social media communities a sense of utility. If our content could be used to better understand the industry or tackle a common problem, it was more likely to be shared and discussed.

4. **Publish content.** This was when we had the opportunity to do what we had been advising our target group to do the whole time: publish on exploreB2B (*https://exploreb2b.com/*). Not only did we publish articles on our platform, but we guest posted on active and relevant sites and blogs.

5. **Distribute content**. Publishing content was only one step of the battle. Distributing the totality of our content through our social communities served to create leads to our platform and, in turn, grow these subsidiary networks.

6. **Continue to grow online communities**. This was one of the largest factors in our spike in traffic and referrals. Once we'd grown our Twitter accounts and initiated daily interaction in LinkedIn groups, whole communities of like-minded people were exposed to—and became familiar with—our brand name. Growing our Twitter account from miniscule to five-figure follower numbers brought about a powerful increase in our visibility. Even though we are B2B, this kind of "social branding" played a large role in our growth.

Through a campaign of trial and error, we learned that social media and content marketing success is not immediate—and that it is not the result of one magical post. The persistence of our actions and the combination of the different measures resulted in a social media following, trust in our content, visibility, and stable platform growth.

What Were Our End Results with PR?

1. A spike in traffic during April 2012

Yes, that's it. And it was smaller than our current (steady) growth rates.

What Were Our End Results with Content Marketing?

1. Brand awareness
2. Connection to key industry influencers
3. Large and active social media followings on more than one network
4. Trust in our useful and engaging content
5. An increase in weekly visits by a factor of 10
6. An increase in registrations by a factor of 10

In the few months we have spent content marketing, we have achieved something that gives much more value to our company than traffic spikes created by media coverage. We have an ongoing dialogue with our users, a network base that constantly returns to our site, and consistently grow our traffic.

Results from our content marketing campaign far outweigh any benefits we gained from being covered in the press.

We have survived by making ourselves the leaders of our own movement, utilizing the platform we created, employing the marketing strategy we recommend, and connecting to thought leaders in our field.

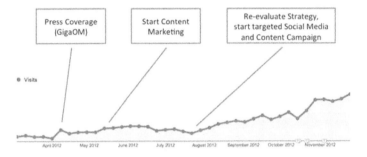

Though our content marketing results were not instant, we were able to use this time to build trust and establish a reputation in "social business."

With positive feedback from users and a steady increase in their own article production, we now sense real stability in our social media and platform interactions.

At This Point in Time, Our PR Still Sucks

But maybe that is just the point. It was due to the fact that our PR efforts were not successful that we attained something that has proven more valuable in the end: steady, self-achieved, and sustainable growth.

The Fate of Your Brand

My advice for startup growth is to not rely on the press to determine your market reputation. Instead, formulate a connection to your target group members by telling your own stories and sharing knowledge that defines your industry leadership. This provides a foundation for your own means of security and growth.

Using methods such as social media and content marketing, figure out where you can reach your target group and pursue them in helpful and entertaining ways. It's not the tech journalists, bloggers, and authors covering your competitors who protect and ensure the bottom line of your company.

In the end, it comes down to the people who trust *you* and find value in your ideas to decide the fate of your brand.

Some Tips for Interacting with the Press

Chris Dixon (http://cdixon.org/)

Here are a few things I've learned over the years about the best ways for entrepreneurs to interact with the press (by press I mean blogs as well as traditional media):

- Don't be afraid to ask what the rules are. Is this on or off the record? If they are writing an article about your company, do they require exclusivity? What is the angle of the story?

- Don't use a PR firm unless you are so successful that you need someone to help you manage inbound press interest. Most journalists, when talking candidly, will tell you they'd vastly prefer getting an email from the founder of a startup than a PR firm. If you're Bill Gates, it is understandable that you have someone reaching out for you. If you are a small startup, having a PR rep contact a journalist says, "I'm not competent enough to reach you" or "I don't respect your time enough to reach out directly."

- Treat journalists with respect. Tech/business journalists often interact with rich and powerful people, some of whom treat them disrespectfully. Like entrepreneurs, journalists are usually interesting people with diverse interests. You'll probably like them if you talk to them, and you might even become friends.

- Unless you're a super-hot startup, the existence of your company is not a news story. Exclusives of launches, financings, and acquisitions are usually news stories. Trend stories that you are part of could be news stories. Relating your startup or data your startup generates to something already newsworthy (journalists call this "pegging") can dramatically increase your chances of getting covered.

- Whether you like it or not, the press will put your company into a category, and might run "horse race" stories comparing how the companies in your category are doing. The best you can do here is to try to choose which category you'll be put into. Arguing that you have no competitors or are creating a new category is pretty much impossible.

- Try to put yourself in the mindset of the journalists. How will this story get them on Techmeme (*http://www.techmeme.com/*) or featured by their editors? What were their most successful recent stories? Do background research on any reporter before talking and read a bunch of his/her articles.

- Don't just contact reporters when you need them: try to be helpful even when you don't. Sometimes I get calls to talk about, say, the state of the venture market or asking for some background on a tech sector that is new to the journalist. My guess is that they appreciate this and are more responsive when I contact them about a possible story.

30

Startup Branding: A Practical Guide for Entrepreneurs

Mike Troiano (http://bit.ly/onstartups-branding)

1. What does startup branding really mean for an early-stage company? Is it just picking a name and a logo?

"Brand" is one of those words everybody uses and nobody really understands, so I'll start with a definition.

It's important for entrepreneurs to understand that their "brand" is the collective emotional response to their product or service. A brand is not a logo, and it's certainly not a URL. Those things are the stimuli, while the brand is the response. It's something out there, in the hearts and minds of the people you hope to sell to.

So... do I think it's important for startups to be thoughtful about the nature of the emotional response that might serve their interests, and try to build a graphic identity designed to elicit that response? Abso-freaking-lutely.

2. Any favorite startup examples that you think are particularly clueful about brand and drawing out the right emotional response?

Sure, a few come to mind right away.

Zipcar (*http://www.zipcar.com/*) is a brand we've played a role in since the beginning—it isn't about urban lifetstyle, or being green, or collective commerce, really. From day one it's been about Freedom, from both the hassles of car ownership and car rental (wheels when you want them). Focus on that emotional value proposition has guided everything from brand identity to vehicle selection at the company, and Zipsters around the world have responded with not just loyalty, but advocacy.

Path 1.0 (*https://path.com/*) was a decent execution of an interesting idea: that you could derive more value from a smaller social graph of actual friends than you could from Facebook's comparatively industrial-sized cohort. The problem was, there wasn't anything in the original UI to inspire an emotional response, and the service foundered. While much has been made of the radical turnaround in user experience for v2.0, for me the result of those improvements is a kind of easy intimacy on the mobile device, something that distinguishes Path from other networks and is the root of users' newfound enthusiasm for the product.

Instagram (*http://instagram.com/*) is interesting because they got it so right in the product, and so wrong in the messaging. Does anybody really love Instagram because it offers fast, beautiful photo sharing on the iPhone? Really? I think Instagram helps us notice and share more of what we find beautiful in the world (*http://scalableintimacy.com/what-instagram-does/*). And I know that promoting it that way would help them grow faster.

3. Speaking of names, how do I pick a great name for my startup? Does it really matter all that much?

I've always thought it matters less than people think.

10% of names are great, and that helps a business at the margin, and 10% of names are crap, and that hurts a business at the margin. The implication is that 80% of names are not a material driver of brand impact or business success, so sometimes it's just best to get on with it.

For proof of this, there's a great story George Lois (*http://scalableintimacy.com/the-real-don-draper-me/*) once told me, about the first time he heard about a client called "Xerox," in the '60s.

"It sounds like a Chinese laxative," he said. I bet it did to most people, and they did OK.

The point is you can make just about any name mean something to people with great product execution over time. Spend some time getting the tactical fundamentals right—URL-friendly, sticky, distinctive, that kind of thing—then pick something three of your cooler friends think is decent, and move on.

4. What about logos? Can I just hack something together? Use a crowdsourcing service like 99designs? Or is that a waste of time?

I think logos and the graphical identities of which they are a part matter a lot. They're something the West Coast– and NY-based guys seem to care about and do way better than Boston-based startups, and that's always bugged me.

Look... in the early going perception is reality for a startup. So is it worth investing a little dough to encourage the perception that you're professionals; that this is a serious and professional undertaking; that you care about design and brand response? I guess there are a few businesses where it isn't. But for the vast majority I'd say it absolutely is, that it's worth investing in a professional identity.

If you're among this vast majority, you want to work toward something smart, not just something pretty. What I mean by that is you want to start by being thoughtful about your brand, meaning the emotional response you want your product to elicit as well as any practical ideas or metaphors that will help people understand what you do. Armed with that, you should sit down with a reasonably priced freelance designer to brainstorm some treatments, and keep at it until you hit on something you and others seem to like.

In my experience great design comes from the collaboration between someone with a clear vision for a problem (a thoughtful entrepreneur), and a professional with the talent and craft to create something great (a real designer). You just don't get that interaction using the crowdsourcing guys, which is why I think you get what you pay for there.

5. Any tips on where to find a great freelance designer for a startup logo? And what would you consider reasonably priced?

Try checking the portfolio sites, like Carbonmade (*http://carbonmade.com/portfolios/ logo-design*). Find someone whose work you admire, then call them to talk about your project. Look for someone with whom you have chemistry, who can bring ideas to the table and not just pictures. And take their advice when they offer it—they do this for a living.

Expect to pay $50–75/hour, and to be glad you did.

6. How do I decide what category my startup falls into? Is it better to find an existing category, or blaze the trail of a new one?

The short answer is, it depends, but on balance it's better to pick a category that already exists.

From a marketing communications standpoint, a category is a frame of reference for the buyer. If you think of it that way the value of one becomes clear, as does the time, hassle, and expense of creating your own.

That's not to say that sometimes it doesn't make sense to create a new category, and I've used HubSpot (*http://www.hubspot.com/*) as an example of a company for which it was necessary. For entrepreneurs enamored of that idea, I often follow my HubSpot observation with the question, "So how's your book coming?" That question is usually met by a blank stare, but the truth is that level of commitment to IP is what it's going to take to create a category.

If the opportunity cost of doing that is too much for you, just hold your nose, pick a category, and focus on communicating your distinction within that category in a way that resonates with your target.

7. How much does good branding matter when trying to raise capital? Is smart money really fooled by that kind of thing? Will I look foolish for having invested in branding?

I'll say it again: perception is reality for an early-stage startup. One can argue that the world would be a better place if this were not so, if Excel drove more decisions than PowerPoint. But that argument is a waste of time, my friends.

VCs invest in the companies that win over their hearts and their minds, usually in that order. If you're trying to raise money it's important to remember this, and to invest the time and energy you need to court a little loving, and not just a good first-look scorecard.

And the same is certainly true for customers, so sooner or later you're going to need to spruce up a bit and look like a brand they want to be a part of. Why not start now?

PART VI

Product Management/ Product Design

Sometimes It's Not the Change They Hate

Laura Klein

There has been a lot of discussion in the design world recently about "change aversion." Most of the articles about it seem to be targeting the new Google redesign, but I've certainly seen this same discussion happen at many companies when big changes aren't universally embraced by users.

Change aversion is a real thing. Often people don't like something different just because they're used to the old way. Once they get used to the new way, they discover all the wonderful new features and are happy with the new change.

But sometimes your users' rage isn't change aversion. Sometimes your new design actually sucks.

So, before you blame your users, you should figure out if it's change aversion, or if you really screwed something up. Ask yourself the following questions.

Did You Do Any Sort of User Testing Before Launch?

This is an important one. Sometimes people complain about a product because it has changed. Other times they complain because the product makes them feel stupid or it prevents them from doing what they want to do.

Most often, products make people feel stupid because the products are hard to use.

It's very possible that the changes you made to your product have made common tasks that the user is used to performing harder to do. Yes, the user may eventually learn to perform the tasks the new way, but that new way may be legitimately more difficult! You may even be reducing the amount of time the user spends performing that task, if you make it hard enough.

To pile onto the Gmail redesign for a moment, I can tell you right now that I am constantly hitting the folder button instead of the label button now that they are icons rather than text. I am still occasionally doing this probably a month after I switched to the new look. It's not a deal breaker for me, but it annoys me every time it happens. The new icons, for me, are honestly harder to use than the old buttons, and they build up a certain amount of unhappiness every time I use them incorrectly.

The interesting thing is that this is exactly the kind of problem that you can surface very easily by simply doing some observational testing of people using prototypes or early versions of the product.

Hell, you could probably even figure that one out with metrics. How often are people hitting the Undo button now compared to previously? If people are undoing their actions more frequently, you can bet that your new design is causing them to make mistakes.

Did You Test with Current Users or Just New Ones?

When you have millions of users, it's not cool just to test on people who have never seen your product before.

New user testing gives you really valuable feedback, but it's just one kind of feedback. It doesn't give you any insight into how your current users (often users who are paying you money) are using your product right now.

It may be that your users are doing something surprising with your product. They may be using it in ways you never anticipated. Making major changes without understanding your users' work styles can destroy something they were relying on.

It's not a matter of their relearning how to do a task in the new interface. You may literally have removed functionality for people who were using your product in innovative ways.

Similarly, if you're only testing with internal users (that is, users internal to your organization), you're not really getting the full idea of how all sorts of different people are interacting with your product. The more types of people you can observe, the clearer your understanding of real use cases and behaviors will be.

Did You Add Something Useful to Users? Really?

Sorry, improving your brand is not particularly useful to users. Even a nice new visual design tends not to be a big enough improvement if you're also changing functionality that users rely on.

Here are some significant improvements that might be enough to counteract a tendency to change aversion:

- Making your product noticeably faster or more responsive

- Adding a great new feature that users can understand and start enjoying immediately
- Fixing several major bugs that people have been complaining about

That's pretty much it.

The problem here is that often companies mistake doing something that is good for the company with something that is good for the user. That can be a tricky thing to spot, but a good way to handle it is to always ask yourself, "What real user problem is this change solving?" If the answer is, "How to get them to give us more money" or "Well, there's more visual breathing space," you might want to brace yourself for the inevitable shitstorm when you launch that change.

Do You Mind Losing a Portion of Your Users?

This is a 100% legitimate question to ask. Sometimes you make changes to your product that you know will piss off a certain subset of your users, and that can be okay.

I've often advocated for prioritizing changes that help your paying customers over changes that help your non-paying users. But there can be other reasons to make changes that annoy certain groups of your users.

The thing is, you have to know that you're making this trade-off and be okay with it. If you've gone into the change knowing that you might lose a certain percentage of your users, but hoping that you will make up the loss by making other users very happy or attracting new users, that's a fine choice to make. Just be sure that your metrics show this actually happening.

Have You Honestly Listened to Your Users' Complaints?

Let me give you two common examples of user feedback:

- "I hate it! It's terrible! I want the old way back!"
- "I'm constantly hitting the folder button when I want to hit the label button, and I find it really hard to tell which emails are more important any longer. Also, every time I try to 'Reply to All' in the middle of an email thread, it's just ridiculously difficult to do."

Can you spot why they are so different? That's right, one of them is completely non-actionable. There is nothing you can really react to with the first one. You can't fix this user's problem. Yet.

The second one is significantly better because you're starting to get at *why* the user hates the change. You know that the user is having trouble performing specific tasks. You can follow up with the user and have her show you the things that you have made harder to do. You can then figure out if those are things that are done frequently enough and by enough users to justify making them easier to do.

Here's the trick. You can turn the first type of feedback into the second type of feedback by following up with users and asking them for specific things that they hate about your change. If they just keep saying, "It's different!" then they may get over it when they get used to it. But a significant portion of them probably have specific complaints, and writing those complaints off as change aversion is really kind of a dick move.

Have You "Fixed" the Problem by Letting Users Change Settings?

Stop it. Seriously. Just stop it.

The vast majority of your users don't know how to change the default settings.

It's not a failing. They're not stupid. They just don't know nearly as much about your product as you do, so they don't have a great understanding of the million different ways you've allowed them to customize their experience. They probably don't even know that those settings are there, and even if they do, why are you making them work that hard?

If you are going to include a few settings that they can change, make them obvious and easy to understand, and don't bury them in a thousand other settings that are incredibly confusing to everyone who isn't in tech and half of us who are.

32

What You Will/Won't Learn from Usability Testing

Cindy Alvarez

You will (probably) learn:

- Is it usable? Can people figure out how to navigate through your product?
- Are your calls to action visible? Do people notice the buttons or links that you want them to click on?
- Are the steps to use a feature clear? Can someone figure out how to complete a task that you set them?
- Is your copy clear? As people scan the words in your product, are they comprehending and moving forward smoothly? Or are they frowning and hesitating?
- Is your product intimidating/jarring/confusing/threatening? As people are going through testing, is their body language indicating discomfort? (Do they have furrowed brows or tense shoulders, are they fidgeting or hesitating, are they frowning?)

You will not learn:

- Is it useful? Would they bother if you weren't there in the room watching them?
- Are your calls to action compelling? Will people actually click them?
- Do people understand what your features are? It doesn't matter how "easy" a feature is to use if people aren't aware that the feature exists (or why they'd want to use it).
- Is your copy convincing? When a person comes to your product with behavioral/purchase intent, do the words in your product help push them to action?

- *Why* is your product intimidating/jarring/confusing/threatening? Because body language is at least partially subconscious, people may not notice that they are reacting to your product. Even if they do, they often can't articulate what is bothering them or how it could be resolved.

33

Product Marketing Contribution

Martina Lauchengco (http://www.svpg.com/articles/)

Jane is supporting the launch of Product X, a new release her company is really excited about. She is on the marketing team. Armed with her launch checklist, she schedules a meeting with John, the product manager. At the meeting, John answers all of her questions, draws a market segmentation on the whiteboard, and talks about the key features and why they are important. Jane takes lots of notes and asks John to review what she sends him.

The first thing John gets is a press release. The features are mixed up. There is no positioning—just announcing it's "now available!"—and the quote sounds like it came from a Web 2.0 robot. John inserts corrections. There are so many it's like a rewrite.

Next, John gets the copy from the website. His corrections from the press release aren't in it. The feature descriptions are wrong in an entirely new way because "the copywriter" took a pass. John is starting to worry that Jane and the rest of the marketing team don't get his product.

John asks the head of marketing, Bob, "Are we all on the same page about the product launch?" Bob assures John, "We're in great shape." Bob says this because when he reviews the launch checklist, everything is on schedule. John assumes Bob meant the marketing of his product is part of some grand strategy connecting it with what the market needs to hear.

Assured, John accepts Jane's next meeting request to "review product positioning." "At last," he thinks, "I'll see it all come together." Jane shows up to the meeting and asks, "Now tell me, how do you want to position Product X and what features do you want us to talk about?"

Does this confusion or frustration feel familiar? You are not alone, and are probably suffering from the need for product marketing.

The Problem

What makes product marketing distinct from corporate marketing is its specific focus on using products—most technology companies' greatest asset—to drive market strategy and growth. When a company is a startup with one product, "marketing" and "product marketing" are often one and the same. The need for product marketing as a distinct discipline becomes much clearer when a company branches into multiple product lines or is highly technical or complex.

The Job

My partner, Marty, has written elegantly about the necessity to split product management and product marketing into two separate roles (*http://www.svpg.com/ product-management-vs-product-marketing/*), and this discussion assumes that model.

I have yet to find a company that practiced the two roles as systematically and well as Microsoft, where I began my career. Microsoft recognized that the two jobs generally required different skills and people to be done well. Product management (which goes by the Program Manager title) defined the products to be built. Product marketing (which goes by the confusing title Product Manager) made sure the world knew about the products and why they should care.

It's the "why they should care" part that requires far more product and communication skill than most realize. To hone a compelling strategy and messaging requires deep customer understanding, an analytical mind, broad understanding of the industry and business, and—most important—a really good understanding of the "why" of a product.

It's insufficient to just know a feature set or the business concerns of a C-level executive. If you get the in-depth "why" for a customer as well as the "why" for a product, you can dynamically position your product based on the specific goal or activity at hand. It's this skill—the strategic application of product to achieve marketing goals—and the ability to communicate about it in a clear way that's lacking in many companies. This is the domain of the product marketer.

Product Marketing Responsibilities

Good product marketers have command of:

- Competitive analysis (what is the competition saying and how is it shaping perceptions in the marketplace?)

- Market and customer research (what matters in and beyond our category, what's the engagement model of the people influencing product conversion or the perception of our product?)

- Product positioning (what is it, why is it different, and why should the world care?)

- Product communications/PR/social media (what can we say that will make others do the talking about us?)

- Marketing communications and campaigns—advertising, email, interactive, search-engine, events, etc. (when to use each and to what end)

- Sales support, sales tools (this includes demos and the product knowledge required to build a compelling one)

- Vertical/affiliate/evangelist programs

- Measurement of marketing programs (ROI and mapping to business goals)

In consumer companies, product marketers focus on enabling activities driving acquisition, activation, retention, and referral.

In enterprise companies, product marketers focus on shaping the product's perception in the business and competitive domain and enabling sales channels.

Product marketers' work also bridges product and corporate marketing teams, ensuring new product enhancements shape company messaging and strategy.

What to Do?

In all the companies I work with, when we look at product planning through a product-marketing lens, the what and when of features inevitably changes. Having product marketers participate in product planning discussions ensures every product effort has the maximum market leverage at its back. Remember, if the world doesn't know about a product, believe it is important, or care, it doesn't matter how useful or useable that product is.

Even in organizations with existing product marketers (typical of most enterprise companies), the edges of the relationship between product mangers and their product marketing counterparts varies—due to skill differences, product maturity phases, or often simply the lack of shared understanding of expectations. Don't let old habits get in the way of improving roles. Make sure product managers and their product-marketing counterparts talk often so both feel invested in and understand market strategy.

Adapt until things work well, as each company and group has to find a groove that works for its teams. The ideal relationship is one in which the product manager feels like her product marketer is an essential part of the team. That's also how a product marketer knows he is doing his job well.

However you get there, make sure the world knows why your product matters and invest in great product marketing.

34

Time-Boxing Product Discovery

Marty Cagan (http://www.svpg.com/articles/)

In this article, I want to talk about time-boxing product discovery. First, for those that are not familiar with the term, *time-boxing* is not the same as *time-limiting*. Time-limiting is what we did in Waterfall development—teams would plan a schedule with 2–4 weeks of time to do "requirements and design," and then development would proceed after that.

In contrast, time-boxing simply says that we will decide what we want to focus on in a given iteration, then work for that fixed period of time, and then reflect on our progress and see if we can't improve how we work the next iteration.

This is at the heart of Scrum as a method, and it is especially well suited to delivery because of our critical need to have frequent, consistent release vehicles.

But product discovery is not about delivery. It is about coming up with something that is worth building and delivering. Very specifically, the output of product discovery is a validated product backlog.

The product discovery team (product owner, lead designer, and lead engineer) are working in product discovery to come up with the product backlog, and the delivery team is busy building and delivering the items on the backlog. This model of working is often referred to as *dual-track Scrum*.

I have been reluctant to advocate for time-boxed product discovery because with time-boxing the pendulum can easily swing too far toward output rather than outcome (just get something done, also known as "feed the beast"). Also, for good teams the velocity of product discovery is on the order of multiple iterations per day, in which case time-boxing breaks down.

However, the reason I wanted to discuss the concept of time-boxing product discovery is that I occasionally run into product teams that take far too long and go too slow in product discovery—not a little too slow, *way* too slow. And I know that if they continue to move this slowly, they simply will not get enough iterations produced and validated, which will almost certainly lead to wasted time and money, and failed efforts.

Note that this is not about working harder or longer hours. It is about techniques, and especially about mindset.

The overarching principle in selecting the best techniques for product discovery is: "What is the fastest, cheapest way to validate the idea?" Actually building production software and deploying it live is among the slowest, most expensive ways to validate an idea.

Most of our techniques—including many flavors of MVP tests, user prototyping, and live-data prototyping—are about validating in hours or days rather than delivery sprints (typically measured in weeks and months).

One technique to help teams improve on the speed at which they do this ideation and validation is to time-box product discovery. Let's say that you decide on a one-week time-box for product discovery. On Monday you meet in the morning and decide what you are going to work on (hopefully by taking the highest-priority opportunities from the opportunity backlog). Then you ask yourselves, "What is the fastest possible way we can flesh out this idea and validate it?" The product discovery team then spends the next several days doing exactly that. The purpose of the week is to generated validated product backlog items. At the end of the week, you would then reflect on how things went, and ask yourselves if there may have been even faster ways to ideate and validate these ideas.

For those that want to try time-boxing product discovery, the key question is the best duration for the time-box. Unless you're working on hardware, to me this duration is never longer than one week. One week is a long time for product discovery, and good teams will explore and validate many iterations in a week. On the other end, I haven't seen a duration shorter than one day. So, the answer is likely somewhere between there.

Product discovery depends on establishing a rapid ideation/validation rhythm, and short-duration time-boxing may help the team to move to this mindset.

If you're not moving fast enough in product discovery, consider trying to time-box product discovery and see if this discipline can't help the team to get the feel of a much more rapid test and validation mindset.

35

Product Management Then and Now

Marty Cagan

Occasionally in my work with technology product teams around the world, I run into product managers that are still practicing the role as it used to be defined back in the PC era of technology. These organizations are inevitably frustrated, as the role is not terribly effective and often not respected.

There are many possible reasons why these organizations have never moved forward. Perhaps the leaders are simply perpetuating what they learned many years ago. Perhaps the organization received "training" from one of the many non-technology firms that try to apply their models of the past to Internet-era companies. Perhaps the old role has been institutionalized in a formal corporate product development process.

In any case, after I explain the new role to the team, I find that it sometimes helps to highlight the key differences.

I think this probably works better in person, but I want to try this in written form. Let me say up front that this is a little bit exaggerated (but not much), to shine a light on the key behaviors.

Organization:

> Old: Marketing
> New: Product (product management plus user experience design), a peer to technology and marketing

Education:

> Old: MBA
> New: Computer Science or User Experience Design

Spends days:

> Old: Writing requirements documents

New: Working on product discovery/pursuing minimum viable product

Learns about customer behavior:

Old: With focus groups
New: With user testing and A/B testing

Makes case for project funding based on:

Old: A business case
New: Customer and product discovery

Reads:

Old: The *Wall Street Journal*
New: TechCrunch and GigaOM

Deep knowledge in:

Old: How to use Excel
New: His customers

Loves:

Old: To be the boss
New: To apply technology to solve problems

Sits with:

Old: "The business"
New: The product team (designers and developers)

When things don't go well:

Old: Blames the developers
New: Blames herself

Strives to please:

Old: Stakeholders
New: Customers (because he's learned that's the only way to really please the stakeholders)

Makes decisions based on:

Old: Opinions
New: Data

Communicates with stakeholders:

> Old: With PowerPoint
> New: With prototypes

Attitude:

> Old: Believes her ideas are great
> New: Knows at least half of her ideas won't work

Worries about:

> Old: Competitors
> New: Taking care of customers

Secret weapon:

> Old: Killer features
> New: User experience

Strives to create:

> Old: Profit
> New: Value (because it's the best path to sustained profits)

Live-Data Prototypes Versus Production

Marty Cagan

I have written (*http://www.svpg.com/product-discovery-with-live-data-prototypes/*) about the differences between user prototypes (simulations intended to test the user experience) and live-data prototypes (actual code intended to send live traffic to in order to test real behavior).

We use a live-data prototype (usually in the context of an A/B test) to prove something works, and we perform user testing to understand why it doesn't work, and what we can do to correct.

I'm happy to see so many teams now doing live-data prototypes. However, I often find that teams confuse live-data prototypes with production software. The purpose of this article is to clarify the difference.

First, let's be clear for those that do not necessarily know what is meant by the term "production software."

Generally, this means that this is software we can run our business on. But specifically, this means:

- All of the critical use cases have been implemented and tested.

- The necessary level of test automation is in place.

- The software has been architected and engineered so that it can work at the necessary scale and performance.

- The associated SEO work that may be necessary based on the changes is complete.

- If the product is a global product, the software has been internationalized and localized.

- Activities like code reviews have been done to ensure that the software is something the team can maintain and stand behind.

- The sales, customer support, and marketing organizations have been briefed on the differences between live-data and production prototypes and trained if necessary.

Many nontechnical people often wonder why it can take real time to go from something that's just working to something that can sustain the business, and in large part, these are the reasons. Especially for consumer Internet companies operating at scale, these can be very nontrivial activities.

While I would argue that the items in the list above are critically important, I would also argue that most of these items are not necessary for the purposes of a live-data prototype, and in fact work against our pursuit of the minimum viable product.

Remember that the general principle of product discovery is to find the fastest, cheapest way to validate our hypothesis. We use a live-data prototype to prove that our idea works. Anything beyond that purpose will very possibly prove to be waste.

Confusion about the difference between a live-data prototype and production software can lead to a couple of significant problems.

The first issue is that if the team is not very clear that it is building a live-data prototype rather than production software, it may overengineer the live-data prototype. This is bad because it hurts their ability to iterate quickly and can lead to significant waste. So, we must be very clear with our product team and with the items on the backlog whether this is normal production software–quality work, or whether this is a live-data prototype.

The second issue is that because the live-data prototype is live in the sense that there is something on the site that some people can see and use, others in the company can easily become confused as to its status. Is this something we should be selling? Is it something we should be advertising? Did we even agree to do this? Companies, especially those with direct sales forces, can end up selling something prematurely. Nobody wants to go back to a customer and explain that it was all a big mistake. We must be very clear with the company when something is simply a live-data test, and when it is something we can sell and support.

So clearly there is a big difference between a live-data prototype and production software.

While I don't want you to think of a live-data prototype as anywhere near as expensive to build as production software, I also don't want you to view it as trivial.

It must work enough to handle the live traffic. It must have enough analytics in place that we can understand how it is being used to measure its success. It must run well enough that we're not causing problems for our customers. As just a rough guide, I find creating a live-data prototype to involve somewhere between 20% and 50% of the work of building production software.

There is one special case I run into occasionally in certain types of companies, such as ecommerce. Sometimes the performance of an idea is essential to accurately assessing whether or not the idea actually works. In other words, it might be an otherwise very effective idea, but due to slow performance, the benefits are overshadowed. In this case, some amount of the performance engineering may need to be done during the live-data prototype work in order to ensure a fair test of the idea.

One final note: remember that if your live-data prototype proves to be a good idea, the team will still need to "productize" the live-data prototype, which means turning it into production-quality software. So, you'll need to plan on that work. The good news is that you'll have the evidence and confidence that this hard work will not be wasted.

37

Continuous Discovery

Marty Cagan

I have written recently about how product teams do product discovery in parallel with product delivery. I have also written about how teams sometimes like to time-box their product discovery work.

What I'd like to write about in this article is an increasing trend I am seeing towards both continuous delivery and continuous discovery.

Continuous Delivery is an increasingly popular notion today. The concept has been talked about by many teams for a few years now, but now there are actually quite a few teams really doing it.

Nearly all product teams today do continuous build. The principle here is that if there are build problems, it is really good to find them sooner rather than later, so typically builds are initiated the moment changes are committed.

Many product teams have taken this principle to the next step and have learned that integration problems are time consuming, and that by integrating early and often (rather than a "phase" before testing), they can significantly speed up their overall throughput by minimizing the time that they are working in isolation.

Similarly, instead of testing everything in a phase at the end of a release cycle (even a 2-week release cycle) and finding all the problems at once, it is much better to run automated regression test suites continuously to find newly introduced issues as soon as possible (which significantly reduces the possible sources of the issue and hence the time to correct).

Quite a few teams now are taking this principle to its logical conclusion and releasing continuously (known as continuous deployment). This means that each logical change (or sometimes groups of changes) are released in small "micro-releases" as soon as they are ready. There are a couple pretty significant benefits to this. The first is that this is the ultimate form of an incremental release strategy which is our key mechanism for gentle deployment – good for our customers and good for us. The second is that detecting and correcting issues in production is much easier when you are just changing one thing, or a small number of things, at a time.

However, everything I've described thus far has to do with product delivery. What about product discovery?

I have long argued for exactly the same principle in terms of how we come up with product backlog items. Rather than a "Product Discovery Phase" where we come up with several weeks of validated product backlog items and deliver them to engineering, I encourage teams to do continuous product discovery – where we are constantly identifying, validating and describing new product backlog items. Some discovery work takes a few hours and other things can take longer, but it is an ongoing process of ideation, validation and description.

In the dual-track analogy, the discovery track is continuously generating product backlog items, and the delivery track is continuously building, testing and deploying these items.

With the continuous discovery and delivery trends, many teams are finding that Scrum as a process can be limiting, and that Kanban tends to fit this continuous discovery and delivery model better.

Even short of moving to Kanban, I have found many Scrum teams that have adapted Scrum in a Kanban direction for exactly this reason. The most common adaptation is that rather than releasing at the end of each time-boxed two-week sprint, they just release features and other changes as they are ready – often doing many micro-releases per week. In this case, they are mainly using the time-boxing of Scrum as a way to structure work and encourage a frequent retrospective.

In general, moving to continuous discovery and continuous delivery is a really good thing and many of the best teams I know are doing this. However, as with everything else, there are trade-offs. In the next articles I will talk about the impact of continuous discovery on release planning, and the impact of continuous delivery on product marketing.

38

The Role of Product Managers

Ben Yoskovitz

Recently, I came across an interesting discussion on Branch (*http://branch.com/b/ does-the-world-need-product-managers-any-more*) about the role and future of product managers. I'm not a member there so I couldn't respond directly, but I figured I'd put my thoughts here instead.

One of the comments posted after I read the post is very similar to what I was going to say. Satya Patel (*https://twitter.com/satyap*), who recently left Twitter in a product-related role, wrote:

> *Product management isn't a role or a function, it's a set of skills. Those skills help remove obstacles and grease the wheels so that the functional experts can do their jobs best. Product management also balances the needs of users, the business and the team and makes the difficult tradeoffs needed to keep pressing ahead. In that way, Product Managers are very similar to CEOs. Very few would argue that a company doesn't need a CEO. Product managers are simply CEOs of their products. No organization should be without someone who has "product management skills" and works to make everyone else's lives easier.*

Nabeel Hyatt (*https://twitter.com/nabeel*), venture partner at Spark (*http:// www.sparkcapital.com/*), then wrote:

> *An excellent product manager is keeping in mind the long term vision while driving short term results, has the customer intuition to get there, and has the authority/integrity to lead the team along the way —very much a mini CEO when it's done right.*

"Mini CEO" is the phrase I'd use for a product manager. Actually, I'd say a product manager is a CEO without all the "other crap" you have to deal with in running a business. CEOs are pulled in millions of directions, whereas product managers are given the mandate to focus.

I see my role at GoInstant (*http://www.goinstant.com/*) (I'm VP Product) as *a conduit between the outside world and the inside world.* That doesn't mean developers, engineers, designers, and others shouldn't interact with customers and be exposed to the outside world; that's extremely important, so people aren't doing things in a bubble or through a broken telephone. But I focus on having a bigger and more holistic view of the business. I take more input from the outside world, process it, and translate that to the team.

Product managers shouldn't micro-manage. You're not there to stand over people's shoulders, watching what they do and giving them specific instructions to the Nth degree on how they should do their jobs. I also don't think product managers should be solely in charge of designing products. That's a team effort. Even with a broader perspective on the business and more input from the outside world, I don't have a monopoly on the truth when it comes to the product and how it should look or work. I may be the one that makes the final decision—*and I am the one ultimately responsible* (and I believe you need someone in that role)—but I don't design the product top-down.

Decision making isn't solely in product managers' hands either. While you own the product, you don't have to own every single decision about it. You own the bigger decisions on product direction, for example, but thousands of decisions go into a product every single day. You own the responsibility for those decisions, but you trust your team to make them.

"What do you think?" That's one of the most common questions I like to ask. I want to know what others think, and I want to make sure others are involved in the product design and development process. Lean Startup as a methodology helps with this, because it provides a framework for how everyone communicates and evaluates progress. It also closes the gap between engineers and customers. Many startups are now founded by two technical people, and the best ones excel at speaking with customers and serving as great product managers. I wrote about this to some degree in a post titled "The Death of the Business Founder (*http://www.instigator blog.com/the-death-of-the-business-founder/2010/11/24/).*"

Product managers should own prioritization of deliverables. But at the same time, product managers have to take into account what a development team is telling them. You can't force-feed priorities without feedback. You may push a client deliverable in a crunch, but then you need to react when a developer tells you that you've accrued a lot of technical debt and it should be resolved.

Product managers should get their hands dirty. You can't be a good product manager without the ability to roll up your sleeves and get dirty. That may mean coding —but I'd rather leave that to the experts, or to those that are dedicated to that task. More so, it means being able to do paper prototyping, wireframing, quick hacking, etc. It means being good at testing. Even if you have a QA team in place, you're ultimately responsible for everything, and if you can't dig into your own product and find the edge cases, ferret out the bugs, and identify problem areas, you're in trouble. Product managers are not puppeteers pulling strings from on high.

Product managers are leaders. Leaders stand in front of their teams and shield them from the shit. They motivate (understanding how each person on the team responds to different types of motivation), and keep everyone as focused as possible. They reward when appropriate, and identify when there are issues that need resolving. Like a good CEO, product managers have to adapt and respond quickly; they're not sitting back in a reactive mode, they have to be proactive and aware of what's going on at all times.

Of course, there are crappy product managers. And I think a part of the discussion we're seeing about this recently is a result of developers having bad experiences with managers. Like in any profession, there are always crappy people. There are crappy designers. Crappy developers. Crappy teachers. Crappy doctors. But you can't judge a profession or the need for something by those who are bad at it. Judge by those who are great at it and encourage others to move in that direction.

39

Why Companies Should Have Product Editors, Not Product Managers

Andrew Chen (http://andrewchen.co/)

One of the most compelling organizational things I've read about lately is Square's *(https://squareup.com/)* practice of referring to its product team as product editors and the product editorial team *(https://twitter.com/msquinn/status/146402788702818305)*, rather than the traditional "product manager" title. I wanted to share some quick thoughts about this.

Product Manager: One of the Toughest and Worst-Defined Jobs in Tech

The role of "product manager," "program manager," or "project manager" is one of the toughest, and worst- defined jobs in tech. And it often doesn't lead to good products. The various PM roles often have no direct reports, but you have the responsibility of getting products out the door. It often becomes a detail-oriented role that are is as much about hitting milestones and schedules as much as delivering a great product experience.

Thus PMs sometimes end up in the world of Gantt charts, 100-page spec documents, and spreadsheets rather than thinking about products. Now, all the scheduling and management tasks matter, but it's too easy for PMs to lead with them rather than leading with products first.

Bad Ideas Are Often Good Ideas That Don't Fit

In the context of literature, books, and newspapers, it's the job of the editor to pick the good stuff and weave it into a coherent story. You remove the bad stuff—but "bad" can mean it's a good idea but just doesn't fit into the story. It's a compelling and important distinction for the consumer Internet.

Cohesion and consistency are difficult. When you have an organization with lots of very smart people all with their own good ideas, it's difficult to decide which path to take. So often, products are compromised as the product "manager" doesn't feel the responsibility to build up that cohesion as an end in itself, and instead just tries to do as much as possible with the product given some set time frame. Focus, people!

Jack Dorsey in His Own Words

In a recent talk at Stanford, Jack Dorsey described his idea of editors:

> I've often spoken to the editorial nature of what I think my job is: I think I'm just an editor, and I think every CEO is an editor. I think every leader in any company is an editor, taking all of these ideas and editing them down to one cohesive story. And in my case my job is to edit the team, so we have a great team that can produce the great work, and that means bringing people on and in some cases having to let people go. That means editing the support for the company, which means having money in the bank, or making money, and that means editing what the vision and the communication of the company is. So that's internal and external, what we're saying internally and what we're saying to the world—that's my job. And that's what every person in this company is also doing. We have all these inputs, we have all these places that we could go—all these things that we could do—but we need to present one cohesive story to the world.

You can also watch a video (*http://www.youtube.com/watch?feature=player_embedded&v=fsoR-UvZ-hQ*) of Jack Dorsey talking about the concept.

Lead with Product

What's compelling to me about this is that it really orients the role of product to be about cohesive experiences first and foremost. OK, yes, there are still schedules first, but they don't drive the thing—great products drive the process.

Similarly, you don't just jam lots of characters and plot points into a story just because. Even if they are good characters, it can bloat the story. Same with features —sometimes you have many, many good ideas for your product, but if you come to do all of them, you ultimately make it a confusing mess. Instead, you have to "edit" down the feature list until you have a clean, tight experience.

Anyway, I hope to see this trend continue in the tech industry—it sets the right tone for where we should all be focused.

40

Five Outsourcing Mistakes That Will Kill Your Startup

Jayson DeMers (http://bit.ly/VB-outsourcing-mistakes)

Several months ago I was on the phone with the CEO of an SEO agency in Utah who was looking for white-label SEO link-building services for her clients. She wanted to know how my agency was sourcing the work; when I told her that the manual labor was largely performed overseas in the Philippines, she scoffed. "How can you offshore jobs when the American economy is so awful right now? There's no way I would ever consider doing that."

Needless to say, that conversation ended quickly. But the reality is that outsourcing has not only allowed the business to operate efficiently, but has also actually enabled the business to create dozens of American jobs. Without outsourcing, those American jobs wouldn't exist.

Creating American jobs makes us feel warm and fuzzy, but if you're launching a startup, there's one thing you're definitely interested in: money. And you know that to make money, your business is going to need to separate itself from the competition—you're going to need a competitive advantage.

Outsourcing is one way to optimize efficiency and achieve that competitive advantage, but there's a minefield of potential mistakes that can severely hamper your efforts or even kill your startup.

Mistake #1: Outsourcing Something That Shouldn't Be Outsourced

The lure of sending work overseas to cheap labor is enticing, but you need to tread carefully when outsourcing. Mission-critical tasks, tasks that require creative thinking coupled with experience, and tasks that "touch" the client should all be kept in-house. Call centers are routinely outsourced and significantly touch the client/customer, but the impression left on the client is often less than stellar.

So, what are some of the types of tasks that should be outsourced?

- Pieces of your online marketing strategy (SEO link building, social media marketing)
- Research and development
- Software development
- Graphic design
- Data entry

Mistake #2: Not Sufficiently Vetting Your Staff

As a busy CEO of a new startup, there's nothing worse than training an employee and having them disappear on day two. To prevent this, hire an employee and, before you train them, give them an extremely difficult task. This task should be something that they can figure out how to do if they're resourceful. One of my favorites is to ask them to set up a WordPress blog, make it look good, and post content to it. Most overseas workers will have no experience doing this, but there's plenty of information on the Web explaining how to do it. If they accomplish the task, then you know you've got a keeper.

Mistake #3: Hiring Based on Technical Skills Rather than English Proficiency

One of the most common mistakes I see (and have been guilty of, myself) is hiring based on technical skills listed on a resume rather than English proficiency. This mistake will lead to miscommunication, incorrectly performed tasks, poor company representation, and major headaches for you. Rather than grill prospective employees on past experience doing X and Y tasks, just chat with them for a half hour. Take note of the following:

- How's their grammar?
- How's their spelling?
- How fast do they type?

Those are the qualities that you can't train but that will pay dividends in the end.

Mistake #4: Insufficient Management

American employees are accustomed to working from home with little supervision, but trying to do the same with an overseas employee (or team of employees) could kill your startup. I learned this lesson the hard way. I thought I was being a great boss and allowing my employees autonomy. Instead, when it came time to report to my clients, I was faced with a mountain of work that either hadn't been done or hadn't been done properly.

Ideally, you should set up an office and hire a manager to supervise your staff. If you don't have the budget for an office, require daily work reports from your employees so you can monitor their work. Consolidate your employees under one manager that you hire and supervise, or assign management to an assistant stateside. Use Dropbox and Google Docs to organize and visualize the work.

Mistake #5: Failure to Award Responsibility and Reward Good Work

Every entrepreneur eventually faces the need to let go and entrust certain responsibilities to their employees. This can be especially scary when you're assigning work to an overseas employee who you've never even met, but failure to do so will likely result in you losing your employee altogether.

Assign meaningful work and educate your employee on the importance of the work and the role in the business. After promoting one of my employees and assigning her managerial work, she told me that she now looks forward to every day because she loves the sense of responsibility and importance in the overall business that her job has.

Give raises regularly and reward good work. A simple tip of $50 on one month's paycheck will build loyalty and mean much more to your employee than you probably imagine. Failure to do so will result in employees disappearing or getting lured away by other firms looking for trained overseas workers.

Conclusion

Whether you embrace or cringe at the thought of outsourcing, it's worthwhile to remember that you have an opportunity to support the lives of entire families for a fraction of what you'd pay to keep those jobs stateside, all while creating additional American jobs and achieving the competitive advantage you need to foster your new startup. Avoid these mistakes and you'll reap the benefits of outsourcing.

PART VII

Business Development and Scaling

41

Who You Gonna Call? Partnering with Goliath: A Tale of Two Announcements

John O'Farrell (http://john.a16z.com/)

SUNNYVALE, Calif., June 2, 2003

HP and Opsware Inc. Join Forces to Deliver Enhanced Automation for HP's Utility Data Center

SUNNYVALE, Calif., Feb. 13, 2006

Opsware Announces Worldwide Distribution Agreement with Cisco

These two headlines sound pretty similar—"Small company partners with giant company to reach a bigger market"—but they led to two very different outcomes. Our 2003 deal with HP didn't generate a single dollar in revenue, whereas our 2006 agreement with Cisco drove tens of millions of dollars in sales and helped to make Opsware the uncatchable leader in data center software. Why did one succeed spectacularly while the other never took off?

As a startup with the best product, your challenge is often getting it in front of enough customers and getting them to buy. In theory, striking a deal to have an HP or an EMC or a Vodafone sell your product to their customers is the way to cover the market and exponentially increase sales velocity. In practice, however, most "David-Goliath" distribution deals turn out like our 2003 HP deal: great PR, but not much else. Here's the way it typically plays out:

1. The deal is announced with great fanfare and high internal and external expectations.

2. Goliath needs product changes, training, and lots of help to even attempt to sell your product.

3. Goliath deluges your already overloaded people with feature and support requests.

4. You can't justify assigning dedicated people to support Goliath because you can't bank on any new revenue.

5. Goliath sells nothing, or even worse, ends up competing against your sales team for customers you would have won directly at a higher margin.

6. The "partnership" quietly withers away, leaving a damaged relationship with Goliath and a bad taste inside the company.

The temptation for some startups is to try to "make it up in volume"—sign as many distribution partners as possible on the basis that none of them are likely to deliver much on their own. While that degree of over-coverage might feel temporarily reassuring, it only multiplies the challenges exponentially in practice. The only thing worse than having no partners is trying to manage multiple ineffective partners competing with each other in the market and drowning the company with their demands.

In my experience, one well-constructed, high-impact partnership is better than a hundred run-of-the-mill arrangements. Distribution partnerships take an enormous effort to make work. It's just not realistic to have many of them, which is why picking the right one and constructing it intelligently is fundamental. At Opsware, we only had one significant distribution relationship over eight years, but it had a massively positive impact on the company.

Time to Find a Partner

It was early 2005, and things were starting to go pretty well for three-year-old Opsware. We had just closed our $33 million acquisition of Rendition Networks, giving us a lightweight but powerful network automation software product that we christened Opsware NAS (Network Automation System). NAS would allow us to penetrate and rapidly deliver value to new accounts, then up-sell them to our considerably heavier and more expensive Server Automation System (SAS). (Our average NAS deal size was $115k and took a month to sell and a couple of weeks to deploy, whereas SAS deals averaged $765k and could take a year to sell and 6 to 12 months to deploy.)

It made sense to market and sell NAS as aggressively as possible—but we faced a challenge: our direct sales force was small, only covered the US and UK, and had few relationships with network buyers. We needed a big partner with the buyer relationships and global coverage we lacked.

THE RIGHT PARTNER

The right partner was obvious: Cisco. So was the product: NAS.

Thanks to our investment in strategic business development (see the previous posts in this series, "Who You Gonna Call? Navigating the Existential Crisis" (*http://john.a16z.com/2012/01/09/who-you-gonna-call-navigating-the-existential-crisis/*) and "Who You Gonna Call? Strategic M&A" (*http://john.a16z.com/2012/01/27/who-you-gonna-call-the-importance-of-strategic-business-development/*)), we'd been calling on Cisco since the founding of Opsware, from the C-suite to mid-level data center managers. Now we finally had something to talk about. For all its preeminence in router and switch hardware, we knew from customers that Cisco's management software capability was weak for its own devices and nonexistent for, say, Juniper devices in the customer's network. We had the market-leading, cross-platform product. Within days of closing the acquisition, we visited the Cisco SVP responsible for management software and offered him the solution his customers were demanding.

MISSION CLARITY

Before you can construct a high-impact deal, you have to be crystal clear on what you want to achieve. We spent a substantial amount of time up front to achieve internal clarity and consensus across the company on what we wanted from a partnership. These were our main objectives:

- A real commitment by Cisco to market and sell a lot of NAS product, at an attractive margin to us
- Opsware's right to target every Cisco NAS customer for an Opsware SAS sale
- Opsware branding on the Cisco NAS product
- Minimal product changes and a single code base
- Enough assurance of financial potential to allow us to invest in the support Cisco would need to succeed

In a seemingly endless series of meetings in Cisco's blue-gray conference rooms over the spring and summer, we gained a good understanding of Cisco's main objectives. They wanted:

- The ability to sell NAS to any Cisco account, with active support, not competition, from Opsware
- A Cisco-branded product
- Freedom to sell at any price they chose, including throwing in the NAS software free as part of a big equipment sale
- "Insurance" against a surprise acquisition of Opsware by a competitor
- Access to Opsware NAS source code, and even the ability to make derivative works (as you might imagine, this one caused us a lot of heartburn)

All through the fall and early winter, we shuttled back and forth between Tasman Drive and Opsware's office on Mathilda Avenue, alternately negotiating a deal structure with the Cisco software team and updating and strategizing with our sales and product organizations to make sure we were staying true to our objectives. Some issues, like source code, were extremely complex. Nonetheless, like a figure emerging from the fog, a compelling deal gradually took shape.

On February 13, 2006, a year after closing the Rendition acquisition, we announced a worldwide distribution agreement with Cisco. Cisco's enterprise sales force would sell our NAS product, rechristened Cisco Network Compliance Manager, to their worldwide customer base. Opsware's sales force would follow their Cisco counterparts, supporting their efforts to sell the network product and in the process building the relationships and laying the groundwork for a subsequent million-dollar-plus server software sale.

BEHIND THE HEADLINES—A DEAL WITH TEETH

While the press and public endorsement by Cisco were valuable, what made this partnership work unusually well in practice was a smart deal structure designed to achieve both sides' objectives:

- *Minimum revenue commitment*: It took us almost nine months, but we persuaded Cisco to make a binding three-year quarterly revenue guarantee that totaled almost as much as we had paid to acquire Rendition. We helped our Cisco counterparts to understand that this would be a win-win: guaranteeing several million dollars a quarter to Opsware would give Cisco huge motivation to drive sales. In turn, it would give us the assurance we needed to back off on our own

NAS sales efforts and do everything—including assigning some dedicated sales and product headcount—to make our partner successful.

- *Substantial revenue share*: We secured a revenue share and pricing floors that made a Cisco NAS sale almost as financially attractive to us as if we had sold it directly—because Cisco could actually charge more for the software than we could.

- *Co-branding*: The product was marketed as Cisco Network Compliance Manager, "built on Opsware automation technology."

- *Channel-neutral compensation*: To motivate Opsware's sales people to support their Cisco sales counterparts instead of competing with them, we compensated them for every Cisco sale in their territory. While this cost us real money, it made sense because every Cisco sale opened the door for us to sell a much bigger, higher-margin product.

- *Acquisition insurance*: We committed to give Cisco advance notification of any agreement to sell the company, and the opportunity to enter the bidding if they wanted to. (Note this is very different from a right of first refusal.)

- *Source code license*: We gave Cisco a three-year license to view our source code and build on it, but came up with an innovative licensing approach that protected us fully and even generated millions in additional revenue. In any case, we bet they would never actually do anything with the code, and we were right.

GOLIATH DELIVERS...

Within nine months, Cisco was selling large network software deals into accounts like DHL, Costco, Sprint, USPS, and Telstra, and a short time later, they were selling enough to exceed the quarterly minimum revenue guarantee to Opsware. The Cisco deal would go on to generate over 25% of our bookings. Cisco's massive distribution power vaporized our NAS competitors. Just as important, every NAS sale opened the door for our SAS product in accounts we had never penetrated before, providing a major thrust to our high-margin server business.

Figure 41-1. Seen in a Cisco corridor

... WITH A LITTLE HELP FROM HIS FRIEND

Of course, there were many challenges along the way. Cisco people needed lots of training and support to sell the product. There were occasional conflicts over accounts that had to be arbitrated. We ran a separate weekly pipeline call with Cisco to track and drive their sales and direct our follow-on server sales calls. Product change and bug fix requests from Cisco had to be triaged and folded into our roadmap.

However, we were able to handle these demands with equanimity, because we had a couple of dedicated heads in sales and product management to handle them, and a large guaranteed revenue stream that helped the whole company to realize this was a deal worth supporting.

In Summary

Like Opsware's 2003 HP deal, the vast majority of David-Goliath type distribution deals don't deliver beyond PR.[1]

On the other hand, like Opsware's Cisco deal, the right distribution deal with the right partner can be truly transformative. In formulating your partner strategy, consider four golden rules:

1. **Quality trumps quantity.** One well-constructed partnership will have far more impact, and be far more supportable, than lots of toothless arrangements.

2. **Mission clarity is key.** Invest the time up front to get crystal clear on your objectives and those of your partner.

3. **Demand hard commitments.** Big companies are easily distracted. Binding commitments focus the mind and create incentive to deliver long after the deal is signed. (Note: this means finding a senior executive sponsor with the authority to commit.)

4. **Make hard commitments in return.** You will need to invest substantially in making your partner successful. Commitments like sales and product support and channel-neutral compensation are worth making in return for the right commitment from your partner.

Only a few startups invest in the ongoing BD effort to systematically cover the landscape of potential partners and create that game-changing partnership when the opportunity presents itself. For Opsware, that investment paid off three years after our start as a software company. Like the Loudcloud-EDS deal and the M&A campaign that followed, the Cisco partnership provides another example of the power of strategic business development.

---

[1] Note that our objective (and HP's) for the HP deal was in fact PR, so it met its objective. It may well make sense to announce lots of lightweight "partnerships" to demonstrate integration and gain market credibility—just don't expect them to generate revenue, and make sure the company understands that too.

42

A Recipe for Growth: Adding Layers to the Cake

Jeff Jordan (http://jeff.a16z.com/)

Businesses don't grow themselves. One of the most important jobs of a CEO is to aggressively define and pursue a growth agenda for his or her business. Why is this important? Growth typically improves a company's competitive position and provides increased scale and leverage, and investors clearly value growth.

The pursuit of growth continues to be important regardless of the lifecycle of the company. Obviously it's critical early in a company's life... or it won't be a company for long. But it continues to be important as a company develops. Virtually all businesses, even hyper-growth ones, inevitably experience slower growth as they get larger, with their growth rates falling relentlessly back down to Earth over time. I call this effect "gravity," and it will weigh down even the most promising of companies—unless a CEO can find a way to accelerate growth and positively change the long-term growth trajectory of the business.

The first real operating job I had was managing eBay's US business in mid-2000, which included the *ebay.com* website. Virtually all the revenue—and more than all of the profits—of the eBay company came from the US unit at the time, and despite the bursting of the bubble, eBay was still trading at highly robust multiples. So you can imagine the terror I felt when the US segment failed to deliver month-over-month growth for the first time ever in my first month on the job. The heavy weight of sky-high growth expectations was showing the first signs of a potential collision with the brutal effects of gravity.

It was clear we needed to quickly define a growth agenda that had the scale to fight gravity's impact. We quickly narrowed the options down to a few: spend more marketing or spend it more efficiently, innovate the product, or buy a company to help us grow.

Marketing had some leverage, but it was limited. eBay was already one of the biggest marketers on the Internet, and efforts to optimize spend were already underway. M&A, on the other hand, felt desperate and was controlled in a separate part of the organization. So we quickly turned our attention to focusing on product innovation.

One of the first places we looked for growth was in buying formats. *ebay.com* at the time enabled the community to buy and sell solely through online auctions. Many in the community thought this was the magic of the site, and it clearly helped propel the company to a very strong start. But auctions intimidated many prospective users, who expressed preference for the ease and simplicity of fixed-price formats. Interestingly, our research suggested that our online auction users were biased toward men, who relished the competitive aspect of the auction. So the first major innovation we pursued was to implement the (revolutionary!) concept of offering items for a fixed price on *ebay.com*, which we termed "buy-it-now."

Buy-it-now was surprisingly controversial to many, both in the eBay community and in eBay headquarters. But we swallowed hard, took the risk, and launched the feature... and it paid off big: buy-it-now complemented auctions well, brought new users and new listings to the site, and became a very important driver of growth for many years. These days, the buy-it-now format represents over $40 billion of annual gross merchandise volume for eBay, 62% of their total.

With an initial success, we doubled down on innovation to drive growth. We introduced stores on eBay, which dramatically increased the amount of product offered for sale on the platform. We expanded the menu of optional features that sellers could purchase to better highlight their listings on the site. We improved the post-transaction experience on *ebay.com* by significantly improving the "checkout" flow, including the eventual seamless integration of PayPal on the eBay site. Each of these innovations supported the growth of the business and helped to keep that gravity at bay.

I came to call this process of layering in new innovations on top of the core business "adding layers to the cake." Much of the natural effort in the organization is spent on chasing optimization of the core business. This makes sense, as small improvements in a big business can have a meaningful impact. But there is huge potential leverage to adding layers of new, complementary businesses on top of the core (aka "cake"). In the *ebay.com* case, buy-it-now, stores, features, checkout improvements, and PayPal integration were all new initiatives that layered on top of the core business but added something new to it.

The eBay company in its first decade is a good illustration of the impact of "layers on the cake." eBay US was the company's original business, and my team worked tirelessly to optimize it and add layers on top of it. And at the company level, the eBay Inc. management team also looked to add layers. Our first was international expansion, which started in earnest in the early 2000s. We followed with payments, facilitated by our acquisition of PayPal (and it's worth noting here that PayPal's early growth was primarily as the payment functionality on the eBay marketplace). Here's what the result looked like at the company level:

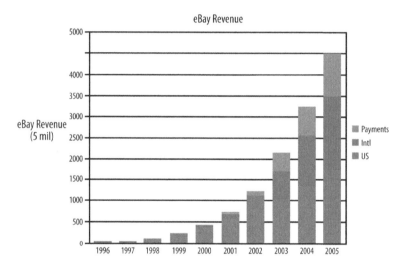

Figure 42-1. eBay SEC filings 1996–2005

eBay US clearly was a fantastic business in and of itself, and it demonstrated strong, sustained growth. At the same time, the international and payments layers grew from virtually nothing in 2000 to around 60% of the company's revenue by 2005. As a result, the overall company grew dramatically faster than its original core business and successfully fought off the impact of gravity for a decade.

And the market rewarded the company handsomely for this growth. Here's what happened with eBay's stock price during the period:

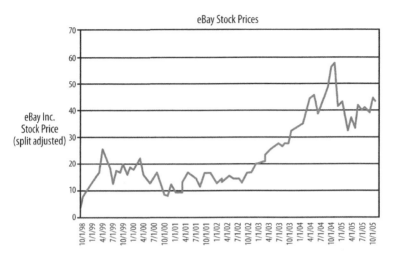

Figure 42-2. Quarterly closing prices for eBay on NASDAQ

After eBay, I continued to deploy the layers-on-the-cake approach at the other Internet companies that I've managed. At PayPal, the key layers we implemented were international expansion, improving PayPal's offerings for merchants who wanted to sell outside of the eBay platform (called "Merchant Services"), and starting to offer credit on top of our payments business. We even trialed a text-based mobile payments product in 2006, although the market wasn't quite ready for it at that time (I'm convinced the product's developers and I were the only people who ever used it).

During my time at OpenTable, the key layers we introduced included building a robust set of mobile applications that expanded diner use cases, expanding internationally (again), introducing a new "Connect" product that meaningfully increased the addressable market of restaurants, and developing yield generation products that helped restaurants attract additional diners. These initiatives helped OpenTable overcome gravity. For example, year-over-year revenue growth rates accelerated from 23% in 2009 to 44% in 2010.

Two other illustrations of the success of this layering approach are provided by two of the most successful growth companies of the past decade: Apple and Amazon. Steve Jobs and the Apple team relentlessly added new layers at Apple that sat on top of their original core business of computers, including the iPod, iTunes, the iPhone, and the iPad. And Amazon in recent years has innovated incredibly skillfully beyond its core physical merchandise business, adding layers such as Prime, digital goods, Amazon Web Services, and the Kindle and now Fire digital devices.

These very large companies demonstrated explosive growth pretty much entirely through brilliant innovation.

Innovation clearly is the success model on the Internet. It explains how Google emerged as the dominant player in search, despite being relatively late to market and competing with established companies like Yahoo! and Microsoft. It explains how PayPal buried the other online payment sites that started around the same time, including *billpoint.com* and *accept.com*, despite these companies having preferred access to the massive eBay and Amazon platforms, respectively. And it explains how Facebook has come to dominate social networking, even though it was very late to market relative to Friendster and MySpace.

These winning Net companies are incredibly strong at product innovation. They invest in it, they create cultures that support it, they prize it, and they reward it. The other companies that failed to capitalize on their early success arguably did not. The best innovations improve and complement the core business of a company, taking advantage of and enhancing its most valuable assets. Diversification outside of the core business is a much more challenging strategy. The further a company strays from its core in its innovation, the longer the odds of success.

I'm a huge believer in the potential for innovation to drive results for all companies, but particularly for technology companies. Core to the CEO's job is to rise above the day-to-day requirements and to keep his or her vision far out on the horizon, proactively delivering new innovations today that have the impact to materially boost the long-term growth of the business in the future.

PART VIII
Funding Strategy

43

Micro-VCs and Super Angels Two Years Later: Looking Back and Some Predictions for the Future

Rob Go

I was surprised to find that it has been more than two years since my post summarizing the state of the seed stage market (*http://robgo.org/2010/06/29/making-sense-of-micro-vcs-and-super-angels-a-primer/*), and trying to bring a balanced view on the rise of Super Angels and Micro-VCs.

The venture capital market continues to be in transition, and a lot of changes have occurred in the early stages of the market. In some ways, many of the forces that drove the rise of Micro-VCs are as strong as ever. But there are also a whole host of new questions that have arisen. Here's my take on the state of things as they stand at the end of 2012.

The Dedicated Seed Strategy Continues to Have Strong Benefits

I call "dedicated seed funds" ones that, at their core, make seed investments. These are not funds that "do seeds but pile in on the winners." Those are what I'd call more traditional "life-cycle funds." Overall, I'd say that if your model is to "lead" the Series A of your best seeds, that is not really a dedicated seed strategy. To do that means that you have a large enough fund to write a $3–$5m Series A check, which is great, but creates a lot of misalignments that true dedicated seed funds have.

Given this definition, we continue to see dedicated seed funds providing strong benefits for founders, including:

Minimal signaling risk at the next round of financing

Chris Dixon has written (*http://cdixon.org/2012/04/02/revisited-big-vcs-investing-in-seed-rounds/*) most articulately about this, but many others have as well. What's interesting is that the threat of signaling seems to die down and then flare back up when a bunch of young companies that have been "seeded" by large funds (sometimes many large funds in the same round) hit a brick wall when none of those funds aggressively leads the Series A. This risk is alive and well and makes dedicated seed funds a compelling option for founders.

Flexibility of exit options

This continues to be true, but as seed funds have increased in size and become more institutional, these managers are realizing that it's hard to make a living hitting singles and doubles and moving their funds. For the most part, I think seed funds are still fairly founder-aligned when it comes to early exit options. But at this point, I think most investors realize that they need their best companies to pursue big outcomes to drive real returns. Math, however, continues to favor seed funds, many of which can return significant portions of their funds with $100–$200m exits. A $40m seed fund with 7% ownership can return 25% of the fund in a $200m exit, whereas a similar outcome for a $500m fund with 20% ownership only returns 8% of the fund.

Willingness to lead

Seed rounds in good markets tend to have lots of investors who are eager to participate, but there often needs to be a catalyst to set terms and make the round really happen. Many of the leading seed funds and early adopters of the strategy are perfectly happy to lead and have been doing so for years. In addition to our fund NextView, we often (or usually) see funds like First Round, Founder Collective, Softech, Floodgate, and others fighting for lead positions. But many funds that used to only occasionally lead are starting to do so more and more often, which is overall a good trend, I think.

Partner time

This is one factor that I think may have gotten less favorable in recent years. One of the pitches of seed investors is that they both have the relevant experience needed to really help companies and are incentivized to spend more time helping founders than the very large funds. In many cases, this is still true. But I'm noticing this value being diluted somewhat, for a few reasons. First, many of the funds were extremely prolific in their early years, and didn't have a well-established model for managing their time and capacity. Only a few funds have really found ways to create meaningful leverage for themselves as they scale and build large portfolios over time. First Round is a great example of one fund that has started to do this. The second issue is that many seed funds have expanded their teams to address capacity constraints. In some funds that have a strong "alpha" investor, there is a dilution of the value proposition to founders if the new team members aren't as strong, and/or the new team members do not have the full authority to "speak for the fund." Some funds have done a wonderful job of adding human capital to their teams, but some have not done as good of a job. Time will tell how this evolves, but adding team members always adds new risk that both small and large funds face.

Evolving and Converging Strategies

As this segment has evolved, another trend has been an evolution, institutionalization, and overall convergence of strategies. This is not a surprise. In general:

- **We've seen seed funds becoming more focused on ownership and minimum investment sizes.** Because time is often the most precious resource for seed funds, it is increasingly important to make every investment more "impactful" in the case of success. This means greater focus on ownership, pre-money valuations, and dollars in. We're seeing more and more funds "walk away" if they can't get the numbers they hope to get. Having a really teeny piece of a hot company is good for the brand and the website, but unless the company is an absolute monster, it's hard for those investments to really move the needle.

- **As a result, we've seen seed funds reserve more capital for follow-on rounds.** It's a similar argument. You need to own more of your winners, and you want to put more capital into those winners. So, you need to reserve more. I'd bet you'll see that for every seed fund that is in their Fund II or III, their % capital in follow-ons/initial rounds has gone up, maybe by a factor of two or three.

- **As a result, we've seen seed funds raise larger funds to make this happen.** In some cases, seed funds have decided to reduce the number of investments they make per fund to concentrate capital better into winners. But for the most part, I don't think the reduction in portfolio sizes overall balances the increase in reserve capital. Put another way, you don't see funds simultaneously tripling reserve capital while also cutting the number of core investments they make by a factor of three. As a result, fund sizes must increase.

I should say that a small handful of funds continue to pursue a high-volume, small-check-size strategy. Groups like 500 Startups and SV Angel continue to build very large portfolios. The strategy behind that is that there is a much higher probability of catching a super-outlier if you cast a wide net. Ironically, although some folks pooh-poohed this strategy early on, as more seed funds are concentrating capital, I think the strategy has increasing merit.

If you've been following this logic, you will see that it's circular. As ownership matters more and fund sizes get bigger, this will only create more pressure for seed funds to write bigger checks and own more, which will create more pressure to raise larger funds. Oh, and by the way, once you have a big fund, you start to say, "Maybe we should go ahead and just lead this Series A of the really terrific company we just seeded. And maybe we'll start passing on seed rounds and think, 'If this really takes off, we'll just lead the A anyway.'" This is on top of the existing motivation to raise large funds to increase fees. This leads ultimately to...

A New Normal?

These changes beg the question of what the future holds. There are a couple ways to think about this:

- **Same old story?** One could look at the past several years and say that this is just the continuation of the same old story. Successful funds get too big, which leads to the formation of new funds that have success, which leads to the small funds getting bigger... rinse and repeat. By this logic, the seed funds of today are essentially the mid-size life-cycle VCs of tomorrow, and the most successful will be the monster mega-funds of the day after tomorrow. This is already starting to happen in some cases. But there are also admirable cases of funds that are sticking to their knitting even though they could probably raise 3–4x the capital they have in their current funds.

- **A new normal?** One could also argue that rather than a repeat of the same movie, what we have is a new normal in a new environment. This view purports that dedicated seed funds are a fundamentally new category that will continue to exist and thrive in capital-efficient sectors, along with life-cycle funds and mega-funds. Signaling risk won't go away, and the perils of fund math won't go away either. Perhaps many of the elite funds will maintain a dedicated seed strategy and realize that their deal flow and competitiveness will be significantly degraded if they increase fund size.

- **The institutional seed as the new Series A?** Perhaps a blended view of the two perspectives is that because of capital efficiency, the $500k–$2m seed is essentially the "new" $5m Series A that used to be the bread and butter of the venture industry. So, essentially, we'll see that the $100–$300m "early-stage funds" and the $30–$75m "seed funds" will converge and become the same category.

A Few Predictions

Although I am not an unbiased observer, let me offer a few predictions for what we will likely see over the next couple of years:

- **At least two high-profile "seed funds" will become lifecycle funds.** These funds will start to invest more than $35m/partner, have a greater than 3:1 follow-on to initial investment ratio, and will noticeably start doing fewer and fewer seeds (or will noticeably start following on to fewer and fewer companies).

- **Some seed funds that have grafted on new team members will break apart.** Creating partnerships is really hard, and I think many funds that haven't seen institutional partnerships at work before (and even some that have) will have a hard time keeping teams together. Again, I'd predict that at least one high-profile team will break apart.

- **We will hear a lot less about the "Series A crunch" and also about "investor signaling" in two years.** I predict that most large lifecycle funds will scale back their seed-stage promiscuity, because they've realized that it's just not a great product for founders. Instead, we'll see most large funds doing a small handful of seeds only when there is very high conviction. This, coupled with greater discipline among dedicated seed funds, means that the difficulty of raising seed capital from good institutional investors will increase. And if the top of the funnel shrinks, the crunch in the middle will be less pronounced.

44

Why Do VCs Have Ownership Targets? And Why 20%?

Rob Go

Ownership is a relatively puzzling concept in venture capital. It seems like almost all institutional investors have an ownership target, and many stick to that number pretty religiously. But why, and where does that come from? I remember when I first started learning about the VC business, I found the number to be completely arbitrary.

A related pet peeve of mine is that some funds often dismiss other, usually smaller funds with a statement like, "Well, they have no ownership in any of their deals." I think that is a false statement because in my view, ownership does not mean anything without thinking about fund size.

Ownership targets are primarily set based on some internal calculation of how an investment can generate "meaningful" returns to a pool of capital. The theory is that it is a poor use of time and effort to make an investment that, in even a very good scenario, is unlikely to yield a return that makes a difference to one's fund. This means that the right ownership threshold is largely dependent on fund size and/or dollars under management per investment partner. A secondary consideration is investment pace and time allocation among investments, but I'll talk about that some other time.

The traditional VC model is optimized around 20–30% ownership. Usually, this is for a fund that has $50m/investment partner who makes ~2 new investments per year. Let's assume we are talking about a fund that has $400m under management and eight people making investments. That means that if they get an exit of $500m and own 20%, they return $100m. Pretty good—that makes a real dent in returning their fund.

But if that same fund only owns 5% in that $500m exit, it returns $25m, which is pretty modest relative to $400m. But, if you take a much smaller fund, 5% could be great ownership. For example, if you are a $40m fund and own 5% of a company, that same $500m exit returns more than half the fund!

From a limited partner's perspective, it's a huge difference. If you have invested $5m in the $400m fund, and they get three $500m exits at 20% ownership, that returns $300m. You haven't even made back your initial investment yet. But if you are a $5m investor in a $40m fund, and they get three $500m exits at 5% ownership, then you have come close to doubling your money. Five percent ownership is quite good in that situation! Now, as an LP, you just have to be comfortable being a concentrated investor in a small fund to put a meaningful amount of capital to work—but a number of LPs have been showing more comfort in doing this recently.

So, hopefully this sheds some light on ownership and how it is linked to fund size. But this also begs the question of why ownership thresholds exist at all. Besides, shouldn't investors just try to invest in the best companies as early as possible and own as much as they can? It's a reasonable argument, and there are a number of investors that I respect that take this point of view. For me, ownership thresholds are pretty important because they impose a discipline to our investing. Having rules and targets is really important, because it becomes blatantly obvious if you start breaking those rules, and you have to ask yourself "why" if it becomes a common occurrence. With no rules, you essentially have no strategy. It's just like running a business. I always encourage even early-stage companies to make basic plans, have milestones, and have product release targets and revenue or customer usage or engagement targets. This isn't about trying to force a company to be myopic about short-term milestones. But it is about putting a stake in the ground, and forcing yourself to ask yourself why you were or were not able to achieve those goals, and adjust accordingly.

45

How to Evaluate Firms for a Seed VC Syndicate

David Beisel (http://genuinevc.com/)

There are essentially two distinct basic strategies for startup entrepreneurs to raise a seed round of capital:

Subscription approach

> An entrepreneur sets a structure (usually a convertible note) and recruits individual angel investors who subscribe to the round, all without a term-driving lead investor.

Term-driving investor approach

> An entrepreneur finds a lead (quasi-)institutional venture investor to price and set the structure/dynamics of the round, working together to bring in additional syndicate partners (either/both other funds and individual angels).

(Sometimes the subscription approach works to include venture capital firms, but only for a very "hot" company or in a competitive environment, like at a Y-combinator demo day.)

Reaching a decision between the above two options is a post for another day, but when entrepreneurs select the latter route, they are then faced with the daunting task of navigating the murky waters of the myriad of firms who at least market themselves as active seed venture capital investors. While we've seen an increasing amount of information and transparency about the players in this market, it can be challenging to embark on a set of meetings raising seed venture capital without a structure to think about potential funders. *Every firm, whether it follows a dedicated seed venture strategy or a full life-cycle approach or somewhere in between, has a set of qualities that affect how it would fit into a seed venture round syndicate:*

Check size

> Some firms have a typical seed check size that is their standard bite size (as low as five figures or as high as seven); some are agnostic and therefore very

flexible, because it's just about the option on the following round; and some have different processes/decision making for different check sizes within a seed round. Unfortunately, this figure is rarely (if ever) on a firm's website, and must be asked about during the first meeting.

Willingness to lead

This leadership dynamic is especially important when talking with seed-only-focused funds, as many have an explicit strategy of only participating in a round coming together with a third-party lead syndicate VC partner. I've seen many entrepreneurs find themselves with numerous parties "interested to follow" but without a firm willing to catalyze the process. There is some correlation here, but not complete alignment, with check size (i.e., larger check writers have a greater tendency to lead rounds).

Active partner involvement level of lead partner post-financing

Venture firms approach involvement after a seed round wildly differently. For larger life-cycle firms that make a myriad of seed investments, partner involvement can be little to none after a seed round. Or, it can be meaningful if the company "counts" as a full investment within the partnership dynamics. Similarly, for smaller dedicated seed firms, partner involvement can vary depending on strategy. In both cases, the amount of time spent is generally inversely proportional to the number of new seed investments the firm does as a whole each year.

Board seat requirements

Partner involvement post–seed financing can, but doesn't always, require codification with a board seat. The board seat dance at the seed stage can be a challenge in either direction, with occasionally no firms wanting to designate someone's time for the role and sometimes more than one looking for an official board role that isn't a fit at this stage. This dimension moves in a similar direction as the previous point of partner involvement (i.e., more time spent translates into more desire for a board seat), but some firms are satisfied with "in-between" measures like official board observer status and defined information rights.

Additional systematic value-add after investment

Strategic venture investors can add a unique set of benefits, firms with large portfolios have network effects where many institute systematic sharing among the companies, and some larger VCs offer a "full-service" range including PR and recruiting and other functions. There are many ways that venture firms can help their portfolio seed CEOs in lieu of or in addition to partner involvement, which can be a real plus but aren't immediately obvious.

Geography

It's always easiest for an investor to make an investment in her own backyard, and especially at the seed stage, with partner involvement, geography becomes a more acute issue. So as a general rule, seed-stage firms have more of a tendency than larger firms to follow a strategy that limits geography to a particular city or region. Of all the firm attributes, geographic preference one is the easiest to discern from a portfolio company list on a VC's website. But actions speak louder than words—sometimes VC firms would like to market geographic focus or agnosticism, but in practice it deviates. No matter what a VC says, the proverbial bar is higher in making an investment outside his typical geography, however that's defined.

Sector focus (or lack of it)

Like geography, sector focus can be more readily gleaned from a portfolio company list than from other marketing, with the two sometimes meaningfully differing. *Where a firm has been and where it wants to go are two different things.* Some funds promote themselves as completely focusing on a particular space, while others take a broader approach. It's important for the partner and the firm to have some background in the area of a new investment, but extremely heavy investor concentration in particular space may have both risks and rewards for an entrepreneur.

Follow-on capital and strategy

Many people have covered this topic in the blogosphere about the perils of venture firms' signaling in follow-on financing subsequent to seed rounds. It's not worth rehashing here, other than to say that signaling issue of larger lifecycle VCs is real. Period. We've seen it directly in our portfolio companies raising successive rounds. That being said, there are indeed clear benefits to having deep pockets at the table immediately from the seed round. I think that the most important aspect of this issue is for a venture firm to state a clear follow-on approach and be consistent in implementing it. *The most trouble comes when a player's intentions are unknown (or undefined) or inconsistently applied, so that there are surprises in the subsequent follow-on process.*

Conflicts of interest in existing portfolio

Especially given that some seed-only funds follow a rapid deployment strategy in making dozens of investments annually, competitive conflicts of new investments and even existing investments with others within a portfolio can be a real factor. Some firms are lax about these conflicts (which indeed are sometimes inevitable when startups pivot), while others are very strict about not having more than one company in a general space. I have observed VC firms intentionally invest in competitive offerings.

Prestige

Nobody explicitly talks about it because it's implied, but prestige matters. It matters in a lot of things, all the way from recruiting to (especially) attracting that next round of financing. On the margin, higher-prestige seed investors attract higher-quality Series A investors.

Institutional LPs and standard VC fund structure

Why their investors' fund structures matter to entrepreneurs isn't immediately obvious. The more traditional plain vanilla the structure of the VC fund is, the more consistently financially motivated the investors are going to be. That is not to say that these VCs are not going to behave badly... just that even the bad behavior should be consistent in trying maximize return. At least you know the driving force motivating actions. In contrast, less-formalized sources or nontraditional structures of capital can *sometimes* (only sometimes) *risk* exerting more erroneous and erratic non-financially motivated behavior. This dimension is about structural bounds and consistency in investor actions and avoiding surprises further down the road.

Personal dynamics

Last on this list, but certainly not least, is personal dynamics. This is about answering the extremely important question: do you want to work with both the person and the partnership on the other side of the table? Are you merely holding your nose because the money is green, or do you truly want to work alongside this person for the months and years to come?

Dedicated seed firms often have fairly set and consistent answers to most of these questions, as participating in seed rounds is their bread and butter. But surprisingly, this is not always the case. And sometimes larger life-cycle VCs aren't as consistent in their approach to the above because the exact parameters of a seed investment aren't clearly defined internally.

Putting together a seed VC syndicate of one or more firms is like fitting together many puzzle pieces. There are different "right" attributes for a startup's round depending on the situation, and then those characteristics can be assembled by selecting the one firm that most closely matches or by aggregating a series of participants that each bring a couple of those attributes to the table. *The key in building the optimal seed VC syndicate is to figure out what qualities should be present and then to construct a scenario that includes them with one or more partners. Without doing easy homework and asking the right questions up front, entrepreneurs can miss out on including valuable investors in the round—or add too many nonvaluable or "redundant" constituents, which just complicates the composition and communication going forward.*

46

A Choir of Angel Investors Sing Different Parts

David Beisel

We at NextView Ventures (*http://nextviewventures.com/*) often invest in a startup's first round alongside other funds; either seed-stage-focused ones like ourselves or larger traditional firms. Just as often, however, we're investing alongside individual angel investors who are participating in the round as well. *Angel investors come in many shapes and sizes, however. And it's not always easy to recognize the pros and cons of taking money from individual investors, or even how to seek them out in the first place.* Addressing both of those issues requires a view about motivations: that is, why someone would want to put their hard-earned cash into a risky early-stage startup in the first place. Along those lines, the world of individual angel investors is easier for entrepreneurs to navigate when they can recognize the categories that those investors fall into based on their incentives and actions. The choir of angel investors out there is comprised of a number of players that sing different parts:

The Super Angel

Much has been written about this category, so I won't belabor the description beyond saying that the defining characteristic is the large number of investments that the Super Angel makes. *Pros* of taking his angel money are the feeder system to venture financing of the next round and the vast network of portfolio CEOs that can be tapped into for connections and help. *Cons* of an investment from a Super Angel include potential lack of "value-add" because his time is spread so thin amongst many portfolio companies.

The Domain Angel

Investors in this category are usually operating executives who have spent their entire careers in a specific industry vertical, like Internet travel, for example. They will have the ability to "see" the opportunity that the startup is going after unlike anyone else, save the entrepreneur herself, because they inherently "get" the space. *Pros*: Industry-insider who serves as a validator for the rest of the investment syndicate, offering extremely helpful advice and network connections. *Cons*: May be more proactive in "offering" advice that is uninvited.

The *Previous Colleague Angel*

Having someone involved who the entrepreneur(ial team) has worked with before can be a good validator to other syndicate investors and future investors that they will all work well together. *Pros*: Nice signal value. *Cons*: Potentially not much value-add beyond the initial financing round.

The *Friends and Family Angel*

These are the proverbial first-commit investors. *Pros*: Known quantities who are usually the first people to be willing to write a check. *Cons*: No value-add subsequently, and can potentially needlessly interject into operations or future financings that are destructive for the company.

The *Grouped Angels*

Especially here on the East Coast, angel investors have formally grouped themselves together for various reasons. This can benefit entrepreneurs because of a one-pitch/many-investors process, but it can be challenging too. Elaborating on both the pros and cons is probably the topic of another post.

The *Fellow Entrepreneur Angel*

Entrepreneurs know other entrepreneurial endeavors best and can be great backers of other businesses—they're likely to be one of the first to take the leap of faith *and* the first to help, which are just two of the *pros*. *Cons*: depending on the size of their previous wins, they may not have a large checkbook; if the relationship is more of a peer than an advisor, they may not be constructively critical.

The *"True Believer" Angel*

These angels are as difficult to find as a diamond in the rough, but there are those angels out there who hear a startup's story, instantly believe, and want to invest immediately, sometimes in spite of the financial risks. *Pros*: Over-the-top encouragement and support, a cheerleader as a balancing voice amongst what-have-you-done-for-me-lately investor syndicates. *Cons*: Lack a critical eye and may challenge to push an entrepreneur after the investment has closed.

The *Financial Angel*

There is a small cadre of angels out there who are diligently and intentionally, but also quietly, building a diverse portfolio of early-stage startup investments through the lens of a portfolio allocation model. Rather than investing in a fund manager to do the work for them, they are instead doing it themselves for the purposes of disbursing their personal capital into a portfolio purely aimed at financial return. *Pros*: Validation for other financially savvy syndicate investors, lack of intrusion (they tend to let the entrepreneurs run their own businesses). *Cons*: often very little help or involvement with the company post-investment, if any.

The "Sport Fisherman" Angel

These mega-wealthy individuals, sometimes not from the startup world, invest an extremely small portion of their net wealth into early-stage startups so that they have something to talk about with their friends at cocktail parties. They do it merely for the entertainment value of participating and care very little if their investments actually yield a return (though that would make for even better conversation fodder). *Pros*: Sometimes these individuals are well connected or have a public persona that can be helpful to the business. *Cons*: Potential lack of concern for the entrepreneur or the company, as there is always another fish to try to catch.

The Foolish Angel

Often bucketed with others above into a "Friends, Family, and Fools" category, I think that the truly naïve blind supporter angel deserves his own category. *Pros*: Money is money. *Cons*: Many, as a foolish owner of your business can influence it in foolish ways.

If, as an entrepreneur, you're currently seeking and pitching angel investors, and they don't fit into one of the above categories, there's a good chance it's going to be tough to get them over the line and make them commit to writing a check. All of the people in the above categories have their own, different motivations, but they at least have those as drivers toward investing. Without a specific rationale, it's an uphill battle to convince an angel investor to part with his own personal capital.

Conversely, when starting a financing process that includes raising money from individual angels, using the above schema as a guide to thinking about who within your network (and your network's network) might be interested in participating as an early investor is a good first step.

At the end of the day, all money is green. But if you have the fortunate ability to be oversubscribed in a seed round and are selecting who you are going to let into the limited space within the round, it's important to think about composing a syndicate of angel investors who come from a deliberate range of the above categories so that you can maximize the benefits and hopefully diffuse some of the potential drawbacks. Here at Next-

View, we welcome investing alongside individual angels, especially when they're going to be constructive in some way. A vast majority of the seed rounds in our portfolio have angel participation; and as my partner Rob explained in a recent overview *(http://robgo.org/2012/01/09/a-stroll-through-the-nextview-portfolio/)*, a third of our initial investments are syndicates comprised of just the NextView Ventures fund plus individual angel investors.

47

Super Pro-Rata Rights Aren't Super

David Beisel

I recently received a email from an entrepreneur I know with a genuine question about the terms of his financing: "How do you guys at NextView feel about one of our investors holding super pro-rata rights for the next round?" We at NextView Ventures have recently seen super pro-rata rights introduced by other investors in a couple of the rounds in which we've participated, and we have started to see a pattern emerge of the consequences of this insertion.

On the subject of super pro-rata rights, a couple of months ago Brad Feld wrote a blog post called "Just Say No," (*http://www.feld.com/wp/archives/2011/09/entrepreneurs-just-say-no-to-super-pro-rata-rights.html*) and Mark Suster (after detailed explanation of both pro-rata rights and super pro-rata rights (*http://www.bothsidesofthetable.com/2011/09/25/why-super-pro-rata-rights-are-not-a-good-deal-for-entrepreneurs/*)) summed up that the reason not to take them is that "you might make it difficult for you to get your company funded in the next round." Mark's argument is essentially that they make the entrepreneur's next fundraise more difficult because of the signal value associated with whether or not the existing VC investor is going to exercise those pro-rata rights.

But the reason that super pro-rata rights aren't super goes beyond just how the VC with those rights acts as the next round approaches. These rights fundamentally misalign incentives on how the company is operated, which is bad for both an entrepreneur and the VC. *The rationale for the negative effects of super pro-rata rights comes down to VC math, in which the latter of the three dimensions for the next round —valuation, amount raised, and dilution %—already become artificially fixed.* So, in order to successfully raise at a higher $x valuation, the resulting math requires the round size to be larger. An entrepreneur can be forced to raise more capital (which the business may or may not need) if she is going to be rewarded with a higher valuation.

This scenario presents a number of troubling incentives. Prior to the next round, the startup risks being run at a higher burn-rate so that it looks positioned to need the larger financing. Second, an entrepreneur is more likely to be compelled to put a larger dollar-amount "ask" on the cover of his next round's pitch deck, which can hurt his chances of a successful fundraise if the business isn't ready yet for a large financing (but would be for a successful smaller one). With super pro-rata rights in play, if an entrepreneur is going to give up a specific % of his company in this round anyway, he's motivated to make that as large a round as possible—which might not be the right thing for the business, as well as decreasing the chances for a successful fundraising process. And lastly, even if the larger amount is raised, again, it can over-capitalize the company, which changes the dynamics of how the business is run subsequently. All of these scenarios are not just detrimental to the entrepreneur/startup, but also to the VC funders themselves, who want to eagerly invest in a company that is doing well.

I see super pro-rata rights as another VC term-sheet bell and whistle that stems from genuine and legitimate intentions (allowing a VC to own more of a company she likes a lot) but that results in misaligned incentives between an entrepreneur, an investor, and what is "right" for the business. As a general rule, deviation from a simple and elegant term sheet (especially in early rounds of financing) can cause strain, and super pro-rata rights are just another (new and emerging) example.

PART IX

Company Culture, Organizational Structure, Recruiting, and Other HR Issues

48

Getting Promoted Too Quickly

Bijan Sabet (http://bit.ly/sabet-promotions-quickly)

"He's a star. Thank god he's on the team."

"He's not scaling, it's time to find a replacement."

I've heard both of those lines from too many CEOs about someone on their management team.

In a hyper-growth company, those two sentences can be just a year or two apart. So what's happening here?

Sometimes it's just that the person that was given the management job was a bad hire. Mistakes happen.

But the more common thing I'm seeing is the bad promotion. In this case bad promotion means premature promotion.

In the early days, when the company is small, the 10x achiever stands out. The founder/CEO looks at that person and appreciates all of the contributions. Then the next thing you know, that one person goes from being the first UI person or first iPhone developer, to being in charge of a soon-to-be-built team.

And that's when it starts. All of a sudden you find that that person, who used to be an amazing individual contributor, doesn't know how to manage a team. His team misses deadlines, quality of work suffers, and the biggest red flag of all happens—he can't get amazing people to work for him.

It's easy to see why this happens when you look at it from the outside (outside is defined as anyone not working full time in the company). The CEO wants to promote the stars, and there is something special about promoting from within. And the killer individual contributor may be ambitious and asking for the bigger job as well.

But being a fantastic individual contributor doesn't mean automatically becoming a fantastic manager.

Ultimately, the CEO has to decide if that promotion worked out or not.

The biggest tragedy resulting from the bad promotion is that more often than not it means that person has to leave the company if he can't scale. And that's always very sad to see. It's sad to see someone so special that made so many contributions not have a role in the company. Once you promote someone it's almost impossible to then demote that person to make room for the new manager.

The very best way to reduce the chances of a bad promotion is to take your time before you take the leap of faith and promote the person. Think about what it means if the person doesn't scale. Think about the different skills between doing the day-to-day job vs. leading a team. Can that person staff a team? Will fantastic people want to work for that person? Can she organize a team to prioritize all the things on her plate?

I've seen some startups try to get ahead of this issue by getting the team leader a coach or a mentor. I like that approach a lot. Invest in your team, help them become better managers. And most of all, be very careful about promoting too quickly.

49

Recruiting Developers? Create an Awesome Candidate Experience

Dharmesh Shah (http://onstartups.com/)

If you're trying to attract awesome developers, you need to create an awesome candidate experience (CX). Something that makes them go, "*Wow!*" It's like UX—but for the people interviewing to join your team.

It seems that every startup I know out there is trying to grow its development team. But given that there are always a hundred things going on, few startups spend the time thinking about their interviewing process (because we're all busy building products and delighting users).

Yesterday, I sat in a HubSpot (*http://www.hubspot.com/*) "Tech Talk." The topic was "Technical Interviews." The idea was to share ideas and best practices across the product team so that we can better find and recruit great developers for the team. HubSpot has had a bit of an unfair advantage when it comes to technical recruiting. We're fortunate to have Paul English, founder/CTO, as a friend (he's hands down the best recruiter I've ever met). Paul was kind enough to be "CTO for a day" at HubSpot. And because Google Ventures is an investor, we've been able to have a Googler from the recruiting team spend a few hours with us, reviewing our practices and giving us tips for how we can improve them.

Ideas for Creating an Awesome Candidate Experience (CX)

Here are some ideas for what I think would make a great candidate experience. Many of these ideas are implemented at HubSpot—and I'm hoping the others will get adopted too. We have some work to do ourselves, but we're passionate about building an amazing product team in Boston (*http://onstartups.com/tabid/3339/bid/37790/HubSpot-s-First-Shot-in-Boston-Battle-For-Talent-Diabolical-or-Desperate.aspx*).

1. **Decide to do it.** The first step in creating a great candidate experience is deciding that it's important. Just like you'd commit time and energy to creating a great UX for your product, you need to devote some calories to iterating on your CX and working hard to make it exceptional. There are a number of reasons you should do this. For example:

   a. Recruiting great people is hard—and competitive. All things being equal, on average, if you can make the candidate experience better, you win. People will often take positions with lesser-known companies simply because they had a great interviewing experience.

2. **Focus on the entire experience.** Designing a great candidate experience is not just about doing interviews well. A great CX starts from the moment a person connects with your company (like your website) and continues all the way through the point that person is delivered a decision—and every step in between.

3. **Measure it to improve it.** It's not possible to create a great CX without getting feedback from candidates. What I'd suggest is a simple Net Promoter Score or NPS-style survey at the end of the candidate interviewing process. The survey asks exactly two questions:

   a. On a scale of 0–10, how likely are you to recommend that a friend or family member interview here?

   b. Why did you give us that score?

   You don't have to use these specific questions—the benefit of NPS is that it is simple and widely used as a way to measure customer satisfaction (or more accurately, customer delightion). We use NPS in a variety of ways at HubSpot —including measuring the happiness of our customers and team members.

   Some quick notes on collecting this feedback: first, it should be collected before a final decision is delivered, so you get unbiased data; second, it should be made clear to the candidates that they are doing you a favor. There's no harm in telling a candidate exactly why you're asking for this feedback. In almost all cases, the candidate will likely see this as a positive signal. It shows that you care.

4. **Interviews are both a buying and a selling process.** One of the mistakes inexperienced interviewers often make is behaving as if their job is only to "be convinced" by the candidate that she'd make a good hire. As a result, they often

have an "edge," aren't particularly friendly, and don't do enough to make the candidate feel comfortable. That can be a bit disconcerting for the candidate, and it creates a suboptimal candidate experience. As an interviewer, your job is twofold: one, make a rational judgment as to whether you think this person would be a good hire for the team; and two, ensure that the candidate wants to work at your company. It's both a buying and a selling process (not just buying). As it turns out, great people always have options. Even if they're not a good fit and you decide not to hire them, you want them to leave with as positive an impression as possible. They may have friends or family that are better fits.

Note

Quick mental hack: Pretend every candidate you don't hire is going to become a future potential user/customer.

5. **Be at least a bit organized**. Yes, you're a startup. Yes, everyone's already working away furiously and interviews are often an unwelcome irritant. But that's our problem—not the candidate's problem. Spend some time devising at least a simple process to ensure that meetings are scheduled appropriately, make sure the candidate knows what the process is (and how long he'll need to be there), and always, always, always make sure the candidate is feeling comfortable and welcome.

6. **Make speed a feature**. Just like a great UX, a great CX is about speed. Faster is always better. I've never met someone that thought, "Boy, am I glad those folks took two weeks to get back to me with an answer...."

7. **Have a "guest" tablet available for candidates**. Make sure it's already on your WiFi network, and that the home page in the browser is your company website. The idea is to give the candidates something productive to occupy their time with while they're waiting. They can even play Angry Birds, if they want. Nothing's worse than sitting in reception, not knowing what the guest WiFi password is, and having to twiddle one's thumbs before an interview.

8. **Don't repeat the same topics**. Be organized enough that if the candidate is going to go through multiple interviews, you don't have her cover the same topics multiple times. That's annoying and a waste of time. If one interview focuses on the candidate's frontend development skills and how well she really understands jQuery, then perhaps the other interview should be more about work style and thoughts on team collaboration.

9. **Have a clear feedback/rating system.** You need to have a clear internal rating system so that interviewers can express their overall take. If the person is an absolute no-hire, that should be clear. So, your scale could be: absolutely don't hire, leaning against, neutral, leaning in favor, absolutely hire. One important point while we're on this topic: the rating scale is not about the person; it's about whether this person should be made an offer at this point in time. I've sometimes seen people give a "high" rating (because the candidate was really, really good, and interviewed really well), but then later heard "but I wouldn't hire him." The reason for the interviews is to *make a hiring decision.* Said differently, *the ultimate return value of the function is a Boolean hire/no-hire NOT awesome/good/not-so-good person.*

10. **Learn something.** Make every effort to *learn something* from every candidate. Just because you're on this side of the hiring table and just because you may be more experienced does not mean you can't learn something from every candidate. You can. Try to draw out a particular passion that the candidate has. Perhaps a recent epic debugging victory, or why her editor is the One True Editor to Rule Them All. Doesn't matter what the topic. Find what they're passionate about, and genuinely get them to teach you something about it. (If they're not passionate about anything, you've got a problem.)

11. **Teach something.** Whether the candidates get an offer or not, they should have learned something from you. They need to walk out smarter than they walked in. (However, this does not mean you spend 50% of the interview telling them about the proper Pythonic way to do something!)

12. **Be transparent.** Make the conversation open. Let the candidates ask questions that are on their mind. They could be about team dynamics, work style/hours, financials (growth, cash, etc.), product strategy, dev philosophy, whatever. Be honest. If there are some things you can't answer, be honest about that. But try to be as transparent as possible—it makes for a much better candidate experience.

13. **No leading of the witnesses.** If you're having multiple people interview a candidate, you need to make sure that the early interviewer(s) don't unduly influence the later ones. This is important for a couple of reasons. First, you want *multiple viewpoints,* not the same viewpoint multiple times. Second, from the candidates' perspective, if they feel like they got off on the wrong foot in the first interview, you want them to have a reasonable chance of showing off their awesomeness in the subsequent interviews.

Warning: Controversial idea coming up! One of the top areas of debate regarding technical interviewing is whether you should "fail fast" (or not). Let me set this up with an example. Suppose you invite a candidate in for four hours for a series of interviews. And after the first interview, the interviewer is absolutely sure that this candidate is a no-hire. What do you do?

a. Thank him for his time and stop the interview process? The advantage here is that you're not expending further (very precious) developer time, when a decision is already made. The downside is that this is kind of disheartening and deflating for the candidate. If he was scheduled for four hours and you send him home after the first hour, that just doesn't feel good.

b. Continue the interview process? The advantage here is that it's (arguably) a better candidate experience. It's also possible that the later interviewers might like the candidate so much that they convince the first interviewer to change her mind.

My general leaning is not to completely cut off the interview process. Having said that, there are a few things I'd try:

a. When inviting candidates in, make it for a time range instead of an absolute number of hours. For example, "Please schedule 3–4 hours for your visit." That way, you can reasonably end the interviews without going through the full "maximum" time.

b. Build a reputation for being super-selective, but fair. Be honest and open about this in the early conversations.

c. ~~Consider offering a $100 Amazon gift card for "early exits". Be transparent and honest. "I just don't think we have a good fit here and it doesn't make sense to put you through more interviews."~~ *Update*: I reconsidered this one. The more I thought about it, the cheesier it sounded.

14. **Get them to code, but let them pick the language**. Coding exercises are a critical part of the interviewing process. There is no substitute for getting a candidate to do a quick coding exercise (either on a computer or on a whiteboard). The intent of this exercise is not to test proficiency with a particular language, but to see if the person can "think in code"—and how he goes about doing it. My advice is to let the candidate pick whatever language he's comfortable with (amongst the mainstream languages available, like Python, Java, Ruby, PHP, JavaScript, etc.). Any of these mainstream languages are more than powerful enough for a coding exercise, and even if you're not completely proficient in

that language, you'll still get a sense for how the person goes about thinking about a problem and manifesting a solution in code.

15. **Do a friendly follow-up after the offer.** Generally, you'll have someone extend the offer in some formal or semi-formal form. In addition to that, have one of the designated interviewers follow up with a quick email (perhaps with a "cc" to the others they met). Something like: "Hey, thanks for visting HubSpot. We'd be thrilled to have you join our merry band. If you ever want to grab a coffee or a bite to eat, just drop me a note. I should probably tear myself away from the computer every now and then anyways...."

50

Startups: Stop Trying to Hire Ninja-Rockstar Engineers

Avi Flombaum (http://bit.ly/onstartups-ninja-rockstar)

Hiring technical talent is often cited as one of the most difficult parts of scaling a startup. Great companies are built by great teams, so naturally, when it comes to technical talent, companies are competing harder than ever to entice the best of the best. The rationale you'll typically hear is along the lines of "a great developer is 10x as productive as a mediocre one." That might be true, but it is an impractical startup hiring strategy.

While companies fight tooth and nail over engineers with MIT or Stanford degrees with years of experience, as CTO of Designer Pages (*https://www.designer pages.com/*), my best hires were consistently entry-level developers that I developed on the job. Some companies, like Zendesk (*http://www.zendesk.com/*) and General Things (*http://generalthings.com/*), have already realized this and are working with schools like Dev Bootcamp (*http://devbootcamp.com/*) in San Francisco, the Flatiron school (*http://flatironschool.com/*) in New York (of which I'm a cofounder), and Code Academy (*http://www.starterleague.com/*) in Chicago to hire their newly minted web development graduates. Aside from the fact that they're significantly easier to attract, there are tremendous benefits to the company.

These benefits include:

Cost

Starting salaries for senior developers have skyrocketed in the past few years. The average starting salary for a senior Ruby developer has climbed to $94,000 ($107,000 in Silicon Valley). Compare that with the average salary for a junior Ruby developer, $70,000 ($80,000 in Silicon Valley). At that rate, you can give a junior developer a 10% raise every year for three years, at the end of which you'll have an experienced senior employee who's been with you that long and is still costing less than a new senior hire.

Attitude

Anyone that gets courted the way a senior engineer does today is at risk of developing a sense of entitlement (to put it lightly). When I hired "rockstars" at Designer Pages, the requests became increasingly ludicrous. Senior engineers had four-day weeks, required conference budgets, and refused to adhere to the language and technology standards the company had established. They always knew best and felt that we were lucky to have them. Junior devs, on the other hand, are hungry. They want to prove themselves and are eager to learn. And assuming you're fostering the right culture, they are excited to be part of your team.

Turnover

High turnover is the easiest way to kill a product. In *The Mythical Man-Month* (*http://www.amazon.com/The-Mythical-Man-Month-Engineering-Anniversary/dp/0201835959*), Frederick Brooks discusses problems inherent in a system designed by a succession of leaders, each with his own style and ideas:

"I will contend that conceptual integrity is the most important consideration in system design. It is better to have a system omit certain anomalous features and improvements, but to reflect one set of design ideas, than to have one that contains many good but independent and uncoordinated ideas."

Great companies need great engineers who want to solve complex problems. But the majority of work being done on a typical web application does not require a team full of PhDs with 10 years' experience, making it no surprise that senior engineers quickly get bored and seek out other opportunities. By hiring junior developers and ensuring they're getting the continual training and development that they need, you can ensure that they stay engaged and derive as much personal and professional value from your company as your company derives from them.

Culture

A prerequisite for being a great programmer is a love of learning. Unfortunately, many senior engineers come with a lot of baggage; they want to work on specific problems, in specific languages, and have little patience for the inexperienced noob. By hiring junior engineers and giving them the training and development they need to flourish, not only can you align everyone's technical styles under a cohesive vision, but you can more easily create a culture wherein it is expected for the senior employees to mentor and coach new hires, just as they were coached when they first started.

To be clear, this isn't true in every case. I happen to know plenty of incredibly humble, loyal, and generous (though not cheap) senior engineers. And if you're trying to build a better search engine, or solve the world's most complex data problems, you probably do need to recruit from the top 1%. Most companies, though, just need great leaders who can help their teams think through the difficult questions, and team members who are willing to work together to implement creative solutions. The bottom line is that *for most products, seeking out rockstar senior engineers is like hiring Picasso to paint your apartment.*

So what's the best way to put this plan into action? Here are some things I've found to be effective when developing junior engineers at Designer Pages:

- **Deploy on day one.** Making engineers deploy code on their first day is the single best way to get them feeling great about their ability to acclimate and impact change in your organization. Companies like Etsy actually have a hard-and-fast rule (*http://codeascraft.etsy.com/2012/03/13/making-it-virtually-easy-to-deploy-on-day-one/*) that all engineers should deploy to production on day one.

- **Assign mentors.** Lots of companies say they mentor their employees. I've found that unless this is systematized, senior employees get too busy to dedicate the necessary amount of time. Make sure every new hire has a mentor to pair with basically all day for at least the first two weeks.

- **Foster productivity early.** The best way to sharpen a programmer's skills is to write code. Junior engineers shouldn't be trying to learn legacy systems when they first arrive—let them work in as fresh a codebase as possible so they can get cranking right away.

- **Invest in training.** Nothing will give you a better ROI on your time than making sure your employees are well trained. Create a learning plan for each hire for the first three to six months, complete with recommended reading, that applies to the projects they are working on.

- **Be patient.** :)

At the end of the day, when you hire junior developers, you are investing in people. You are creating a culture of growth, promotion, and learning that will pay for itself multiple times over. And it will also help you recruit the ninja-rockstars when you actually need them ;).

What do you think? What's been your experience in terms of bringing on junior members to the team vs. the almost mythical ninja-rockstar engineers?

51

How to Hire Hackers: A Realistic Guide for Startups

Iris Shoor (http://bit.ly/onstartups-hire-hackers)

Call them hackers, "ninjas," or "rock stars" if you'd like. Other than being very talented developers, they all share one thing in common—it's unbelievably hard to bring them onboard in your company. And as if competing with other companies for the same talent was not enough, being a startup just adds more challenges to the equation. Your startup may turn out to be the next Google/Facebook/Instagram, but until then, how can you convince the best developers out there to join a company where the CEO's office is an IKEA desk? Here's one answer—recruit like a startup, in a creative and agile way, doing things the way big companies can't. During the last five years I've interviewed over 250 candidates and recruited dozens of great engineers. The first interviews took place in our tiny office's kitchen, and we still managed to convince some of the best candidates to join. There aren't any magic tricks involved, but here are some tips and methods that helped us get ninjas, rock stars, and other highly talented people onboard.

You're a Startup—Have the Founders Make the First Contact

We lose many potential candidates even before the starting line—we fail to bring them over for a first interview. Some are already talking with too many companies, or decide after a brief visit to your website that your startup just isn't their thing. That's the point where you can make a difference. Our cofounders (including myself) are in charge of sending the first email to potential candidates. We've kept this habit even as we've grown. At first, I was worried some candidates might think we had too much free time on our hands (sadly, we don't). But I soon found out that when candidates receive a personal and flattering email (important when it comes to star developers) from a cofounder, it sends a message that this startup is all about its employees. Here are some helpful points for writing the first email:

- **Link to your online profile when introducing yourself.** This might be your personal blog, an interview with you, or a YouTube video. When there's a face behind the email, you're more likely to get a positive response.

- **Add a personal touch.** Have other employees who went to the same college? Mention it. Grew up in the same town? Write it down. It might sound irrelevant, but it creates the first hook, enough to have them come over for a meeting.

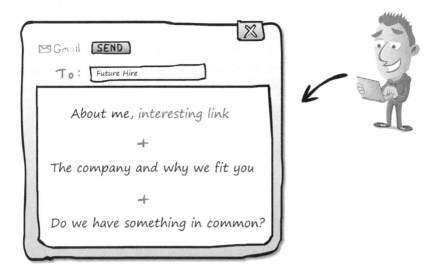

Interviewing: It's Not Just About the Role, It's Also About Who They Will Have Lunch With

While we tend to tell candidates everything about the role, the managers, and the company, there's one part that's usually missing—who will they work with? One of the most common answers I get when asking people why they've chosen one job over another is knowing other employees there. Let candidates know who'll be sitting next to their (IKEA) desk and sharing their 9GAG jokes.

- **When candidates come for an interview, try to have them meet at least one future coworker.** A candidate asks a good tech question during the interview? Refer him to the engineer working on it instead of answering yourself. Found out the candidate has something in common with one of your current employees (likes skydiving, grew up in Ohio, has a thing for ASCII art)? Introduce them. It's not something we plan ahead, but given the opportunity, having the candidate stay at the office after the interview chatting with other employees is considered a success.

- **Don't interview too early or too late in the day, when the office is empty.** If the only time your future star can come in for an interview is 8 a.m., make sure some people come in early. You want to paint a full picture of what it will be like working at your startup.

Figure 51-1. You don't need a fancy office to make good impression—the small details do the job. Our entrance door has code on it, and these are our meeting room's custom coasters.

Interviewing: Choose Carefully Which Opportunity to Pitch

There truly are great things about joining a startup—new technological challenges, opportunities for moving up the ladder more quickly, learning about the business side of things, stock options, and more. Don't sell them all at once. Pitching becoming a manager to an engineer who just wants to experiment with new technologies? Bzzzz, wrong move—and one that might send her elsewhere.

- **Look back.** When we first started interviewing, we used to ask candidates what they were looking for. Instead of sharing their true motivations, they answered with what they thought was the "right" answer: "I just want to work on interesting stuff." After a while we discovered the magic trick; instead of asking what they're looking for now, we began asking how they'd made previous job decisions. When asked about past decisions, people tend to share what really matters to them.

- **Don't pitch, give examples.** You can't really promise someone that he will become a manager in the future, or only work on interesting stuff. Instead, I tell candidates what talented people who joined the company a year ago are doing now. This could be how an engineer with no previous management experience is already heading a small team, or how a developer straight out of college is doing such a great job we've put her in charge of some very key algorithms.

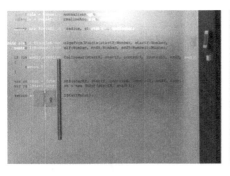 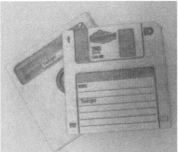

Signing: How to Make Candidates Sign an Employment Agreement More Quickly

You've reached the home stretch. The candidate you really liked said yes, and now all that's left is to sign the employment agreement. This can turn into a very risky period. The current employer is likely to come with a counter offer, and so can other companies.

- **Avoid having your future star waste time on legal issues.** To help with this, we've decided to have the exact same employment agreement for everyone in the company. Other than the terms themselves, everything is the same, from the number of vacation days down to the small letters. It's a super-friendly agreement and we never change it. Once I tell candidates that everyone—the CEO, the engineers, and myself—have all signed the exact same contract, and therefore we can't change it, it usually takes them only a day or two to sign it. There's much less need to re-read every part.

Note

Scott Weiss from A16Z shares a great tip (*http://scott.a16z.com/2012/06/04/ guerilla-recruiting-combating-the-counteroffer/*) about the pre-signing period with the "Welcome basket".

HOW TO HEAR "NO" AND HOW TO SAY "NO"

- **Hearing "no"—stay in touch with good candidates who chose a different company over yours.** When a candidate I really like accepts a different offer over ours, I always get the feeling I was dumped. True, I can't honestly say I don't understand how someone can pick a great job at Google over a job at a small and unknown startup, but it still hurts. While the easiest thing to do after hearing a "no" is, well, nothing, I try to make one last effort to stay in the picture. There are two main reasons for this:

  — Startups grow quickly. You might have a good candidate who decided a 10-employee company was not for him, but a year or two later, as your company grows, it may become much more attractive.

  — Receiving a negative answer usually means you've reached second place. Sometimes, the first choice doesn't turn out to be the dream job the candidate was hoping for. Some candidates don't feel comfortable getting back in touch after they've given you a negative answer. By making the first move, you're saying that everything is fine and that you're still interested.

Yes, it's very much like dating. How do you keep yourself in the picture? I like to send Facebook friend requests to candidates, and that's something that you can do only as a startup (it can get pretty awkward when done by someone from a large company). Facebook is a great platform to share how well your startup is doing over the years. I also like sending an email once every 4–6 months, sharing how we're doing and asking how everything's going. I've found that most people find it friendly (and somehow flattering) rather than annoying.

- **Saying "no"—giving a smart negative answer will help you reach other great engineers in the future**. I often ask myself how I would have liked to receive a "no." My answer is that I would like to hear the truth. Instead of using the default answer of "We've decided to continue the process with someone else," I write the (sometimes hard) truth: "You didn't pass the technical test," "You don't seem like a startup kind of guy," "It seems like you're more interested in managing and that's something we can't offer right now." I also make sure to write some of the things I liked about the candidate. True, there are some cases where you can't write the real reason, but in most cases you can. I was terrified when I sent the first 100% sincere email, but I soon found out that candidates embrace this, and usually agree with the reason. Now comes the interesting part—instead of feeling rejected, most people (rightly) feel that they interviewed for the wrong role. Once you don't "break up" with them, you can ask them to recommend friends or coworkers they think could fit the position. Yep, it sounds crazy, but it's true. Even if you don't get a new lead, rest assured you'll have a past candidate saying good things about your company, and that's something great in itself.

52

MBA Mondays: Best Hiring Practices

Fred Wilson

Hiring is a process and should be treated as such. It is serious business.

The first step is building a hiring roadmap, which should lay out the hiring plan over time by job type. This should be built into your operating plan and budget. You want to be very strategic about how you invest your scarce resources into hiring and think carefully about when you need to add resources.

Once you have done that, you want to have a system for opening up these positions for hire. This should not be done lightly because each position will require a fair bit of work by a bunch of people to hire for. Don't open up your hiring process lightly.

The first step in opening up a position for hiring is to define the position you are looking for. Most companies call this a job specification (or spec). The spec should outline the role that is being filled and the characteristics of the person who will be successful in the job. Check out this job spec (*https://twitter.com/jobs/positions?jvi=orLdWfw5,Job*) for a brand strategist job in Twitter's office in NYC. It starts with a high-level description of the role within the context of the larger Twitter organization. Then it gets into what it will take to be successful in the role. Then it lays out specific responsibilities, and finishes with the background and experience that Twitter is looking for in the candidate.

The manager who is directly responsible for the person being hired should draft the job spec, and it should be signed off on by the CEO and whoever is in charge of HR (which could be the CEO in a small company). Once this job spec is published on your jobs page, this position is officially open for hire and the process begins.

Your company should have a jobs page. Even if you are a five-person startup, you should have one. It should articulate what it is like to work at your company and list any open jobs. It should be linked to at the bottom of your web page, right next to the link to your about page. This is important. Don't put it off. Etsy's "careers page" (*http://www.etsy.com/careers/?ref=ft_careers*) is a good example of what you want to do on your jobs page.

There are web-based solutions to get your open positions onto your jobs page, track the candidates through the hiring process, and provide workflow for your hiring team. In the industry vernacular, these systems are called Applicant Tracking Systems (ATSs). Many of our portfolio companies use Jobvite (*http://recruit ing.jobvite.com/*), but there are plenty of other options out there as well. You do not need to build this stuff yourself.

Once the position is open, you want to crank up the sourcing process. I talked about where to find strong talent (*http://www.avc.com/a_vc/2012/05/mba-mondays-where-to-find-strong-talent.html*) in an earlier post. Do not take the "put the job opening up and let the applicants come" approach. That will not get you the best people. You must go out and find the talent you want to hire. You can use your existing team—that is where the best leads always come from. You can use your network. You can use recruiters, both contingency and retained, and you can use services like LinkedIn and Indeed. You want to cast a wide net and work hard to source the best candidates you can. This is a time-intensive process. Many companies will hire an in-house recruiter to help with this process, particularly when recruiting engineers, designers, and product talent. I've seen companies as small as 10 employees bring on in-house recruiters. I am a big fan of making that investment because it pays dividends in terms of better talent.

Once the candidates start coming in, you will need to vet them to determine who gets an interview and who does not. Someone inside the company must lead this process. If there are HR resources, this vetting process starts with them. But the manager who is hiring for this position must be directly engaged in this vetting process. An HR professional can identify the candidates who don't come close to meeting the requirements of the job and filter them out, but the hiring manager should go through the applications of everyone who is close to being a viable candidate. He knows best what the job entails and can make the kind of "gut calls" that often lead to the best candidates.

You will want to interview a decent number of folks for every position. There are no hard rules for this, but the more people you meet, the better job you will do with the hire. Of course, you can't meet everyone. Many companies like a 15-minute phone call (the phone screen) as the first filter into the interview process. A Skype video call is also a good way to do this. At USV we have experimented with a video application (using a service called Take the Interview (*http://www.taketheinter view.com/*)), with good results. The phone or video screen is an efficient way to identify the small group (a half dozen to a dozen) that you will want to do a face-to-face interview with.

Once you get to face-to-face interviews, you will want to figure out how to get as many folks in the company to meet the candidates as possible. Our portfolio company Return Path (*http://www.returnpath.com/*) has each candidate meet with four to eight employees during the interview process. That is a lot, but Return Path makes a huge investment in its team, culture, and employees and feel it is worth it. It may be worth it for your company as well.

Many employees don't know how to interview, and you should teach them the basics as well as educating them on what you are looking to learn from their interviews. Some training on interviewing as well as a quick feedback form for each employee to fill out will provide consistency and clarity from the employee interview process.

Most CEOs I know interview every hire their company makes until they get to be bigger than 100 employees (or more). Even if you have a head of HR and a top-notch recruiting team, the responsibility for hiring is yours and yours only. A bad hire is your fault. A good hire is your success. So do not abdicate your responsibility to make the final call on each hire until your company is developed enough and strong enough to start making these hires without you. This is how you build a great team, a great culture, and a great company.

Once the successful candidate is identified, you will want to do some checking on the person. I am a fan of making reference calls on everyone. They are not that hard to do and you will learn more from them than any other source of background checking. LinkedIn is particularly good for this. If you connect to the candidate on LinkedIn, you can quickly figure out who you know that knows them. Call those people and do your homework. It is also pretty easy to do a simple background check for criminal or civil information. We don't do that at USV, but I know a lot of companies that do it as a matter of good corporate practice.

When you are ready to make the hire, you must prepare an offer letter. The offer letter will outline the compensation you are offering and any other salient terms of the employment offer. Have your lawyer help you draft the first one you send out and use it as a template for all future hires. Offer letters are written agreements between you and the employee—treat them as such. Sign the employment offer and have the employee sign it to acknowledge that she is accepting it.

That's the hiring process. Done right, it involves a huge investment in each and every position. So many startups cut corners on it because they simply don't have the time or the resources to do it right. I would encourage everyone to take a step back and think about the costs of not doing it right and commit themselves and their companies to doing it right. You will see the benefits in time. And they are large.

53

How to Design a Successful Interview Process for Hiring Top Talent

Ben Yoskovitz

Most companies don't have a serious, repeatable interviewing process for hiring.
Instead they wing it, bringing people in for interviews, asking a few questions, turning it into a fireside chat, and then hoping for the best. In my experience that's not good enough.

At Standout Jobs (2007-2010) we hired some great people. I still consider them friends today, but more importantly they've all gone on to bigger and better things. And many of them still say that their experience at Standout Jobs was a fantastic one, even though the company wasn't a success (*http://www.instigatorblog.com/ postmortem-analysis-of-standout-jobs/2010/10/05/*). They learned a lot, grew as people, and found teammates that they genuinely respect and appreciate. A few of the guys went on to work together in other projects and startups, and I'm sure some of them will re-connect in the future.

That feedback is a testament *-in part-* to the effort we put into hiring and interviewing people. I've seen a lot of different hiring strategies, from the nonchalant to the super intense (even more than our approach, which I've shared below.) I can't say there's one approach that works for every company, or that our approach is even "the right one" for you, but I do know that everyone we hired that went through the process was successful and stayed with us; those that we bent the rules for (often to expedite the hiring process) didn't pan out quite as well. So for us, the interview process we implemented was a very good filter.

Note: Most of the hiring we did was in 2007-2008. That's a few years ago, and my memory of every specific detail is a touch fuzzy. I wish I had kept more notes on the specifics, questions we asked, etc. There are those out there that may be able to fill in some details...

1. Reviewing Resumes

The process typically started with a resume. The resume isn't dead, but the format should change, especially for developers that have plenty of resources (like Github) for sharing their work and demonstrating their capabilities. Resumes still contain some nuggets of information that are helpful, and we went through them all. Here are some of the things we looked for:

- Spelling errors (almost an automatic "thanks but no thanks")
- Lots of short hops between companies (a potentially bad sign)
- Open source contributions, side projects or other work shared in a portfolio
- Twitter account and/or blog (so we could take a look at what people were interested in, talking about, etc.
- Previous startup work and the quality of those startups

Both my co-founder (Fred Ngo) and I reviewed resumes. In some cases we shared resumes with other team members to get their opinions as well. If we were rejecting someone, I'd email them. Every single one. I did my best to make sure everyone that applied heard back from us at least once. This is a tough process, but I encourage every company (*http://www.instigatorblog.com/the-resume-black-hole/ 2012/01/13/*) to do it. After reviewing and filtering resumes, we'd screen the remaining candidates over the phone.

2. Screening Candidates

We put a lot of effort into screening candidates. Given that the next step (in-person interviews) lasted almost a day, we didn't want to go through that with too many people.

Screening candidates was mostly about:

1. Verifying the validity of their resume (i.e. how much did they exaggerate?)
2. Testing for role fit (i.e. do they understand the role, and is that a good fit?)
3. Testing for cultural fit (i.e. do we think we'll get along well?)

I tried keeping screening calls to 30 minutes, but they'd often go longer. It was always interesting to see what people talked about (specific work they'd done, accomplishments, interests.) I also gave people an opportunity to ask questions, which was also instructive on their personality and what they cared about.

We had a standard set of fairly open-ended questions, but I wasn't too concerned if we got through all of them. The goal was to have a conversation and see how it went. Some of the questions I asked included:

- Tell me about [pick something on the resume]...
- What did you learn at [pick company name]?
- What are you looking for in a new company?
- Tell me about the [pick a side project s/he's worked on]... (or: Have you ever thought of doing a side project of some kind? If so, why haven't you? What would you do?)
- What's an ideal work environment for you?
- Do you read Hacker News? (i.e. Are you genuinely interested in startups and new technology?)

Some of the gotchas I came across:

- **Lying.** A lot of people lie on their resume. They drastically overstate their contributions to things that were successful. You expect some exaggeration (or even lack of clarity because it's hard to measure how valuable a specific person's code was to a project's success, for example) but lying is a no-no.
- **Dissing past / existing employers.** There are a lot of crappy employers out there, and a lot of crappy jobs, but spending 30 minutes complaining about them isn't the right approach. It's better to be more politically correct, tease out the positives (you must have learned something, met someone, had your eyes opened up to different ways of doing things) and move on. Badmouthing people isn't going to win you points with potential new employers.
- **Not having any questions.** A candidate without any questions is most likely a disinterested candidate.
- **Not having done any research on the company.** Unfortunately a lot of candidates barely looked at our website when we screened them, so they really didn't know

what we were about. When you'd ask, "What interests you about Standout Jobs?" and they didn't have an answer, it was definitely a bad sign.

Once screening was complete, we'd decide if the candidate should come in for the in-person interviews. If not, we'd let them know. If so, we'd ask them to block off half a day or more and we'd explain the process to them (verbally or via email) so they'd be somewhat prepared.

3. First In-Person Interview (with me)

I typically did the first in-person interview. Similar to the screening process, I'd prepare a list of fairly standard questions (with some deviation based on the specific person I was speaking to) and we'd spend 1-1.5 hours talking. Admittedly, these conversations got too casual at times, and I caught myself talking more than listening, but generally I found them constructive. You could probably be more rigorous here than I was, and make this interview shorter.

Ultimately, I was really looking for a personal connection. *Did I want to bring this person onto my startup roller coaster and ride with them?* It wasn't about being friends (while I'm friendly with many ex-employees, we didn't spend tons of time outside of work socializing), it was about finding a mutual connection and respect. You are going into battle with them, and a lot of it will get ugly, so there better be a real sense of camaraderie and understanding.

4. Second In-Person Interview (with Fred)

Next, Fred took over and did a more technical interview with candidates (assuming we were hiring programmers). If we were hiring for other positions, Fred still did an interview but didn't ask technical questions.

Fred had his own style for interviews. He asked theoretical questions, math questions, and worked through different problems with candidates. He also spent a good chunk of time getting to know the candidates, how they communicated, what interested them technically, etc. So it was a combination of practical (does this person know what they're talking about) and personal. These interviews typically lasted 1 hour.

5. Third In-Person Interview (with the team)

The next interview for a candidate was with a few members of our team. We wanted to give our existing employees a chance to meet prospective employees. This usually lasted 30-60 minutes. The discussions were broad ranging, because the team loved to talk technology and they often found candidates eager to discuss technology as well. I didn't participate in these meetings (neither did my co-founder, Fred) so I can't really go into a lot of detail, but I do like the idea of having candidates meet the team. That's who they'll be working with every single day. **And the truth is that a lot of employees stay at a particular job because of their co-workers, even if they don't like the job, the company or their boss.** That's how important it is for people to really bond with their co-workers.

6. The Practical

After three in-person interviews (now 2.5-3.5 hours in), we'd move to the practical portion of the interview. We used to call this a "technical test" but it really wasn't about testing technical capabilities. Candidates coming in for an interview knew there'd be a practical component, but prior to the interview we didn't provide any additional detail, except perhaps, *"we'll get you to code something."*

Note: This is for developers and technical people, but we did run others (like customer support people) through a practical exercise as well. I'll share some details on that later.

Here's how we designed the practical "test":

(i) The Setup. Fred and I would tell the candidate that we were going to roleplay a scenario, and ask them to participate. At some points during the practical we'd be roleplaying, at other times we'd step out of that and review things. We'd explain the general steps to them – roleplay the initial scenario (where we're a client asking the candidate to build an app), they'd design the app on paper and present it (partially roleplayed), they'd go build the app (not roleplayed), and they'd present the app after (partially roleplayed.)

(ii) The Scenario. Now it was time for a bit of roleplay. Fred and I would pretend we want the candidate to build a photo sharing application for our university dorm. We picked this application for a number of reasons:

1. Everyone understood what a photo sharing app was and generally how it would work (we weren't trying to invent something radically new here)

2. It was a simple enough application, but it had a bunch of important "web" elements (login, user accounts, content management, etc.)

3. People felt like they could build it very easily, which proved interesting later on

Fred and I would tell the candidate, *"We want a photo sharing app for our friends in our university dorm,"* but wouldn't provide a lot of details. It was up to the candidate to ask questions, get information from us and propose ideas. Imagine a scenario where you're doing work-for-hire with a "less than brilliant or clear" customer. That was the scenario.

Ultimately we were testing communication skills and critical thinking. What questions did the candidate ask? What assumptions did they make? How did they approach communication with us as a client? Did they embrace the experience or not?

We learned a lot during this phase.

It was amazing to see how some people dove into the scenario and started designing UIs on paper with us, while others didn't ask very much at all and said, *"OK, I'll go build a photo sharing app."* In some cases we had to prompt candidates with specific cues: *"Um, you didn't ask us about privacy."* Or Fred and I would start talking to each other, *"Do we want everyone to have access? Should people be able to delete photos? What happens if someone starts posting too much junk?"* Good point, good point...then we'd wait to see if the candidate jumped in.

We were also looking to see how people prioritized the steps and things they could do, and how they communicated that to us. Some people were great at negotiating: *"So is A or B more important? A is easier, but B might do more of what you want."* Some were great at brainstorming new ideas and proposing stuff, which we loved (as "clients" and employers!)

Once we were finished with this process (~30 minutes), we'd break out of roleplaying and move to the next step.

(iii) The Design. At this point we'd ask the candidate to design the system on paper. They'd often ask, *"What do you want to see?"* And we'd respond, *"It's up to you. What do you think would be helpful for explaining how you're going to build this for us [as the roleplayed customer], and what do you think would be useful for you as the developer?"*

We saw all kinds of things here, from UML to UI mockups. Some people had reams of paper and they'd walk us through the entire application they were proposing to build (soliciting feedback the entire way), others had one or two sheets. It was very interesting to see how people think, structure things, and again, how well they communicate.

Candidates had 30 minutes. At the end we'd jump back into roleplaying so they could present their work; to help us (as "clients") understand what they were going to do. We'd come to a conclusion with them on what the deliverable should be.

Then we'd move out of our roleplayed roles and ask them about their approach, why they did certain things, etc.

Before they could jump into coding, we'd ask the following question:

"OK, so given the scope of the project, how much of it can you get done in 2 hours?"

(Sometimes we only did 1.5 hours depending on time constraints.)

This was one of the most interesting parts of the interview.

Universally, candidates would say that they could get all of it, or nearly all of it done. We'd dive into specifics and they'd give us a list of deliverables they were prepared to commit to. We knew they couldn't complete all the work, but it was a "just small enough project" to give people confidence that they could. It set the tone: This is going to be hard, stressful and intense, but go for it! Most candidates were eager for the challenge.

Three points:

- Initially we were giving candidates a clean computer. It was almost completely empty, and they could set it up as they saw fit. The idea was to see how well they could stay focused on the task at hand versus setting up the machine to their perfect parameters. It made the situation a bit more challenging. After a couple interviews we stopped doing this. I don't think it really provided us with a lot of valuable information about candidates, and the task was hard enough as it is.

- We always offered people more time if they wanted it, usually 30-60 minutes. Most people took us up on that offer.

- We always allowed people to ask us questions (either as the clients in the role-play scenario) or not. If they had technical questions, or got stuck somewhere, they could come to us and talk. Very few did.

No one ever finished.

We knew this would be the case; candidates did not. And what came out of this experience with candidates was always interesting. Occasionally, a candidate would get almost nothing done, spending all their time setting up the clean computer, or just staring at the screen paralyzed. Others quit halfway through. In one particular case, the candidate admitted to us that he just wasn't ready for a job at an early stage startup (there were personal things going on his life that were just too distracting) and so he bowed out. He was a very good developer, but the timing just wasn't right. And that's OK. He's gone on to be very successful.

7. The Post-Practical

Once the practical was finished, Fred and I would get back together with the candidate and review his or her work. They'd show us a demo of what they'd built (if anything) and talk through their approach, decisions they made, and the places where they got stuck. It was always fascinating to see where people put their energy and limited time: some made sure it looked good even if the functionality was shallow, some wanted to get all the plumbing in place, and others got caught on specific (often minor) details and couldn't adapt.

We always asked them, *"Now that you've gone through the process, where did you underestimate the effort / work required?"* Again, it was fascinating and instructive to hear people's answers. We didn't go back into roleplaying mode at this point, but it was important to see how candidates reflected on the conversations we had in those scenarios. How were they trying to address client needs? How did they shift on-the-fly, while keeping in mind how they would explain their decisions to the client? What assumptions did they make that they could then properly communicate?

We were always looking for clarity and adaptability. How they worked under pressure was certainly part of it, but not the only thing that mattered to us; after all, this was a fake scenario. Their ability to work in this scenario wasn't completely indicative of their ability to work on a deadline, although I believe it was a decent proxy. You also got a sense for who had that special extra gear; the few people with the determination to plough through, take chances and be capable of clearly and confidently explain what they did after the fact.

Once the post-practical was done, the interview was over. All told, the candidate had now spent 5.5-7.5 hours with us. It was a gruelling, but effective process.

Conclusions

Hiring the right people is extremely hard. If you don't take it seriously and put the effort into it, you'll end up hiring sub-par people that don't have the necessary talent or cultural fit. And as we discovered, timing is important as well; if someone isn't ready to make the commitment needed, it's better to find out beforehand.

The fact is you will never be 100% successful at hiring – some hires just won't work out. There could be any number of reasons (most of which are out of your control), but you can reduce your risk significantly with a thorough interview process.

Here are some final thoughts about our process:

- Very few candidates disliked the process. I remember a few of them thought the roleplaying was silly, and some of them couldn't understand why we were bothering with the whole thing, but most of them genuinely appreciated the effort. Even those that fell apart during the process understood why we were going through it in the first place. And many of the candidates were **more interested** in working for us because we put in so much effort.

- The interview process was the best way of presenting our company's culture. Candidates got to meet most of the team, talk to them, learn about them, and then they were put through the gauntlet, and came out the other side with an appreciation for the intensity of the company.

- Technical ability is fairly easy to measure. Communication skills, adaptiveness, eagerness, heart, intensity and culture are much harder to measure and understand. We already knew (or were fairly certain) about a candidate's technical abilities before going through the practical, but we didn't know if they'd be the right coder for us.

- As I've said above, our process is just one way of doing things. I think it was effective, but it won't work for every company. Those that performed the best throughout the interview were definitely some of our best employees. I suppose that could be a fluke, but I don't think so. We filtered a lot of people out, and I know (now looking back with the power of hindsight) that we made the right decisions.

We also used practical tests when hiring for other positions other than developers. For example, we ran customer support candidates through a test (although a simpler one than above.) Candidates applying for a customer support role went through the same in-person interviews (with me, Fred and other employees). They would then spend 5-10 minutes with one of our customer support people. Our employee would walk candidates through our website and talk through our core benefits, as well as some of the frequently asked questions we received from customers. Candidates then had 5-10 minutes to prepare and were asked to present what they'd learned back to us. Watching a candidate present on the benefits of Standout Jobs was very helpful in assessing their communication skills, personality and ability to adapt quickly.

Some candidates had done some research in advance, and they often performed better because they were prepared. That was just fine with me. Customer support candidates were extremely surprised when we told them we'd go through a practical assessment, but it was definitely helpful for us.

Recruiting successfully is crazy hard.

The pool of talent is always smaller than you'd like, there are always competing interests, and it takes a significant time commitment to recruit consistently and well. When interesting candidates do come knocking, there's a temptation to hire them quickly and see how it goes. I've done that before, and it usually didn't work out. You get lucky sometimes, but you're taking a big risk; not just with the one individual you're hiring, but with the effectiveness and culture of the entire company. There's merit in the saying, *"hire slow, fire fast."* Don't be too slow about it (or you'll miss people), but you do need to be extremely deliberate and thoughtful about the process. Put the time into a recruitment and interview process as early as possible in your company's existence, measure the results, learn and iterate as you go along.

54

Snake-Oil Startup Recruiting

David Beisel

Everything in startups is selling. Selling to financiers. Selling to customers. Even for consumer-facing online services, UI and product design is about selling users on what actions you'd like them to take.

Recruiting new employees is one of the most important selling jobs that a founder/CEO does in the first couple of years of a startup's life (and subsequently, for that matter). But earlier in a startup's life there exists a real delicate balance in setting expectations for new people joining the company. With recruiting especially, *it is important to sell reality amplified, not to sell at all costs.*

Unlike with other constituents, where you often have some leeway to sell and then orient your organization to deliver, once you've "sold" someone into in organization, that person becomes part of the organization.

This means any miscommunications or disappointment about factors that were or weren't included in bringing somebody on board are now incorporated into your organization itself. These dimensions of course include roles, responsibilities, and compensation, but they also include culture, working style, and environment. And the smaller and more embryonic the company is, the more meaningful an impact a misalignment can create. The last thing you want is to introduce a new individual into a startup who will soon develop resentment about being sold a misaligned permutation of reality, or worse, an empty bag of goods. It's better to have that person not become a part of the organization at all if he'll only add substantially to it in perfect theoretical circumstances.

While this misalignment can happen at all levels within an organization, the more senior the person joining is, the more the intangible factors matter. This issue is precisely why I've seen many instances where the main hang-up with a very early hire is if this person retroactively receives a cofounder title. At the same time, it's both meaningless and ultimately meaningful—it sets the tone for how she'll be treated moving forward and her role within the company.

For similar reasons, I don't think it makes sense to ever kick the can with any part of compensation, titling, roles, or responsibilities "until there is more clarity within the organizational structure." Of course, things change over time—especially in startups—but without clearly defined parameters at the beginning, there's more possibility for an incongruent set of expectations and further deviation from both parties' conceptions of a situation. It surprises me how many times I hear about people being hired into a startup where their title/role/compensation will largely be decided (or they're promised a real upgrade) after a trial period. What almost always happens is that the new employee has grand expectations about what is to come, and when reality hits he finds himself trapped in a different job than the one he thought he was accepting. In most cases these people don't last long in the company, not because they don't have the capacity to execute, but because there is a fundamental breakdown in trust in their ability to do so and be recognized for it.

So, when recruiting a new employee, by all means put the best foot forward. But ensure that any promises made will indeed come through. It's best to amplify the best parts of reality, rather than conjure up alternative versions of it that sound good but just don't exist.

55

Recruiting and Culture (MBA Mondays Guest Post)

Chad Dickerson (http://bit.ly/avc-recruiting-culture)

When Fred Wilson (*http://www.avc.com/a_vc/about.html*) asked me to write a guest blog post, I told him initially that I was going to write about recruiting and culture. Both are topics that I've learned a lot about in nearly 20 years working in companies of all kinds and contexts: public and private, large and small, struggling and ascendant, on the east and west coasts. As I sat down to write, I realized that how you recruit people and your recruiting approach defines and continually reveals the culture of your company, and it quickly became clear to me that recruiting and culture are yin and yang. In recruiting, a successful outcome usually means a candidate saying yes to your company, and at that moment, the candidate becomes part of the company culture. Below are some of the things I've learned to do over the years when it comes to recruiting and culture.

Make Recruiting a Top Priority at the CEO Level

Former IBM CEO Lou Gerstner wrote a book (*http://www.amazon.com/Elephants-Dance-Inside-Historic-Turnaround/dp/0060523794*) about IBM's late-'90s turnaround and said: "Culture isn't just one aspect of the game, it is the game." The word "recruiting" can easily be substituted for "culture." In my career, I've participated in a number of searches for HR executives and staff. Without fail, the least successful ones were those where the premise was, "We need someone/a team to own the culture and/or recruiting." (This is a similar corporate pitfall to looking for someone to "own innovation," but that's another post.) A great head of HR is critically important, but culture and recruiting are owned by everyone if they are successful. As Gerstner noted, one of a CEO's most important responsibilities is tending to the culture. To that end, a CEO must not only drive recruiting at the executive level, but at any level where it will make the difference in closing a critical candidate.

On a practical day-to-day level, that means that I will drop nearly anything I am doing to help close a key candidate. Talent is that important, and it's always worth my time.

Communicate the Company Vision Broadly and Directly

In his legendary recruiting pitch at Apple, Steve Jobs said to John Sculley, "Do you really want to sell sugar water, or do you want to come with me and change the world?" A strong vision can quickly set your company apart from others. In his pitch, Jobs understood the power of the appeal to something larger than simple manufacturing of goods for a particular market. As Antoine de Saint-Exupéry wrote (*http://en.wikiquote.org/wiki/Talk:Antoine_de_Saint_Exup%C3%A9ry*), "If you want to build a ship, don't drum up the men to gather wood, divide the work and give orders. Instead, teach them to yearn for the vast and endless sea." Jobs's conversation with Sculley happened one-on-one, but the forms of communication available today mean that you can communicate the mission and vision of your company more broadly and directly than ever, which is what I did when I blogged in May about our long-term vision for Etsy (*http://www.etsy.com/blog/news/2012/notes-from-chad-funding-etsys-future/*). It has never been easier to tell your own story and talk about your company directly with the people you want to reach. Talking to the media is good, too, but traditional media outlets have their own publishing schedules, editing quirks, and editorial voices, so you should always keep a direct channel open. On a purely pragmatic level, communicating directly gives candidates a deeper sense of what your company is trying to do and they come into the process knowing what your company is all about, often self-selecting to your mission. I've found that this takes the recruiting process up a level.

Challenge Traditional Notions of Corporate Transparency

A compelling vision is just the beginning of a conversation. To be successful in recruiting efforts, you have to have tangible substance to what you say. Current and potential staff demand greater transparency into your company than ever before. Typically, candidates want to know two basic things about your company: 1) how is the company doing from a business standpoint? and 2) does this company operate in a way that I can believe in? The second is arguably more important than the first, since performance metrics rise and fall, valuations go up and down, and stock prices fluctuate. Culture and values persist.

Most private companies don't disclose any financial information, but for years now, we at Etsy have been publishing key metrics from the Etsy marketplace in a monthly "weather report *(http://www.etsy.com/blog/news/tags/weather-report/)*." Our main goal in publishing this information is to let the Etsy community know how the marketplace is doing overall, but publishing this data also helps immensely in recruiting. When you're trying to convince a candidate to move across the country or choose between you and a company that holds its numbers close to the vest, providing this kind of information can be the deciding factor.

Measuring how a company operates from a values standpoint is much more challenging than reporting financial numbers because it is inherently difficult and there are few standards. Fortunately, new models are emerging to make such measurements possible. At Etsy, we believe that as a community-based business—a business where our company's success is entirely linked to the success of our larger community—our company should hold itself to a higher standard of social responsibility and transparency. We are not alone, and an entirely new form of business—the "benefit corporation," or B Corp—is developing to address the challenges of running for-profit businesses within a values-based framework. The non-profit B Lab *(http://www.bcorporation.net/)* has created a quantitative independent third-party assessment to measure companies' success against rigorous values and responsible practices. Etsy recently took the assessment and qualified to become a Certified B Corporation" *(http://www.etsy.com/blog/news/2012/etsy-joins-the-b-corporation-movement/)*. Any potential employee can see how we measured up by looking at our score on the B Lab website *(http://www.bcorporation.net/community/etsy)*. We passed, but as you can see, there are areas where we clearly could do better. Diversity is one area for improvement, and we're actively and transparently working to improve our score. Recently, we provided scholarships for women to attend Hacker School *(http://www.etsy.com/blog/news/2012/etsy-hacker-grants-supporting-women-in-technology/)* to address systemic issues in bringing women into software engineering by providing training. We also announced our support of Code:2040 *(http://code2040.org/)*, a program to increase minority representation in software engineering. We are doing all of this in the full view of the world. Over time, our community, staff, and potential candidates will be able to see how our company practices measure up to our stated values and where we are making improvements. I believe top talent is going to increasingly expect this type of transparency and companies that provide it will have a recruiting advantage as they compete against companies that are merely selling the metaphorical "sugar water" from Jobs's recruiting pitch.

Be Patient: "Slow Recruiting"

Relationships are the currency of recruiting, and while recruits sometimes appear almost out of nowhere and close quickly, the truly great candidates can take a long time to find. John Allspaw (*http://www.amazon.com/John-Allspaw/e/ B002BMN7XW/ref=sr_tc_2_0*) runs technical operations at Etsy, and I think John is the best in the world at what he does. When I hired John at Etsy in 2009, the near-term recruiting process was a few months, but the actual recruiting process had been going on for a decade. Nearly 10 years earlier, when I was CTO at Salon.com (*http://salon.com*) in San Francisco and John ran the ops team there, he came to me and said he needed to move back to Boston for family reasons, so he had to leave the company. I said, "Why? You can just work from there. We'll keep the same salary and nothing will change except where you work." John went back to Boston, the family situation improved, and John came back to San Francisco a year later. He never left the company, and we made a difficult situation much easier for him. Since then, we have worked together at three different companies. Our relationship has persisted through boom and bust business cycles, massive upheavals in our personal lives, and changes in our business relationship. Looking back, I started to recruit John to lead Etsy's ops team when I found a way for him not to leave Salon in 1999. I call this (with tongue slightly in cheek) "slow recruiting."

Recruiting too slowly for key positions can be a liability in a fast-paced industry, but the larger point is that the way you and your company treat people over longer periods of time has more impact on your recruiting efforts than anything else. Whether it's making a tough situation like John's work and turning it into a win-win, talking patiently with someone at a conference when your time is constrained, or thoughtfully answering an email from a college student seeking advice, recruiting goodwill adds up over time. If you're just entering the industry and expect to be recruiting at any point in your future, I assure you that people will remember things you said to them 15 or more years later. Keep that in mind at all times. It could be the difference in closing a key candidate 10 years from now.

Open-Source Your Culture: Generosity of Spirit

Most people really want to work for successful companies with really smart people where generosity and helping are the cultural norm. There are specific ways to institutionalize sharing in your company and demonstrate that spirit to the world —particularly in engineering, where recruiting is most intense. In early 2010, we launched our engineering blog and named it "Code as Craft (*http://codeas craft.etsy.com/*)," tying the mission of engineering back to the larger culture of craftsmanship in the Etsy community. Several months later, we formally introduced the concept of "generosity of spirit" at Etsy and asked every engineer do one of the following things within the year: 1) present at a conference, 2) write a blog post for the engineering blog, or 3) contribute to open source. Since then, the team has open-sourced 40+ projects (*https://github.com/etsy*), written over 70 blog posts (*http://codeascraft.etsy.com/*), and posted over 50 engineering presentations (*http://www.slideshare.net/etsy*), spawning a Code as Craft speaker series (*http://codeas craft.etsy.com/etsy-speaker-series/*) in the process. The team does these things because they love sharing their work, but as recruiting activities, they are incredibly effective because the software and information we provide helps potential candidates solve real problems. Cold-calling candidates doesn't come close to the warm intro of a candidate using the software you've open-sourced and thoughtfully explained to them.

Kellan Elliott-McCrea (Etsy CTO) says: "If your culture isn't explicitly leaky, if it doesn't aspire to change the world beyond the walls of your business, if it isn't captured in the product you're building and your users' experience, then it probably isn't culture, it's just cheerleading and team spirit burning up expensive inputs of time and company outings. Culture is lived, and it's why generosity of spirit is such a key piece of our team culture" (and therefore a key part of our recruiting philosophy and approach).

Cultivate the Spirit of the Organization

In his 1954 classic, *The Practice of Management* (*http://www.amazon.com/The-Practice-Management-Peter-Drucker/dp/0060878975/*), Peter Drucker devoted an entire chapter to what he called the "spirit of an organization," writing: "Management by objectives tells a manager what he ought to do. The proper organization of his job enables him to do it. But it is the spirit of the organization that determines whether he will do it. It is the spirit that motivates, that calls upon a man's reserves of dedication and effort, that decides whether he will give his best or do just enough to get by." At the end of the day, a candidate will look most closely at the spirit of your company and the visceral sense he/she gets from visiting your office, reading your blog posts, following what members of your team say on Twitter, and reading about you in the press. It's hard to quantify this spirit, but you know it when you've got it, and you know how painful it is when you don't. When it comes to recruiting and culture, a leader is mostly responsible for tending to the spirit of the organization, and for making whatever adjustments need to be made to keep that spirit strong and powerful. In the end, that spirit matters more than anything.

Note

Thanks to Kellan Elliott-McCrea (Etsy CTO) and Randy Hunt (Etsy Creative Director) for their feedback.

56

Firing

Chris Dixon

Firing is awful. You can try to avoid it, but even the most selective founders make serious mistakes. Here are a few things I've observed about firing:

1. **The good people bounce up, the bad ones bounce down**. I was told this by my boss once when he was firing one of my friends. At the time, I thought this just made him feel better about himself. Over time, I've seen the wisdom in what he said. Some people who get fired react by fixing their weaknesses. Others spiral down.

2. **Do it early**. If you think you're going to fire someone over the next six months, you probably will. Don't wait too long. Too many founders do. It's better for management and employees if it happens fast.

3. **It's awful**. You're in control of a situation that will meaningfully hurt someone. It's an awful place to be. The fired person will go home and tell his/her family about how terrible it was. It was your fault. Perhaps your mismanagement caused it. Who knows. You'll question it, and perhaps you are right to do so.

4. **The other choice is firing everyone**. You're the founder of the company. If you run out of money, you're forced to fire everyone. If you don't fire the bad employees, you risk everyone else's jobs. It's an impossible situation.

5. **The feeling is more likely to be mutual than you think**. Most of the time, the person getting fired was already about to quit. The antipathy you feel is likely reciprocated. It's surprising how often this happens and management doesn't see it coming.

It would be great if startups were all about growth, hiring, and success. But the reality is that founding a company is a brutal job and lots of the pain gets passed down to employees. Creative destruction sounds nice in textbooks, but in the real world it means telling friends to go home, stop getting paid, and find new jobs.

57

MBA Mondays: Asking an Employee to Leave the Company

Fred Wilson

I don't like using terms like "fire" or "terminate." To me they have too much emotion attached to them to be appropriate when splitting with an employee. I like to say that "fred was asked to leave the company" or "fred, we need you to leave the company." That works better for me and, I think, it also works better for the person who is being asked to leave the company.

But more than how to say it, I think how you do it is paramount. Here are some simple rules along with some color commentary on each:

Be quick

Once you've made a decision to let someone go, move quickly to do it. Don't procrastinate. Do get things buttoned up (terms of departure, departure date, how it will be communicated, etc) but once you've got things in order, have the conversation.

Be generous

Unless the employee has acted in extreme bad faith or done something terribly wrong, I like to be generous on the way out. I like to give some severance even if it is not required by company policy or contract. I like to vest some stock that may not be required to be vested. I like to paint the departure in as favorable light as possible. And I like to say good things about the person once they are gone. I like to be generous in financial terms and emotional terms. It makes things go easier for everyone.

Be clear

Do not beat around the bush. Start the conversation with the hard stuff. They will be leaving the company. Be clear about when and how. And be clear about the financial terms and other aspects of the separation. Do not mince words and do not say confusing things. Most employees in this situation will ask for reasons. Have them lined up in advance and be clear and crisp when describing the reasons. The reasons for a split do not have to be the employee's fault. They can, and often are, the company's fault. In startups, employees are almost always at will and it is the CEO's right to ask anyone to leave the company for any reason. So just be as honest as possible, be clear and crisp about the reasons, and don't turn this into a long involved discussion.

Get advice

There are some situations where the company has some potential legal exposure in these situations. When you are a small company, ask your lawyer about the specific situation so you know when you have one of them on your hands. When you are a larger company, your HR team should know when you have one of these situations on your hands. But make sure you are appropriately advised about a departure before sitting down and having the conversation. In the off chance you have a tricky situation, you will need to handle it differently and you will need advice on how to do that beyond what is written in this post.

Communicate

Once the employee has been told about their departure, you should immediately communicate it to those who will be affected in the company. For executives and co-founders, that means the entire company. So figure out how you are going to have that conversation immediately after you have the conversation with the departing employee. Be consistent with your messaging. Don't tell a departing employee one thing and the team another. People talk. And they will quickly figure out that you are spinning, bullshitting, or something worse if you give different messages.

When an employee is asked to leave the company there are two constituencies you need to think about. The first is the departing employee. The second are the remaining employees. How you deal with the departing employee will be noticed by the remaining employees. Even if the departing employee was not liked, a bad cultural fit, or worse incompetent, the remaining employees will have some empathy for them on the way out and if you handle it well, that will send an important message to the team. I find that a lot of inexperienced managers miss this nuance and it hurts them. They think they need to "look strong" to the team. They do. But they also need to look fair and humane. This is a big opportunity to do that.

I will finish with a few words aimed at the boss' own psyche and then suggest some further reading on this topic.

Asking someone to leave the company is never easy. I don't know anyone who enjoys doing it. But it comes with the territory. You don't have to learn to like it, but you have to learn to do it well. The thing that helps me and, I believe, helps everyone in this situation is knowing that you are doing the right thing for the company, the remaining team, and all the stakeholders in the business including customers, partners, investors, etc. When you put it in those terms, doing this unpopular chore becomes a bit easier.

If you'd like to read more on this topic, I think <u>Ben Horowitz</u> has written well on this subject a few times. I found these links below from Ben's writings and would encourage you to go and read them.

58

The Board of Directors— Selecting, Electing, and Evolving

Fred Wilson

Every company should have a Board of Directors. At the start it can simply be a one-person board consisting of the founder. But it should not stay that way for long. Because if you are your own board, you won't get any of the benefits that come with having a board. These benefits include, but are not limited to, advice, counsel, relationships, experience, and accountability.

The shareholders elect the Board of Directors. But there is usually a nominating entity that puts directors up for election by the shareholders. If the founder controls the company, then she is usually that nominating entity.

I am a fan of a three-person board early on in a company's life. I generally recommend that a founder put himself on the board along with two other people he trusts and respects. The election of directors in this scenario is simply a matter of the controlling shareholder voting them in.

This situation changes a bit when investors get involved. If the founder retains control, then the situation does not have to change. The founder can still nominate and elect the directors she wants on the board. However, investors can and will negotiate for a board seat in some situations. This is less common for angel investors and more common for venture capital investors.

The way investors negotiate for a board seat is usually via something called a *shareholders agreement*. This is an agreement between all the shareholders of the company. It contains a bunch of provisions, but one of the provisions can be an agreement that the shareholders of the company will vote for a representative of a certain investor in the election of the Board of Directors. The representative can even be named specifically. For many of the boards I am on, this is how my seat is elected. For venture capital investments, this is a very typical provision.

Adding an investor director does not mean that the founder loses control of the board. It can remain a three-person board with one investor director and two founder directors. Or the board can be expanded to five and the investors can take one or two seats and the founder can control the rest. These two situations are common scenarios when the founders control the company.

As a company moves from founder control to investor control, the notion of an *independent director* crops up. And independent director is a director who does not represent either the founder or the investors. I am a big fan of independent directors and like to see them on the boards I am on. Boards that are full of vested interests are not good boards. The more independent-minded the board becomes, the better it usually is.

When the founder loses control of the company (usually by selling a majority of the stock to investors), it does not mean the investors should control the board. In fact, I would argue that an investor-controlled board is the worst possible situation. Investors usually have a narrow set of interests that involve how much money they are going to make (or lose) on their investment. It is the rare investor who takes a broader and more holistic view of the company. So while investor directors are a necessary evil in many companies, they should not dominate or control the board. The founder should control the board in a company he controls, and independent directors should control the board when the founder does not control the company.

When and if a company goes public, the shareholders agreement will terminate and public company governance standards will dictate how a board is selected and elected. There will most likely be a committee of the board that is called the *nominating committee*. That committee will select a slate of directors that will be put up for election by all the shareholders of the company at the annual meeting. Most public company boards have staggered board terms such that a subset of the board is elected every year. Three-year and four-year terms are most common.

It is possible for the shareholders to put up an alternative slate. In theory, this approach could be used in both private and public companies, but in reality it is almost entirely limited to public companies. This will be perceived as a hostile move by most companies and they will fight the alternative slate of directors. This "alternative slate" approach is most commonly taken by "activist investors" who take a meaningful minority stake in a public company and agitate for changes in the board, management, and strategic direction of the company. But it can also be used in a hostile takeover effort. It is very, very rare for an alternative slate to take control of a company, but it is fairly common for a new director or two to get elected in this way.

Boards should evolve. Boards should recruit new members on a regular basis. Board members should have term limits. I like the four-year term, but I've been on boards for much longer. I'm in my thirteenth year on one board and my eleventh on another. These are not ideal situations, but they involve companies I invested in while I was with my prior venture capital firm and I have a responsibility to my partners and the founders to see these situations through.

A much better example is Twitter, where I was the first outside director, taking a board seat when Twitter was formed in the spinout from Obvious and USV made its initial investment. Over time Twitter added several investor directors and then started adding independent directors. By last fall, Twitter had the opportunity to create a board with two founders, a CEO, three independent directors, and one investor director. As a shareholder, that sounded like the right mix to me and I voluntarily stepped down, along with my friend Bijan, who had led the second round of investment.

The point of the Twitter story is that boards evolve. In the first year it was me and two founders and a founding team member. In the second year it was me and Bijan, two founders, and a founding team member. In the third year it was three investors, two founders, and two senior team members. In the fourth year, it was three investors, two founders, a CEO, and three independents. And now it is one investor, two founders, a CEO, and three independents. Many of these changes in the Twitter board happened at the time of financings. That is typical of a venture-backed company.

In summary, the shareholders elect the board. That is the essential truth in every company. But how they elect the directors can be very different from company to company. For public companies, it is largely the same for all. In private companies, as Jeff Minch (known to my reader community as JLM) would say, "You get what you negotiate for," so negotiate the board provisions carefully. They are important.

Most importantly, build a great board. They are not that common. But you owe it to your company to do that for it.

PART X

Startup Failure

59

What Goes Wrong

Jessica Livingston (http://www.foundersatwork.com/blog.html)

It's been more than seven years since we started Y Combinator (*http://ycombina tor.com/*) (YC). In that time we've funded 467 startups, so I've seen a lot of patterns. There's a talk I always want to give at the beginning of each batch, warning everyone about things that I know are probably going to happen to them. I finally wrote down all my thoughts and I'm going to share them with you now.

We all know that a lot of smart and talented people start startups. You see huge numbers of startups getting started, and yet there are actually only a handful of startups that are big successes. What happens along the way that causes such failure?

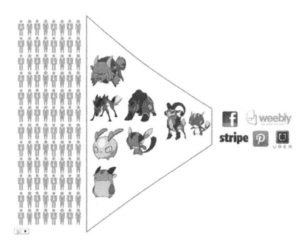

It's like there's a tunnel full of monsters that kill them along the way. I'm going to tell you what these monsters are so you know to avoid them.

Determination

In general, your best weapon against these monsters is determination. Even though we usually use one word for it, determination is really two separate things: resilience and drive. Resilience keeps you from being pushed backward. Drive moves you forward.

One reason you need resilience in a startup is that you are going to get rejected a lot. Even the most famous startups had surprising amounts of rejection early on.

Everyone you encounter will have doubts about what you're doing—investors, potential employees, reporters, your family and friends. What you don't realize until you start a startup is how much external validation you've gotten for the conservative choices you've made in the past. You go to college and everyone says, "Great!" Then you graduate and get a job at Google and everyone says, "Great!"

What do you think people say when you quit your job to start a company to rent out airbeds?

Check out Airbnb's website from when it first launched in 2008. Here's how the company described what they do: "Two designers create a new way to connect at this year's IDSA conference." Have you even heard of the IDSA conference? Also, it was only for airbeds!

This is not the sort of thing you get a lot of external validation for. Almost everyone is more impressed with you if you get a job at Google than if you make a website for people to rent out airbeds for conferences.

Yet this is one of the most successful startups out there. Even if you are Airbnb, you are going to start out looking like an ugly duckling to most people.

When Airbnb did YC back in early 2009, they had already endured tons of rejection. (Check out Brian Chesky's talk (*http://www.justin.tv/startupschool/b/272180383*) from Startup School in 2010. It's one of the most inspirational stories out there.) By the time they came to us, they had maxed out their credit cards. They were eating leftover Cap'n McCain's cereal. They were at the end of their rope.

Everyone thought their idea was crazy at the time—even I did, actually—but they knew they were on to something. During YC, they made some key changes to their site, talked to users, set their goals, and measured everything. And the graphs started going up.

Remember that new ideas usually seem crazy at first. But if you have a good idea and you execute well, eventually everyone will see it.

We funded Eric Migicovsky about two years ago when he was working on Inpulse, the predecessor to the Pebble watch. Eric was a single founder and these watches have a quality that terrifies investors—they're hardware.

Poor Eric had a really hard time getting funding. No one wanted to fund a hardware company. He met with lots of investors who'd say things like, "I love the idea. But I can't fund a hardware company." Some claimed they just didn't fund hardware as a rule, others said that there were too many capital expenses up front. They all said no when he showed them the concept.

He'd been building the Pebble based on a lot of user feedback from the Inpulse, and he felt strongly that people wanted this product. So I remember he talked to Paul and they agreed he should give up on investors and put it on Kickstarter. His original goal was to raise $100,000 to make 1,000 watches. Instead of $100,000, Pebble raised $10.2m in 30 days—the largest amount of money ever raised on Kickstarter. Now they are making 85,000 Pebbles.

Even Y Combinator got rejected when we first started back in Cambridge, MA in the summer of '05. Now there are lots of organizations doing what we do, but trust me, when we first started, people thought we were crazy. Or just stupid. Even our own lawyers tried to talk us out of it.

But eight teams of founders took a chance on us and moved to Cambridge and got their $12,000 per team. I think they'd tell you that they had a great experience. We, too, knew we had hit on something interesting. So we focused on making something that a few people loved, and we just expanded slowly from there.

But it was a slow process. When we came out to Silicon Valley in the winter of '06 we hardly knew anyone, so we decided to try to meet more investors to convince them to come to Demo Day. I got an introduction to the number one angel in the Valley, Ron Conway. Let me show you how he tried to brush us off.

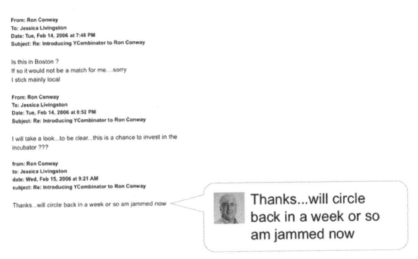

He said, "Is this in Boston? I stick mainly local." I replied, "No, we're in Mountain View and we'd love for you to come to Demo Day." He said, "Is this a chance to invest in the incubator?" I replied, "No, we don't want you to invest in us. It's a chance to invest in the individual startups." Then he told us he'd circle back, since he was jammed. We got the "am jammed now" from Ronco—it was so embarrassing.

It all worked out in the end, though. He did wind up coming to Demo Day, and he was impressed with what he saw. A year later, Ron came and spoke to the winter '07 batch of founders.

Variety of Problems

Remember, there are two components to determination: resilience and drive. We've talked about why you need resilience: because everyone will be down on you. You need drive to overcome the sheer variety of problems you will face in a startup.

Some of them are painfully specific—like a lawsuit or a deal blowing up—and some are demoralizingly vague: no one is visiting your site and you don't know why.

There's no playbook you can consult when these problems come up. You have to improvise. Sometimes you have to do things that seem kind of abnormal.

Rajat Suri was a grad student at MIT when he started E La Carte (*http:// elacarte.com/*). (E La Carte lets restaurant customers order and pay through a tablet.) He was so committed that he got a job as a waiter to learn what restaurants were like.

The Collison brothers founded Stripe (*https://stripe.com/*), which does payment processing online. When these guys got started, they were a pair of young pro-grammers. They had no idea how to make deals with banks and credit card com-panies.

I asked Patrick, "How did you even convince these big companies to work with you?" One trick that worked was to start with a phone call. Then people would pay attention to their arguments without being distracted by their youth. By the time they met in person and the companies could tell how young they were, they were already impressed.

We funded the Lockitron (*https://lockitron.com/preorder*) guys back in the summer of '09—that's them at their YC interview. A year after YC, they were still figuring out their idea. They lived with the WePay (*https://www.wepay.com/*) guys, and one day the WePays had a party for their investors. By that point the Lockitrons were working on a product to lock your door with an iPhone. They were able to impress one of the investors with their prototype, and he asked to have 40 installed in some startup offices he owned. The founders were psyched, but the commercial locks they needed to use cost $500 a pop. They didn't have $20,000 to fulfill an order that big. So they went around to the local locksmiths and scrapyards, buying broken locks for about $10 each. They fixed them themselves and were able to deliver on that order.

Fast forward a few years later: these guys were ready to launch the newest version of the Lockitron and decided go on Kickstarter. And guess what? A day after Lockitron submitted its campaign, Kickstarter changed its policy about hardware companies and rejected them. The Lockitron guys decided to build their own Kickstarter, and they did it in less than a week. They wondered if anyone would even come. Not only did people come, but they've already sold close to $2 million dollars' worth of Lockitrons this way. And they didn't need to give a cut to Kickstarter.

Let me give you one last example of improvising. The Justin.tv (*http://www.justin.tv/*) founders were having a lot of scaling issues in the beginning. One weekend their whole video system went down. Kyle was in charge of it, but no one knew where Kyle was. And Kyle wasn't picking up his cell phone. This was live video, so it was pretty critical that this get fixed immediately.

Michael Siebel called Kyle's friends and found out he was in Lake Tahoe and got the address of the house. So here's a problem for you: you know the address where someone is and he's not answering his phone. How do you get a message to him right away?

Michael went on Yelp and looked for a pizza place near the house, then called them up and said, "I want to have a pizza delivered. But never mind the pizza. Just send a delivery guy over and say these four words: The site is down." The pizza place was very confused by this, but they sent the pizza guy without a pizza, Kyle answered the door, and the pizza guy said, "The site is down." Kyle was able to fix it, and the site was down for less than an hour total from beginning to end.

Cofounder Disputes

Another monster is cofounder disputes. People underestimate how critical founder relationships are to the success of a startup.

Unfortunately, I've seen more founder breakups than I care to count. And when it happens, it can crush a startup.

Be very careful when you decide to start a startup with someone. Do you know them well? Have you worked with them, gone to school with them? Don't slap yourself together with someone just because they are available and seem good enough. You'll probably regret it.

And if you start seeing red flags, do something about it. Don't think that it will go away. It's a red flag when you find yourself worrying whether your cofounder is trustworthy or works hard enough or is competent.

When founders break up for whatever reason, it's a blow to the startup's productivity and morale. If there are three and one leaves, it's not so bad, but if there are two and one leaves, that's very bad, because now you are a single founder and it's hard to do a startup as a single founder.

Investors

Investors tend to have a herd mentality. They like you if other investors like you.

So if no investor likes you until others do, what happens when you talk to the first ones? No one likes you! It's like the Catch-22 of not being able to get a job because you don't have enough experience.

You are essentially starting off in a hole and you have to work your way out. You have to meet with lots investors and hear things like "I'd be interested once you have more traction" or "Who else is investing?"

If you work hard enough, you may be able to find a few people who are excited enough about you and your idea that they aren't put off by the fact that you don't have any investors yet. Then, when you have a few investors, you can start to make the herd mentality work for you instead of against you. Fundraising is slow and hard until it's fast and easy.

But working to convince those first few investors can be really demoralizing. It's a grind. (There are some really good investors who aren't like this, but the median investor is a herd animal.)

Investors will also drag their feet. Left to their own devices, they'll just keep delaying. There's no downside for them to delay, whereas delay will kill you, because while you are fundraising your company will grind to a halt.

It blows my mind how many successful startups had a hard time fundraising at first. If you remember one piece of advice about investors, it's that *you've got to create some type of competitive situation.*

I'll give you what has always stuck in my mind as the most amazing example of this: one of the founders of one of our more successful startups had a long-standing relationship with a VC. When the founder started the company and did YC, this VC kept in touch through the whole three months, not really doing any-thing except keeping a benevolent eye on him. The VC attended Demo Day, but didn't invest. After a few months, the startup got a term sheet from a prestigious VC. When the first VC heard about this, he shifted into panic mode. He faxed the founder a term sheet from his firm with the valuation blank and said, "Fill in what-ever valuation you want and we're in."

There are worse things investors can do to you than just delay. Sometimes they say yes and then change their minds. It's not a deal until the money is in the bank. We've seen some founders learn that the hard way.

I could tell you a lot of horror stories to frighten you, but just remember that fundraising is a bitch.

YC founders get to raise money under the best of circumstances, and even for them it's a bitch.

Distractions

One of the reasons fundraising can be so damaging to your company is that it's a distraction.

We warn everyone early on at YC to be very careful about distractions. Nobody is stupid enough to get distracted by things that aren't work-related, like playing video games. The kinds of distractions founders fall for are things that seem like a reasonable way to spend their time.

We tell people that during YC there are really only three things you should focus on: building things, talking to users, and exercising. Maybe this is a bit extreme, but the point is that early on in a startup all that matters is figuring out how to make something people want and doing it well. Don't spend all your time networking. Don't hire an army of interns. Just build stuff and talk to users.

Note

Fundraising is a distraction, but it is necessary. So just try to spend as little time on it as possible.

One thing that isn't necessary, and is a bad distraction, is talking to corporate development (or *corp dev*) people. These are the people at big companies who buy startups. Often what happens is the founder gets a call from a corp dev person who wants to learn more about what he's doing and explore possible ways of working together, and the founder thinks, "Oh boy, this important company wants to work with me. I should at least take a meeting."

I hate to sound harsh, but what these meetings really are for is for them to see if they want to do an HR acquisition.

HR Acquisitions

An HR acquisition means a company is essentially trying to hire you. (They are such a dangerous distraction that they get their own little monster!)

There's nothing wrong with HR acquisitions, if that's what you want to do. But most founders don't start startups just to go get a job at a big company with what amounts to a nice hiring bonus.

Talking to corp dev early on isn't just a waste of time, it's uniquely demoralizing. I see this cycle happen over and over: the founders go to meet the corp dev people and think the meeting went great. They seemed so friendly and enthusiastic. The founders delude themselves into thinking that their startup is going to be the one that gets bought for $10 million after only five months. They start to think, "Yeah, we'd kind of like to get acquired," and then they start not to work on their startup as much and they lose momentum. Then they get the offer and it's essentially what they would have gotten if they'd walked in off the street and got a job. But by then they've gotten so accustomed to the idea of selling that they take it.

So, going down the corp dev road can seriously deflate your ambitions. HR acquisitions are what you do when you are failing. Don't pull the cord on your inflatable life raft until your ship is actually sinking!

Making Something People Want Is Hard

Now we come to the fiercest monster of all: the difficulty of making something people want. It's so hard that most startups aren't able to do it. You are trying to figure out something that's never been done before.

Not making something people want is the biggest cause of failure we see early on. (The second biggest is founder disputes.)

In order to make something people want, being brilliant and determined is not enough. You have to be able to talk to your users and adjust your idea accordingly. Ordinarily, you'll have to change your idea quite a lot even if you start out with a reasonably good one.

Remember the first Airbnb website? AirBed & Breakfast was a rather narrower idea when it first launched. It started out as a site that let people rent out airbeds to travelers for conferences. Then it changed to renting out airbeds. Then it changed to renting out a room or a couch, but the host had to be there to make breakfast. Then finally the founders realized there was pent-up demand to rent out entire places.

This evolution shows that you may begin with a general vision of what your startup is doing,s but you often have to try several different approaches to get it right.

Sometimes you have to totally change your idea. OrderAhead (which lets you order takeout on your cell phone) was the founders' sixth idea.

Even if you don't need to change the overall idea much, you still tend to have to do a lot of refinement. One of the best examples of this is Dropbox. Drew and Arash were working on something that was obviously necessary, but the reason it was hard to predict early on whether they'd succeed was that there were lots of people doing this. The way to win in this world was to execute well. It didn't just happen overnight; they had to get 1,001 details right. There were a lot of unglamorous schleps between this photo:

and this one:

Roller Coaster

Between starting the company and being on the cover of *Forbes*, you're going to have some dramatic ups and downs. In a startup, you don't have the damping that you'd have as part of a larger organization.

Circumstances fling you about. The process is often described as a roller coaster, because you are up one minute and down the next.

Lots of roller coaster stories involve fundraising. One of the most extreme ones I know happened to some people we funded at their previous startup. It was based in Texas and they got a term sheet from a top-tier VC in Silicon Valley. One of the conditions was that they base the company in the Bay Area. So the founders sold their homes and moved their families into corporate housing in Texas until they found new places in the Valley.

The documents were already signed and the money was scheduled to be wired on a Friday. They were going to start working on Monday out of the VC's office. So

Friday came, and for some reason the money didn't get wired. They called VC to ask if they should come out. The VC said, "Yes. Of course!" They got in their minivan and drove from Texas to Silicon Valley, stopping in Vegas to celebrate (this is the up part of the roller coaster).

On Monday, they set up their stuff in a conference room of the VC fund, with all six of the team working there. By that Wednesday, the funds still hadn't been wired. They had a board meeting planned for that day and invited the VC.

In this meeting, the CEO talked about how signup numbers had gone down temporarily because they'd changed the way they measured them.

You know how this story will turn out... the VC had actually gotten buyer's remorse, and he used this as an excuse to break the deal. Remember, they had signed all the documents, sold their houses, and moved to Silicon Valley, and were just waiting to get the $7 million wired to them. Instead, the VC bails. He kicks them out of the conference room. The founders had to call their wives back in Texas and go back with their tails between legs. They had to lay everyone off. Can you imagine? Just a few days before they were celebrating in Vegas, and then they had nothing.

(Incidentally, to get a story this extreme, we had to use an example of a startup we didn't fund. A VC probably wouldn't do this to a startup we had funded.)

Now let me tell you about the other half of the roller coaster.

We funded the Codecademy (*http://www.codecademy.com/*) team in the summer of 2011. Their original idea didn't work and they kept exploring new ones. It wasn't until late July that they started working on the idea of teaching people to code online. They launched just three days before Demo Day. In those three days, they got over 200,000 users.

They only launched so they could get up on Demo Day and say that they were a launched company. They never expected that in just three days they could go from a startup with an unlaunched idea to a startup that could get up on stage and announce they had 200,000 users (which is just about the most exciting thing you can say to investors).

The theme here is how extreme things can be. Just remember that no extreme ever lasts. Don't let yourself get immobilized by sadness when things go wrong. Just keep putting one foot in front of the other and know it will get better. But don't get complacent when things are going well, either. In reality, things are never as bad or as good as they seem.

What makes the roller coaster even worse is that while you are on it, there's an audience watching everything you do. You'll have trolls and reporters saying outrageous things about you online. So be ready for this, and have a thick skin.

Hard, But Not Impossible

Everyone knows that startups are hard. Yet when we watch people do it they are always surprised.

The reason they are surprised is that they don't realize how bad these specific problems can be. I've seen some very smart and talented people get so demoralized that they just gave up.

Startups are not for the faint of heart. I realize that this is not new news, but I wanted you to at least understand how they're hard early on so that when you run into these specific monsters, you'll know what to do.

60

Why Startups Die

Andrew Montalenti (http://www.pixelmonkey.org/)

Startups die due to a variety of causes. Over the course of the last three years, I've watched many of my friends pour their hearts and souls into companies that, for one reason or another, just fizzled out of existence.

In 2007, Paul Graham gave a variety of causes for startup death in "How Not to Die (*http://www.paulgraham.com/die.html*)." He wrote:

> *When startups die, the official cause of death is always either running out of money or a critical founder bailing. Often the two occur simultaneously. But I think the underlying cause is usually that they've become demoralized. You rarely hear of a startup that's working around the clock doing deals and pumping out new features, and dies because they can't pay their bills and their ISP unplugs their server.*

The other major thing Graham advises startups not to do: "other things." Namely:

> *[D]on't go to graduate school, and don't start other projects. Distraction is fatal to startups. Going to (or back to) school is a huge predictor of death because in addition to the distraction it gives you something to say you're doing. If you're only doing a startup, then if the startup fails, you fail.*

In early 2011 I wrote a post, "Startups: Not for the faint of heart (*http://www.pixelmonkey.org/2011/04/02/not-for-the-faint-of-heart*)," that discussed Parse.ly (*http://www.parsely.com/*)'s survival through a one-year bootstrapping period after Dreamit Ventures Philly '09. Since then, I've witnessed yet more startup deaths, and especially extended "troughs of sorrow (*http://www.avc.com/a_vc/2012/03/the-startup-curve.html*)."

The Process

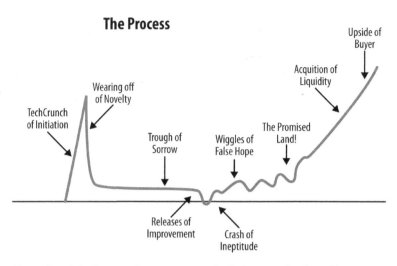

Figure 60-1. The Startup Curve (courtesy of PG (http://tawheed.tumblr.com/post/11329097042/the-startup-curve-courtesy-of-pg))

As a result, I've had a kind of mild survivor guilt (*http://en.wikipedia.org/wiki/Survivor_guilt*), and have started to look for patterns in causes in the deaths I have witnessed.

Post Mortems

Here are some of the patterns I've identified:

Marriage trouble

It has become a kind of cliché that founding partnerships at startups are like marriages. But it's a cliché that refers to an underlying truth. You will see and collaborate with your cofounder more than anyone else in your life during your company's startup period. If that relationship is tense—if you can't work well together and co-motivate each other through thick and thin—then the startup will fail. Unfortunately, the best you can do to avoid this is to make sure you know your cofounder decently well before deciding to embark on the startup mission with that person. I have witnessed startup failures that were due to predictable cofounder conflicts.

No bootstrapping plan

Many startups that come out of an accelerator program (such as Y Combinator, Dreamit, or TechStars) simply do not get funding. If you have the mentality that "without funding, I can't work on my startup," then your startup will likely die. This seems like a straightforward statement, yet many founders I have met don't seem to make the connection. .

Let's say that you just quit your job to work on your startup. I have heard many founders—even in the first few months of product development—expect to raise seed rounds, pay themselves salaries, etc. This simply is not the right attitude. Expect to spend a year or two without external funding. If you are not prepared for that possibility—no matter how grim, financially—then you are not prepared to survive.

Startup as a career move

It may sound lofty, but a startup is your life's work. You have to think about your company as a 10-year project. In your first three years you will get the startup off the ground, establish your core team culture, and fully validate your main product/market through rapid iteration.

In your next three years, you will establish your company as a force in that market, grow your A-team, and scale your business. The next few years may take you in all sorts of directions. You may become a fast-growing business, full of potential and ambition. You may end up a stagnating but still profitable business, looking for exit options. You may end up a company in the difficult position of having to scale back or become defensive, due to market evolution, management blunders, or any combination of factors.

But it will still be your company. Will you still care about the company's mission 10 years from now, no matter what position the company ends up in? If so, you probably have what it takes.

But, if you are treating your startup as a "career move"—a way to move up in the "startup ecosystem" and end up a C-level executive at some other, VC-funded rocketship—then in all probability, your current startup will fail. It'll fail because after year two, you'll start to get antsy and want to move on with your career, and you'll realize you never really cared about the startup mission in the first place. It was just a means to an end.

Refusal to change original idea

It has become yet another startup cliché that "execution is more important than ideas"—even one I've repeated (*http://www.pixelmonkey.org/2009/12/11/ideas-and-execution*). But I've witnessed many founders who were simply too attached to their original ideas.

You should be obsessed with your company's mission, but willing to change your company's approach given new data or circumstances. It's OK—almost every startup changes its ideas several times, especially through its early founding period. An unwillingness to change your original idea can not only waste your time, but also kill your spirits.

Paul Graham (*http://paulgraham.com/growth.html*) recently wrote that a "A startup founder is in effect an economic research scientist." This is the way you should view your company. It's an experiment. You're trying to discover a product that will work for some market, while also being a hugely motivating space for you and your cofounders to work in for (potentially) 10 years. What is that thing? It could be anything. You have to try a bunch of different ideas, until something sticks. No idea is sacred.

Preemptive scaling

This happens especially for startups that are founded primarily by technologists. There is no doubt about it—startups offer some amazing opportunities to exercise computer science and systems engineering knowledge. Engineering friends of mine regularly marvel at the amount of data companies like Google, Amazon, and Netflix (who were once startups, but alas no longer) have to process, analyze, and serve.

Here's the problem: this opportunity doesn't exist for early-stage startups, because, by definition, they have no users or customers. Worrying about "scale" in the early days of your startup is simply a bad investment. You may not have even discovered whether a product or market is worth pursuing, but you will have already invested in scaling that pursuit. Therefore, technical startup founders have to develop a craft in rapid application prototyping. They have to use lightweight tools and build quick-and-dirty prototypes that can be used to validate concepts. They have two choices: incrementally evolve those prototypes into working products, or scrap them in order to quickly rewrite them. Only once they have validated a product direction does it make sense to invest heavily in technical infrastructure.

Founders don't realize how bad an investment preemptive scaling can be. This may be due to watching the occasional downtimes of Twitter and Tumblr and thinking, "I don't want to be responsible for that." What these founders don't realize is that if Twitter and Tumblr had invested all their effort into scaling up front, none of us would have ever heard of them.

Growing too fast

This is, I think, the biggest killer of post-funding startups. It can be very tempting to take in a little bit of seed capital and start to operate as if you're a big company. Chris Dixon wrote a nice list of things startups do and don't need (*http://nonchalantrepreneur.com/post/311546950/things-startups-do-and-dont-need*) that captures this.

Growing too fast can kill a startup in a number of obvious ways, like running out of runway. But it can also kill a startup culturally. The more your company starts to feel like a big company, the slower you will move, and the more you will spend. This, again, feels like an obvious statement, but it's one that's often overlooked. Bigger companies simply move slower. Bigger companies simply spend more.

In order to justify adding another employee to your team, you have to feel confident not only that you have an appropriate core role for that employee to fill, but also that this employee is worth the *added weight* he or she will add to your company. More people does not simply mean additional labor. It also means more disagreement, more communication overhead, and a new branch in your company's cultural tree.

And consider this: when your company is three people (e.g., two founders + employee #1), the single employee at the company is a 33% partner in building the company culture and products. (*Note*: I'm not talking about equity. I'm talking about the amount of influence that individual has in shaping the overall company.) Adding a second employee reduces the first employee's "weight" in the company to 25%. Adding a tenth team member reduces everyone's stake to 10%. So, growing more not only has the effect of adding more weight to the company, but also of diluting each employee's decision-making stake (feeling of overall responsibility) in the company.

It's easier for bigger companies to fail because it's easier for each individual to abdicate responsibility for failure. People don't realize this while things are going well, but they realize it big-time when things go badly. Success has a thousand fathers; failure is an orphan.

Scared of code

This applies mainly to nontechnical founders. In today's market—where technology talent is in high demand—it can seem very, very expensive to rapidly prototype ideas that you will throw away. After two or three of those (and especially without a good understanding of sunk costs (*http://en.wikipedia.org/wiki/Sunk_costs*)) a mentality will settle into the team that "coding is expensive" and thus "must be avoided at all costs."

Founders will start to use every other means at their disposal to avoid it: spreadsheet modeling, potential customer surveys, mockups, etc. Many of these techniques can gather some useful market information. But nothing simultaneously focuses your team in its mission and gathers the most useful market feedback like *actually building* software prototypes.

The other reason I think not writing code can lead to startup death is that without concrete, tangible progress toward a product, it simply becomes too easy to walk away. Startups are all about persistence, and building your product is the way you can rally the troops, even as forces of negativity start closing in all around you.

How to Survive

I've explored various causes of startups death here. This is by no means an exhaustive list, but it illustrates some patterns I have seen over the years. You may wonder if I have any positive advice to offer about survival, rather than just cataloging the diseases I see in autopsies.

Startups are unknown battlefields full of landmines. Studying failures is, in many ways, a positive instruction. It's a map of the landmines. As for concrete advice, I can offer this one suggestion: *be persistent.*

Figure 60-2. Fake Grimlock's "You Must Burn" (image source (http://www.feld.com/wp/archives/2011/10/be-on-fire.html))

In other words, to survive, you must *continue moving forward*. I don't think startups win because they have smarter staff, better ideas, or a clearer understanding of market trends. Surely, those things help, but they aren't the main thing.

The way to win is to keep playing.

PART XI

Exiting by Selling Your Company

61

The Economic Logic Behind Tech and Talent Acquisitions

Chris Dixon

There's been a lot of speculation lately about why big companies spend millions of dollars acquiring startups for their technology or talent. The answer lies in the economic logic that big companies use to make major project decisions.

Here is a really simplified example. Suppose you are a large company generating $1b in revenue, and you have a market cap of $5b. You want to build an important new product that your CTO estimates will increase your revenue 10%. At a 5:1 price to revenue ratio, a 10% boost in revenue means a $500m boost in market cap. So you are willing to spend something less than $500m to have that product.

You have two options: build or buy. Building means 1) recruiting a team and 2) building the product. There is a risk that you'll have significant delays or outright failures at either stage. You therefore need to estimate the cost of delay (delaying the 10% increase in revenue) and failure. Acquiring a relevant team takes away the recruiting risk. Acquiring a startup with the product (and team) takes away both stages of risk. Generally, if you assume 0% chance of failure or delay, building internally will be cheaper. But in real life, the likelihood of delay or failure is much higher.

Suppose you could build the product for $50m with a 50% chance of significant delays or failure. Then the upper bound of what you'd rationally pay to acquire would be $100m. That doesn't mean you have to pay $100m. If there are multiple startups with sufficient product/talent, you might be able to get a bargain. It all comes down to supply (number of relevant startups) and demand (number of interested acquirers).

Every big company does calculations like these (albeit much more sophisticated ones). This is a part of what M&A/corp dev groups do. If you want to sell your company—or simply understand acquisitions you read about in the press—it is important to understand how they think about these calculations.

62

Knowing Where the Exits Are

John O'Farrell

Taking the Exit

On July 23, 2007, HP announced (*http://www.hp.com/hpinfo/newsroom/press/2007/070723xa.html*) it was buying Opsware for $1.6 billion in cash. By any measure, it was a very attractive deal for Opsware shareholders. The acquisition price of $14.25 a share represented a 74% premium over the prior six-month average, and a 40-fold return for anyone who had bet on us at our low point in October 2002, when only an intensive investor relations effort had saved us from NASDAQ de-listing. Almost five years later, the acquisition multiple of almost 16 times trailing revenue still far exceeds that of any other billion-dollar-plus enterprise software acquisition—ever.

The hard work of hundreds of employees contributed to making us the clear high-growth market leader in what was finally an important enterprise software category, but the significant premium we achieved was also the result of a multi-year, strategic business development effort designed to turn a merely good outcome into a truly exceptional one. That business development effort was built around five key principles that you, too, should consider as you build your company:

1. **Always know where the exits are**. Take the time to build relationships with potential acquirers. You never know when you may need them.

2. **Step back from the fray occasionally**. Review the company's strategic situation with the board every 12–18 months and evaluate the alternatives with quantitative and qualitative rigor.

3. **In evaluating your alternatives, ask yourself how you would feel if the environment were to change radically**. Days before we signed the HP deal, the Dow hit 14,087—its highest level ever. Within months, hedge funds and mortgage companies started imploding and we entered the worst recession since the great

depression. Just three months later, a sale at even $8/share would not likely have been achievable.

4. **If you do decide to sell, a meticulously executed competitive process is key to a successful M&A outcome.** The SEC proxy (*http://www.sec.gov/Archives/edgar/ data/1100813/000104746907006048/a2179079zsc14d9.htm*) statement description of Opsware's process details discussions with 10 companies, stretching over nine pages. Every one of those contacts was tightly scripted and carefully orchestrated to drive to the ultimate successful outcome.

5. **Creating and managing the acquirer's psychology is critical.** The key is to subtly convince the acquirer that they have no option but to acquire you, but that you have multiple attractive alternatives—and to reinforce that impression in every interaction, no matter how small, until the deal is definitively done.

"Your Best Exit May Be Behind You"

As I've discussed in previous posts (*http://john.a16z.com/archives/*), the best CEOs leverage strategic BD to cover critical flanks not well covered by other functions— helping to navigate crises, driving acquisitions and strategic partnerships, leading international expansion. No great entrepreneur sets out to build a company to be acquired, but as the company grows, it's important to have options and to understand them well. Perhaps the most important role of a strategic BD exec is proactively to make sure the company always has options and that the CEO and board always know where the exits are. They tell you on an airplane that "your best exit may be behind you," but that's not something you ever want to hear in business.

Stepping Back from the Fray: November 2005

At Opsware, 90% of our board discussions were naturally about the day-by-day work of building a great company: quarterly bookings, wins and losses, product plans and challenges, financials, and so on. However, about once a year we would make a point of stepping back from the daily battle for a more strategic review of our situation. As part of this review, we would address more fundamental questions. For example:

- How do we feel about our market?
- How is our competitive position?

- Who are potential acquirers of the company, and what's their current state of mind?
- What are the major opportunities and risks facing us?
- Bottom line: what's the likely value of staying the course versus exiting?

Prior to these board discussions, we would make a round of senior visits to HP, BMC, Oracle, EMC, and other behemoths to give them an update on the business. While our ostensible purpose was to explore the potential for a partnership, our real objective was to understand (and pique) their interest in our space and to make sure we'd have an open door if we should ever decide to explore selling.

You can find our board presentation from November 2005 here (*https://a16z.box.com/s/94f1b922234b2703db8f*). As you can see, it's a pretty thorough analysis. Here's the executive summary:

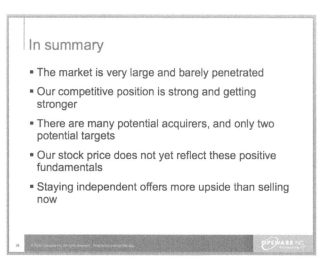

In other words, let's keep marching!

Stepping Back from the Fray: February 2007

In early 2007, Marc Andreessen, Ben Horowitz, and I made another set of visits to the usual suspects in preparation for a new strategic review with the board. We had made major progress since we had seen them last: exceeded $100m in annual revenue, fired up a productive distribution deal with Cisco, added storage automation, expanded internationally. As before, we went through a pretty slide deck that showed a winning company in a strategic category, with a final slide that mused vaguely about partnership. Left hanging in the air at the end of some of the meetings, we could sense the "overwhelming question" in the mind of the big company CEO: "Should we buy these guys before someone else does?" Several of them requested follow-up meetings.

For us, too, the possibility of actually selling the company was of more than theoretical interest this time around. Meeting Wall Street's expectations was still a challenge every quarter. Our one serious competitor, BladeLogic, was about to go public. Despite five years of strong execution, our own stock price seemed stuck in a narrow band around $8/share due to continued heavy investment in R&D and sales expansion. Strategically, we were now at a critical juncture: invest even more heavily in new capabilities like monitoring and enhanced support for virtualization, or capitalize on our current position and the strong interest from acquirers. That exit looked pretty tempting.

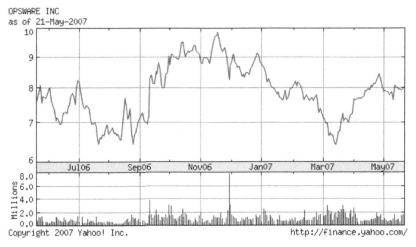

That said, selling for a typical enterprise M&A premium of 25–30% didn't feel compelling to us or the board. We hadn't escaped the jaws of death and worked this hard, for this long, to build a great company, only to sell it for 10 bucks a share. We were resolved: the only way we'd consider selling was for a price much higher than what we felt we could achieve in the standalone case.

Here's the recommendation from our February 2007 board update:

Conclusions and recommendations

- With one or two exceptions, large players' interest in our space remains strong

- Opsware and Bladelogic remain the only acquisition options

- There would likely be multiple bidders if we wanted to sell the company

- Recommendations:
  - Engage with Oracle, Ron, BMC and RedHat to understand the potential
  - Work aggressively to close a partnership with SAP
  - Continue to maximize the Cisco relationship
  - Continue to evaluate our strategic situation

OPSWARE INC

That led us into a dramatic three-month dance with a series of suitors that would test our negotiating and business skills, as well as our resolve. To see what happened next, check out my follow-on post, "Selling the Company (*http://john.a16z.com/2012/06/12/selling-the-company/*)."

PART XII

The Startup Mindset and Coping with Startup Pressures

63

What It's Like to Be the CEO: Revelations and Reflections

Paul DeJoe (http://bit.ly/onstartups-ceo-reflections)

On May 20, 2012, either right before midnight or right after midnight, I can't re-member, I posted my rendition of what it feels like to be a startup CEO to a question on Quora. 1,124 votes later and one last glance at a notification of an up vote from Jia Liu, a social game maker from Zynga, I'm going to close the Quora tab and, at the recommendation of Dharmesh Shah, write what these last few days have been like, some of the cool things I've heard, and some of the great people I've met as well as what I've realized.

With that said, here's the original post that sparked such a fantastic response.

What It Feels Like to Be the CEO of a Startup

Very tough to sleep most nights of the week. Weekends don't mean anything to you anymore. Closing a round of financing is not a relief. It means more people are depending on you to turn their investment into 20 times what they gave you.

It's very difficult to "turn it off." But at the same time, television, movies, and vacations become so boring to you when your company's future might be sitting in your inbox or in the results of a new A/B test you decided to run.

You feel guilty when you're doing something you like doing outside of the company. Only through years of wrestling with this internal fight do you recognize how the word "balance" is an art that is just as important as any other skill set you could ever hope to have. You begin to see how valuable creativity is and that you must think differently not only to win, but to see the biggest opportunities. You recognize *you get your best ideas when you're not staring at a screen.* You see immediate returns on healthy distractions.

You start to respect the duck. Paddle like hell under the water and be smooth and calm on top where everyone can see you. *You learn the hard way that if you lose your cool you lose.*

You always ask yourself, am I changing the world in a good way? Are people's lives better for having known me?

You are creative and when you have an idea it has no filter before it becomes a reality. This feeling is why you can't do anything else.

You start to see that the word "entrepreneur" is a personality. It's difficult to talk to your friends that are not risking the same things you are because they are content with not pushing themselves or putting it all out there in the public with the likelihood of failure staring at them every day. You start to turn a lot of your conversations with relatives into how they might exploit opportunities for profit. Those close to you will view your focus as something completely different because they don't understand. You don't blame them. They can't understand if they haven't done it themselves. It's why you will gravitate toward other entrepreneurs. You will find reward in helping other entrepreneurs. This is my email address: *paul@ec quire.com* Let me know if I can help you with anything.

Your job is to create a vision, a culture, to get the right people on the bus and to inspire. When you look around at a team that believes in the vision as much as you do and trusts you will do the right thing all the time, it's a feeling that can't be explained. The exponential productivity from great people will always amaze you. It's why finding the right team is the most difficult thing you will do, and the most important. This learning will affect your life significantly. *You will not settle for things anymore because you will see what is possible when you hold out for the best* and push to find people that are the best. You don't have a problem anymore being honest with people about not cutting it.

You start to see that you're a leader and you have to lead or you can't be involved with it at all. You turn down acquisition offers because you need to run the show and you feel like your team is the best in the world and you can do anything with hard work. Quitting is not an option.

You have to be willing to sleep in your car and laugh about it. You have to be able to laugh at many things because when you think of the worse things in the world that could happen to your company, they will happen. Imagine working for something for two years and then having to throw it out completely because you see in one day that it's wrong. You realize that if your team is having fun and can always laugh that you won't die, and in fact, the opposite will happen: you will learn to love the journey and look forward to what you do every day, even at the lowest times. You'll learn not to get too low when things are bad and not to get too high when things are good and you'll even give that advice. But you'll never take it because being in the middle all the time isn't exciting and an even keel is never worth missing out on something worth celebrating. *You'll become addicted to finding the hardest challenges* because there's a direct relationship between how difficult something is and the euphoria of a feeling when you do the impossible.

You realize that it's much more fun when you don't have money and that money might be the worst thing you could have as a personal goal. If you're lucky enough to genuinely feel this way, it is a surreal feeling that is the closest thing to peace because you realize it's the challenges and the work that you love. *Your currencies are freedom, autonomy, responsibility, and recognition.* Those happen to be the same currencies of the people you want around you.

You feel like a parent to your customers in that they will never realize how much you love them and it is they who validate that you are not crazy. You want to hug every one of them. They mean the world to you.

You learn the most about yourself, more than any other vocation, as an entrepreneur. You learn what you do when you get punched in the face many, many times. You learn what you do when no one is looking and when no one would find out. You learn that you are bad at many things, lucky if you're good at a handful of things, and the only thing you can ever be great at is being yourself, which is why you can never compromise it. You learn how power and recognition can be addicting and see how it could corrupt so many.

You become incredibly grateful for the times that things were going as bad as they possibly could. Most people won't get to see this in any other calling. When things are really bad, there are people that come running to help and don't think twice about it. Tal Raviv, Gary Smith, Joe Reyes, Toan Dang, Vincent Cheung, Eric Elinow, and Abe Marciano are some of them. I will forever be in their debt and I could never repay them, nor would they want or expect to be repaid.

You begin to realize that in life, the luckiest people in the world only get one shot at being a part of something great. Knowing this helps you make sense of your commitment.

Of all the things said though, it's exciting. Every day is different and so exciting. Even when it's bad it's exciting. Knowing that your decisions will not only affect you but many others is a weight that I would rather have any day than the weight of not controlling my future. That's why I could not do anything else.

Epilogue

In the post, I shared my email with everyone, with the hopes of encouraging anyone that needed any help to reach out to me directly. I was fortunate enough that many people took me up on this offer. The exchanges we had ranged from Skype calls to testing some new products, sharing ideas, and even joining an advisory board. Most of the emails I got, though, were just from people that thanked me for the post, shared their contact information, and said things like David did: "...likewise, if there's any way I can be of help or service, let me know."

For those of you that have reached out to me and shared some of your lives with me, thank you beyond words. It has been flattering, fulfilling, and humbling. For those that have voted up the answer and posted some of the kindest, coolest, and most amazing comments anyone could ever hear, I thank you. And my startup parents, thank you. Suddenly the 80,000lb student loan gorilla with no income to feed him seemed to take the week off and was replaced with elation when reading some amazing comments. It meant a lot. Thank you again.

What might be a surprise to hear, though, is that it felt very uncomfortable to me to say "thank you," and I was doing it a lot. Seemingly overnight, there was a collective up vote from over 1,000 people who shared similar feelings and situations. I started to get the feeling that it wasn't me who had written this and became uncomfortable taking credit. This post gained attention because it was a collective post by everyone who contributed with a comment or a vote, and if I hadn't been lucky enough to come across this question, someone else would have written it. It might have been better, or not, but it would have at least been appreciated in the same way had another entrepreneur written it.

I don't recall seeing too many notifications of a down vote, and that made me realize a few things.

First, this post became an online meetup for a group of people that are committed to changing the world. And rightfully, as well as fittingly so, it's very difficult and sometimes a seemingly insurmountable undertaking. But what was encouraging was that not one person, in the entire comments (go ahead and look) or in the emails that I received, said that they were overwhelmed or going to quit. They all found this inspirational and motivating: just the little encouragement needed to find appreciation for what they do, and a reminder that they're not the only crazy ones.

The most common response I received, however, sounded like: "Thank you for this. I forwarded your answer to my friends and family to help them understand." One person even said that her Mom thanked me for the post (thanks, Renee, for sharing). Unfortunately, and sometimes rightfully so, entrepreneurs are commonly misunderstood by people outside of our networks and by people we love. It's mostly our fault. Although we are not understood most of the time, we take for granted that while we're often misunderstood, we are always accepted and supported. What we don't say thank you enough for, and what we often take for granted, is the very thing that lets us be who we are and chase our dreams. The people around us that love us unconditionally without regard for how badly we might fail are the equivalent of a superhero's cape. Without this, and without someone we can share the ups and downs with, great things do not happen. They can't. The things that are worthwhile to pursue and dedicate a life to involve something way bigger than individuals and have to be completely selfless, or they are not big enough—a goal is not worth celebrating if it does not have the well being of others in mind. A collective thank you on behalf of this group of people that are crazy enough to change the world goes out to you. Thank you. If you are reading this because it has been forwarded to you, please know that you are appreciated, and that it's difficult for us often-quirky introverts to articulate. You don't have to change anything; we don't say it enough, but it's with you in mind that we find motivation. You possess the most scarce resource of all: undying and unnerving support. We thank you for it.

Lastly, undoubtedly the greatest thing that came from this post was an amazing calm that came over me during the most fulfilling, rewarding, interesting, and fun week of this tumultuous journey to build a company. It came at the intersection of being able to interact with all of these individuals and being able to see, all at one time, the collective resolve, ambition, and just how dynamic these people are. Seeing who these people actually are, how many of them there are, and that they actually exist under our noses let my imagination of what was possible wander in a positive direction for the first time in a while. It was powerful enough to spin my negative outlook on what I thought we were inevitably leaving for future generations. What I have just said, you would have not heard me say one week ago. It also made me realize something for which I will forever be grateful to all of those that contributed to this post. I realized what I am supposed to do to be fulfilled and happy in life:

Inspire.

I can tell you firsthand, from over 1,000 data points and messages, that there is no better feeling than when you inspire or when you can help. When you genuinely help, it's a good feeling that is impossible to suppress. It's impossible to suppress for a reason: it feels good in the most selfless way possible. Entrepreneurs will make their own mistakes along the way, millions in fact. They have to learn and improve. Don't discourage them from trying. There's no reason to. It's a useless thing to do, and it might be enough to delay the doctor that cures cancer or the visionary that brings sustainable water to Africa, when a simple word of encouragement was the only push they needed.

Inspire. Help, and do so with other people and future generations in mind. *Wouldn't it be the coolest thing in the world if we were the generation that consistently got punched in the face, didn't complain, didn't slow down, picked up our lunch pails and went out every day to create sustainable opportunities for a generation that we haven't met yet?* If that sounds crazy, ambitious, and delusional, it's because it is, and that's the way we have to have it or it's not worth our time. As crazy as it sounds, I can assure you that it only requires us all to do one thing for it to become real. It requires that we all inspire.

What do you think?

64

How We Fight— Cofounders in Love and War

Jessica Alter
with introduction by Steve Blank

Introduction

I often get asked about finding cofounders, and I usually give the standard list of characteristics of what I look for in a *founder*. And I emphasize the value of a founding team with complementary skill sets—e.g., the hacker/hustler/designer (*http://steveblank.com/2011/12/13/the-startup-team/*) cofounder archetype for web/mobile apps. But Jessica Alter (*https://twitter.com/jalter*), cofounder and CEO of Founder-Dating (*http://founderdating.com/*), pointed out that cofounders did not mean two founders in the same room. She suggested that I was missing one of the key attributes of what makes successful startup teams powerful. She suggested that *how cofounders fight* was a key metric in predicting the success of a founding team. So I asked her to write a guest post.

How We Fight

I think about [cofounding] teams a lot—an insane amount. And, not surprisingly, I frequently get asked what to look for or what to think about when starting the process of finding a cofounder—a true partner to start your next company with.

Like second nature, I start to recite a list of important attributes: complementary skill sets, common visions, the notion of not trying to make someone fall in love with your idea (because the idea will likely change, and then where are you?). There are plenty more, and they are important. But a few weeks ago, after I sat on a panel about cofounders at Startup2Startup, there was a small group dinner conversation to dig deeper into the topic. Garry Tan (*https://twitter.com/garrytan*) (Posterous, YC), recounting his personal experience, said, "success can cover up a lot."

And it clicked in my head—one of the key things to pay attention to in a search for a cofounder is *how you fight*.

TAKING TIME

How you fight with your potential cofounder(s) matters for a lot of reasons, the simplest of which is that you have *time* to fight—meaning you've worked together long enough to hit disagreements or bumps. It's one of the most common mistakes we see. I literally just received an email from someone (that I don't know) asking to me to meet with him so that he could circumvent our regular process, because "I don't feel like I have time for the regular FounderDating process." Quick advice to people that think finding a cofounder is a box to check and that they "don't have time"—you won't find someone, and if you do the relationship is unlikely to last. You're looking for an employee, not a partner.

We tell all our FounderDating members that we're a great starting point to connect with amazing people, all with high intent to start something. But in order to figure out if you can work together you have to (wait for it...) *actually work together*. That could mean starting a side project, heading over to a Startup Weekend (*http://startupweekend.org/*) or other hackathon, working together full time for a few months, or some combination of those options. However you do it, *you need to build something together*. It doesn't ultimately matter it if ends up being the right product; you will still have areas you disagree on throughout the process. Ask yourself: have we had disagreements? If you haven't, maybe you should consider a longer courtship period.

SIMULATING REAL LIFE

Consider what real startup life is going to be like. For a long time (longer than you plan) *things are not going to work*, and you'll have to figure out what to do—together. If you do eventually reach a point where the company is making real progress, you're still going to hit crazy challenges on a regular basis that you'll have to navigate together. This pressure—which is compounded by the sound of the ticking clock if you've taken money—will up the stress levels and hence the propensity to disagree.

If you don't have at least a taste of what that's going to be like, not only have you not done your homework, but you also could be in for a rude awakening. So, let's agree you're going to fight. That, in and of itself, doesn't mean anything. In fact, it's quite healthy. What matters in real life is what the fights are like. Do they escalate rapidly or become knock-down, drag-outs? Can you recover quickly and keep moving? Entrepreneurship and early-stage companies are about moving fast; if you're caught in a disagreement for days at a time it means decisions are not being made and/or people are walking around feeling resentful. Either one will eventually lead to failure. Ask yourself: when we fight, do we get over it quickly and respectfully?

WHAT ARE YOU FIGHTING ABOUT?

Finally, and this is insanely important, *it matters what the fights are about*. Are you fighting about whether a button should be green or blue, or are you fighting about whether or not you want to raise money?

A lot of people approach finding cofounders as just a skill set need and believe once that box is checked, everything will be smooth sailing. Complementary skill sets are important, and if you're fighting about one functional area (e.g., design, product) it might be a sign that you have too much skill set overlap. But if it were just about complementary skill set matching, it wouldn't be very hard.

What's difficult is making sure you're aligned on the softer side. Why do you want to build a company? What kind of company do you want to build? What are your working styles? What are your values? What are your other priorities (family, etc.)? We don't care if entrepreneurs want to build lifestyle businesses or go for IPOs, if they are tethered to their email or check out at 7 p.m.—that's a personal decision. But you'd better *make sure you're on the same page as your potential cofounder about those topics.* These are the issues that break up relationships, not button colors.

Ask yourself: what are we fighting about, and why?

Make no mistake, I'm not suggesting you should manufacture a fight. But every relationship has ups and downs, and the ones that last are able to bounce back from the downs quickly and respectfully and be the better for it. So give yourselves permission and time to fight and reflect on how you do it before you take the leap together.

65

Vision Versus Hallucination—Founders and Pivots

Steve Blank

A founder's skill is knowing how to recognize new patterns and to pivot on a dime. At times the pattern is noise, and the vision turns out to be a hallucination. Knowing how to sort between vision and hallucination can avoid chaos inside your startup.

Yuri, one of my ex-students, started a big data analytics company last year. He turned his PhD thesis into a killer product, got it funded, and now was CEO of a company of 30. It was great to watch him embrace the spirit and practice of customer development. He was constantly in front of customers, listening, selling, installing, and learning.

And that's where the problem was.

I got to spend time inside his company while I was using its software to analyze early-stage ventures. What I saw reminded me of some of the best and worst things I'd done as a founder.

A Pivot a Week

It seemed like once a week Yuri would come back from a customer meeting brimming with new insights. "We're building the wrong product!" he'd declare. "We've got to pivot now." Tossing its agile development process and at times its entire business model in the air, the company would go into fire-drill mode and engineering would start working on whatever his latest insight was.

Other weeks Yuri would be buffeted by the realities of his burn rate, declining bank account, and depressing comments from customers. This time he'd be back in the building declaring, "We're going to be out of business in three months if we don't get our act together." I even heard him say to a customer, "If we don't get your order we'll just have to close up in 90 days."

As a consequence, everyone was afraid to make a decision, because they couldn't guess what Yuri wanted to do that week. Some of the engineers, figuring that if the founder was declaring they were toast in 90 days, were updating their résumés. The company already was gaining a reputation as one without a coherent strategy.

I cringed when I saw this—it sounded like me early in my career. I would come back from customer visits convinced that what I'd just learned was the "real" solution to the company's future, and havoc would reign.

Unfortunately for Yuri's company, while there were three other founders, Yuri was the CEO, and none of them had the stature to tell him that his "insights" were damaging his company.

So when we had a few minutes alone, I suggested to Yuri that he was misusing the word "pivot" and confusing it with "whatever I feel like at the moment." I said, "You've got to realize you're not just a smart engineer anymore; 30 people are dropping everything they're doing when you make these pronouncements."

Pivot as an Excuse

I wasn't surprised when he pushed back: "I'm just getting out of the building and listening to customers. All I'm doing is pivoting based on their feedback." By now I'd heard this more times than I liked. "Yuri," I said, "one of the things that make you a great founder is that you have insights others don't. But like all great founders, some of these insights are simply hallucinations. The problem is you and other founders want *immediate* action every time you have a new idea.

"That's a mistake.

"A pivot is *a substantive change to one or more components of your business model*. You're using 'pivot' as an excuse to skip the hard stuff—keeping focused on your initial vision and business model and integrating what you've heard if and only if you think it's a *substantive improvement* to your current business model. There is no possible way you can garner enough information to pivot based on one customer's feedback, or even 20. You need to make sure it's a better direction than the one you are already heading in."

Sit on It for Awhile

I said, "Sit on your great insights for 72 hours and see if they still seem good after reflection. Better, during that time brainstorm them with someone you trust. If not your cofounders, someone outside the company."

I offered that at Epiphany, my partner Ben's office was the first place I would go when I thought I had new "insights." And *we'd run them to the ground for days before we'd even let anyone else know*. Most of the time, after a few days of thought, we decided these insights were really not much better than the current course the company was on. Or by then, other customers would tell us something quite different. And the rule was we wouldn't change anything about the product architecture until Ben and I agreed. Which required Ben hearing from the same customers I did (*http://steveblank.com/2010/09/27/less-is-more-more-or-less/*).

Change the Value Proposition Last

The second thing that Yuri needed to recognize was that changing the value proposition—the features of the products/services he was offering—was a lot more traumatic for a startup than changing other parts of the business model.

I explained that he should make sure that there aren't other parts of the business model (revenue model, pricing, partners, channel, etc.) that can change before he declares, "we're building the wrong product."

In searching for product/market fit (the right match between value proposition and customer segment), the product should be the last part you think of changing —not the first—as the cost of upending your product development organization is high.

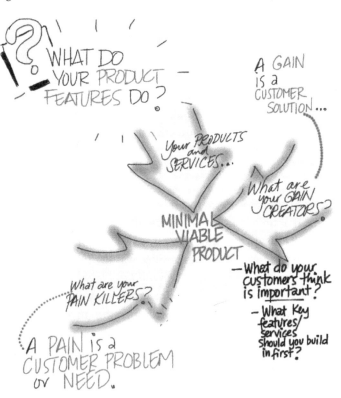

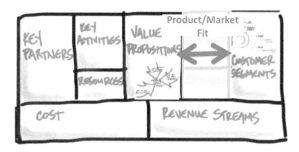

And to make sure everyone knew what he was doing, I offered that he might want to consider letting the entire company know, "Don't worry when I'm talking about changing our business model every week—it's a natural part of searching. Only worry if I ask you to change the value proposition every month."

Find a Brainstorm Buddy

Finally, I suggested that he find someone he respects on his advisory board, who he was comfortable brainstorming with and would tell him when he has a bad idea.

Yuri sat quietly for awhile. I wasn't sure he had heard a thing I said, until he said, "Wait 72 hours? I can do that. Now can I call you when I have a hot new idea?

Lessons Learned

- Founders are great at seeing things others don't—at times it's a vision, most often it's a hallucination.
- Founders want immediate action—often they call it a *pivot*.
- A pivot should not be an excuse for a lack of a coherent strategy or a lack of impulse control.
- Disconnect your insights from your mouth for 72 hours.
- If you can unilaterally overrule your cofounders, there are no brakes on you.
- Your board members are not your brainstorm buddies—find others you trust.

66

50 Startup Lessons Learned in 12 Months

James Maskell (http://jamesmaskell.co.uk/)

Just over a year ago I started work on Vinetrade (*http://www.vinetrade.com/*). Looking back, it's amazing to see just how much I've learned, how many skills I've developed, and what I'd do differently if I were to start another company or build a product today. Inspired by a surge of recent posts by (*http://blog.latentflip.com/post/ 33902095607/startup-lessons-learned*) other (*http://betashop.com/post/32913573235/90- things-ive-learned-from-founding-4-technology*) founders (*http://www.bothsidesoftheta ble.com/on-entrepeneurship/*) on the lessons they have learned, I thought I would post my own.

In no particular order:

1. You need to just get on and build something. It's easy to have an idea—building a product is the hard part. Just getting started is a big leap and will set you apart from so many others who never even get this far.

2. You need a good knowledge of code. It's critical that you know how to build software, or at least what's involved. If you don't have a firm grip on the basics you'll struggle to execute your vision. It is pretty easy to get to grips with the basic concepts, and there's no excuse not to. Sites like Codeacademy (*http:// www.codecademy.com/*) and Treehouse (*http://teamtreehouse.com/*) will help you get to grips with the basics.

3. Don't spend too much time debating which technologies to use. Mark (*http:// www.markmc.co.uk/*) and myself spent a couple of weeks playing with Rails and Django before trying to decide which we preferred and which was the best. In reality, there's barely any difference—just pick what you're most comfortable with and run with it.

4. Your minimum viable product can be much more minimal than you think. We built a Rails app with many features, a nice design, and worried about scalability

and infrastructure. We could have easily gotten away with a much more basic site.

5. User experience (UX) is more important than visual design. A great-looking site is important—but not nearly as important as your customers/users being able to do what they want fast and efficiently. Only hire a visual designer when you've got a grip on the UX.

6. Don't keep your plans to yourself. Put ideas out and get criticism. Feedback is vital, and you'll learn lots. Don't be afraid that people will steal your ideas—they might think about it, but there's a lot of hard work involved, so the risk is small.

7. That includes your site designs and UX. Find people (preferably potential customers) to sit in front of your site and see what works and what doesn't. Where do they get confused? Do they hit any brick walls? Don't give any prompts— just sit and watch. You'll be surprised by what you find.

8. A startup is not a lifestyle business. You're not building something designed to give you a regular income. You're building a company and a business that is designed to grow.

9. You need to pick a large market if you want to raise venture capital investment. A business that makes £10m profit per year may look great to you, but it's small fry for a VC.

10. Banks are a nightmare to deal with. They're almost universally awful and can get away with it because heavy regulation makes the market so difficult to disrupt. They often require more detailed business plans, financial forecasts, and accounts than venture capital investors.

11. Be resourceful and take opportunities. Go to events and network. You'll be surprised by who you meet.

12. Focus on building relationships. Be genuinely interested in other people. Enjoy being sociable.

13. Don't meet people just because you want something out of them. Play the long game and build a relationship. People will be happy to help if you have a good relationship and track record.

14. Meet investors before you need to raise money. It's much easier if they have seen you progress over a period of time and they've gotten to know you. It's about lines, not dots (*http://www.bothsidesofthetable.com/2010/11/15/invest-in-lines-not-dots/*).

15. It's best to meet people through introductions. You can still get there on your own (it's just a bit harder)—but everyone has to start somewhere. Investors are always looking for the best deals and will attend events to meet people. If you've got a product and you're making progress they'll be happy to stay in touch.

16. Focus on the people who show the most interest. If you're looking for customers, focus on those who put their money where their mouth is. Genuine buyers will likely do this very quickly. Same with investors. Lots of people like to talk and many will happily lead you up the garden path with no intention of buying.

17. There's nothing wrong with rejection. If you're getting rejected by different people on a daily basis, you're doing at least one thing right (getting in front of more eyeballs). Focus on those who accept you. They're the people who really matter.

18. Those who initially reject you will likely come running back later. No one wants to be first, and many people want to feel like others are taking away or reducing their risk.

19. Starting and running a company costs way more than you think. If you haven't done this before, find someone who has to check your figures. Factor in the costs of office space, legal fees, events, salaries, taxes, etc. Adzuna (*http://adzu na.co.uk/*) is an incredibly useful site for researching salaries in the UK.

20. Make sure you've got extra cash to use as a contingency. You'll often encounter problems that are easy to make go away if you throw a bit of cash at them.

21. Time costs money. It's often better to be decisive, spend money, and get something done than spend months deliberating and making no progress. Agonise over big purchases, but don't spend an hour deciding whether or not to buy that £20 UX book you saw on Amazon. Just buy it and get on with building your company/product. That hour will cost you more than £20 in the long run.

22. There's a difference between price and value. Price is what you pay, value is what you get.

23. Don't get hung up on things that haven't worked out. If you've spent cash on some design work that bombed, get over it and move on. Fix the problems and forget about the money you spent—you can't get it back. It's gone. Learn from your mistake.

24. Finding good staff takes more than money. Good people are likely to be in stable jobs or have other offers on the table. What else makes you exciting? How much autonomy will they have? What is your culture like?

25. Your first few employees will set the culture. Even just 3–4 people will start to set the tone for the entire company. Cultural fit becomes increasingly important with each employee you add.

26. Don't be scared to say no. This could be to features that customers ask for or requests from employees. Be able to justify your decisions and people will respect you for being decisive.

27. Be prepared to change your mind. You'll learn lots as you progress and the world won't stop changing around you. Be open to changing your mind and take advantage of changing circumstances.

28. Base your decisions around actual data. Learn about metrics and why they're important.

29. As the founding CEO you need to be a good product manager. You need to be able to work with a broad range of people. Read up on agile and scrum methodologies—have a think about how you can adapt them to your business and build good products quickly.

30. Similarly, learn how to sell. You need to be able to get people interested in you, your product, and how it will improve their lives. Learn how to close down objections and get deals done.

31. Don't be scared to ask for money—from customers and investors. If you want to build a company it must be profitable, and this won't happen unless you ask for the cash.

32. Don't get burned out. You don't need to work 20 hours a day, 7 days a week just because you're a startup founder. Some people can do this, but most probably can't. Your health is important. You'll be much more productive and make better decisions when you're well rested.

33. There's always more work that you could be doing. Learn to prioritise and make sure the most important work gets done first. Don't worry if you don't get some minor tasks done. Don't feel like you have to reply to every email—if it's important people will chase and you can reorder your priorities.

34. Choose your investors carefully. Don't take the first deal that you've been offered. Keep going until you find the right people. If something makes you uncomfortable then it's probably a bad sign. Trust your gut.

35. Avoid people who only care about money. Work with people who have genuine passion for what they do. A happy and motivated team is dangerous.

36. You'll have to deal with lots of people who want to make a quick buck out of you (e.g., recruiters). Don't be scared to say no or simply hang up if you can't get rid of them quickly. Your time is valuable and you can't be friends with everyone.

37. Be patient. There's no such thing as overnight success (despite what Tech-Crunch (*http://techcrunch.com/*) may have you believe). It has to be worked for.

38. Be confident. Be clear about what you're doing and why your team is the one that will do it.

39. But don't be arrogant. Be open about what you don't know and mistakes you've made. Ask for advice when you need it.

40. KPIs (key performance indicators) can show hidden progress. You may feel like you've been banging your head against a brick wall, but some of your metrics may show improvements that you weren't previously aware of.

41. Get a good lawyer. The best are expensive but worth the money. Not only will their work be better, but they'll do a better job of making your problems go away and giving you the confidence you need to get on with your job. You'll probably need to work with multiple lawyers before you find (or realize who is) a good one.

42. Don't be afraid to fire (or not return to) people who you're not completely happy with. This rule applies any time you outsource work.

43. Equity should always vest over a period of time. Never give it out up front. It can be worth far more than cash, and it's very difficult to hold people to account if you can't claw it back.

44. The company is bigger than you as an individual. As soon as you have multiple shareholders you're no longer running it solely in your own interests. This can be an odd paradigm shift—while you're executing on your own idea you need to build a machine that is bigger than and can survive without you. If you perform badly, you could be fired.

45. You'll get frustrated and feel like you're not making any progress, particularly when you compare yourself to other startups and their founders. Take a step back to appreciate just how far you've come.

46. Be aware of the long-term vision. Where do you want to be in 5 days, 5 weeks, 5 months, or 5 years? What is your long-term goal and how will you get there?

47. Don't be afraid to admit to your mistakes. Learn from them, put them right, and move on. Don't make the same mistake twice.

48. Read, but don't read too much. Keep an eye on posts over at Hacker News (*http://news.ycombinator.com/*) and cherry-pick the stuff that is useful to you. Subscribe to mailing lists such as Startup Digest (*http://startupdigest.com/*). Reading startup articles is a good way to procrastinate during the day—I've stopped myself from doing this by sending the ones that look interesting to Instapaper (*http://instapaper.com/*) and having an evening or two per week to catch up.

49. This game is not for quitters. Sometimes it can be incredibly tough, and you find it hard to see why you should keep going. But don't do this. Keep going for as long as you possibly can. Remember that there's no such thing as overnight success and that it took many of the most famous founders years to make it.

50. It can be an incredibly rewarding experience, and there's no better way to learn than doing. When you look back on what you've achieved you'll be surprised at the progress you've made in a year. I'm rather pleased that I didn't do a post-grad (*http://jamesmaskell.co.uk/2012/postgrad/*).

67

Advice I Wish I Could Have Given Myself Five Years Ago

Vinicius Vacanti

Since going down the startup path, I've made so many mistakes, struggled so many times, failed in almost every way you can.

But, we turned the corner after a few years of hard work. We're now 25 people (we're hiring!), have raised $7.3 million, and just had our best month ever.

I often fantasize about going back in time and giving myself advice based on what I've learned over the last five years.

I probably wouldn't have listened, but here's what I would have told myself:

- **Teach yourself to code**. After a disastrous experience outsourcing, you'll eventually make this decision. I just want you to make that decision today. Of all the things that will happen, this is the single biggest step-function change you'll experience. Also, I know your outsourcers used Perl, but please *do not* teach yourself Perl. Teach yourself Python/Django or Ruby on Rails.

- **Stop holing yourself up in your apartment**. You think that an hour spent working is more productive than grabbing coffee with another founder. The problem is that you don't yet know what to do in that hour. Talking to other founders, you'll get some valuable advice that will help you save weeks of time. Plus, those founders will eventually introduce you to new hires and investors.

- **Don't be afraid to talk to potential investors**. You keep avoiding it because you know you're not yet ready to raise funding. While you're right, you should still meet with potential investors to get advice. Investors want to have a relationship with you and not just shotgun-fund you. When you finally do raise a round of funding, it will be with investors who have already gotten to know you.

- **Stop worrying about PR.** You spend too much time thinking about it. Your startup won't take off because you got great PR. It will take off because you built a great product. PR is a good way of getting some early test users. It's not how your company will take off.

- **You're not supposed to know what you're doing.** You keep trying to rely only on your instincts. The truth is, your instincts are terrible. You don't know what you're doing, and it's okay. You'll realize this at some point and go out and get advice. You'll eventually stumble into the Lean Startup movement. I just want you to do this sooner.

- **Celebrate the small victories.** That feeling that you're not quite where you want to be won't go away. The way you feel now, hoping to get your first 1,000 users —you'll feel the same way when you've raised $7.3 million and have 25 people working on the team. You'll never be satisfied with your progress, so take time to celebrate the milestones.

- **Don't worry about all the problems you don't have yet.** Focus on the one big problem in front of you. There's a good chance the other problems you're worried about either will get solved on their own or won't be as a big deal as you think.

- **Build your prototype in weeks, not months.** You're going to get lots of ideas. Don't spend months trying to build a prototype. Build something simple to test out the core assumptions of your idea. In a few years, your prototypes will be built in days.

- **Your first few prototypes are going to fail.** You're going to work really hard on your first few prototypes, only to find out that they don't work. That's okay because you'll learn so much that it will make you more likely to succeed with your next prototype. But what's not okay is spending months and months building those prototypes.

- **Lastly, I have an idea for you.** When the iPhone comes out, build a photo-sharing app where you help your users make their photos look better by adding filters. Call it "Instagram." Trust me.

While I have yet to figure out how to go back in time, I hope others who are just starting out can benefit from the advice above.

68

The Only Two Questions Founders Need to Answer

Jason Calacanis (http://blog.launch.co/)

Every day a couple of dozen folks email me asking me to tell them what I think of their products.

When I have the time, or interest, to respond, I generally ask myself a battery of questions:

1. Is the logo iconic?
2. Could you tell me the domain name over the phone once and have me type it in correctly?
3. Is it clear within 10 seconds what the purpose of this product or service is? Does it matter if it is clear?
4. Is the design world-class?

Those are tactical questions that let me know the person has skills. Everyone can pass those tests with a couple of months of hard work.

My two brutal questions, which you can't simply pass with a couple of months of hard work, are how recommendable and unforgettable your product is.

Here is how I ask them:

a. Would I recommend this product?
b. Will I remember this product next month and next year?

If you run an amazing product like Yammer (*https://www.yammer.com/*), Zappos (*http://www.zappos.com/*), Airbnb (*https://www.airbnb.com/*), or Dropbox (*http://dropbox.com/*) through the tactical questions, it quickly becomes clear that these firms have people with skillz:

1. Iconic logos? Yes, yes, yes, and yes.

2. Domain name spelling test? Pass, pass, pass, and pass.

3. Is the product offering clear? Yes: collaborating with your coworkers, big photos of shoes, and finding a place to stay are all super clear. Dropbox takes a little risk by not stating clearly "share files with your coworkers and family." The video is awesome, but that's a slightly risky choice for a home page.

4. Is the design world-class? Yes, yes, yes, and yes. Are Craigslist (*http://craigs list.org/*) and eBay (*http://www.ebay.com/*) world-class? Hell no, but those start-ups were both launched in 1995. They existed before world-class design was the entry fee.

The rubber really meets the road with the two killer questions:

a. Would I tell my friends about Yammer, Zappos, Airbnb, or Dropbox?

Would I? I recommend these products dozens of times each month. Any time someone tells me they have a communication problem in their company I say, "Get Yammer." Any time someone brings up customer service I blurt out, "Zappos!"

People are lamenting the cost of hotels? "Did you try Airbnb?" Need to share files right now? "Download Dropbox."

I've sent tens of thousands of folks to these products. They score 10s on the "would I tell my friends about it?" test.

That test is, of course, based on the Net Promoter Score. We're going to get into that more deeply in a minute.

b. Will I remember this product next month and next year?

The second question is my own invention, and I call it my "unforgettable" test. Is this product so extraordinary that it will haunt me? Is it so well done that I'm not going to forget it?

When David Sacks showed me Yammer during rehearsals for my Tech-Crunch50 show, it burned itself into my brain. An open platform for everyone in a company to communicate. Wow. Twitter or Facebook for the enterprise. That's scary, awesome, and empowering, and as a result it is unforgettable.

Yammer changed corporate culture so meaningfully that dozens of folks copied it.

Zappos's customer service is so unforgettable that people can't shut up about a company that does something as simple as put shoes on your feet. Think about that for a second. They kick ass so royally in customer service that you *want* to talk about buying shoes.

For folks who use Airbnb—and I never have and probably never will—it's a religion. Their life experience has now been broadened because they can travel anywhere at rock-bottom prices and make friends with locals. For folks in need of quick, off-the-books cash, it's saving their lives. It's so compelling that before I go to a city, I find myself looking at search results I'm probably never going to use.

You know you're notable when people talk about your product even though it's not designed for them, and in fact browse it just to keep up with it.

Really, it's genius.

Note

I'm not against renting vacation homes. In fact, I'm renting a kick-ass place in Noe Valley for the rest of the month, and a place in Tahoe for a week this winter. It's just that I can't find those kind of three- or four-bedroom, family-friendly places on Airbnb. They're all on VRBO.com still, it seems. I will keep checking, however.

The promise and name of Dropbox are infinitely memorable. Free storage, works on every platform, integrated into the existing filesystem.... It's so good you ask, "Why didn't this exist before?"

Do You Need to Pass These Tests to Succeed?

Most products and services don't pass these tests. Try and think of an airline, cable company, or wireless provider that's memorable or promotable. Okay, stop laughing and now look at how many billions of dollars these folks make and ask yourself why they don't have to pass these tests to be successful.

The answer is typically that they have a monopolistic, highly defensible, and at-scale business. They don't have to hustle, they don't need to be amazing, and since they have scale, they can actually squeeze additional profits out of their products by cutting down on the delightfulness.

However, if you are a startup, you don't have this luxury. Our (US) government does not give out monopolies and scale anymore. Even space, defense, and health care seem to be becoming more of a meritocracy (e.g., NASA and the USPS are losing their monopolies).

When I Passed These Tests and When I Failed

In all of the big successes and failures I've had in my life, I've passed these tests. Silicon Alley Reporter was memorable, and people recommended it like crazy. A number of our blogs at Weblogs Inc. were notable enough for folks to remember and recommend: Autoblog, Joystiq, Cinematical, Hackaday, and, of course, Engadget.

The LAUNCH Festival (and my previous creation, TechCrunch40/50) created a lot of buzz.

Mahalo 1.0? Well, while I got the product to "good," I'm self-aware enough to know that I didn't exactly get it to "tell your friends" status. I did strike a nerve with "human-powered search," but unforgettable + not recommendable = "nice try."

Now that Mahalo has pivoted to education, in the form of apps and videos, we've been having our notable and recommendable moments.

That's been really, really great for me and the team.

Our educational videos around guitar playing have gotten over 25M views on YouTube to date. Our "Learn Guitar" app has consistently ranked in the top 50 music apps since we launched it three or four months ago.

The Net Promoter Score really is the best way to get there, to my mind.

These days I host meetings with my team where everyone rates a particular video on our semi-customized Net Promoter Score scale:

- 1–6: Bad, and so bad you might tell your friends *not* to get the app.
- 7 or 8: OK and good. I don't feel ripped off by this app, but I'm not so blown away I pull out my phone and show it to someone.
- 9 or 10: Excellent and otherwordly. I'm so enthusiastic about this app I can't stop telling my friends about it.

How do you get to the 9–10 level?

1. Hiring and firing.
2. Iterating.

I know, it's a hard thing to say, but if someone consistently makes an "okay" product, you need to fire them right now. If you make 6- and 7-level content, you suck and you're not doing the world any good.

If you're producing 7- or 8-level content, well, you need to work 30% harder and get yourself to an 8 or a 9. Folks who consistently produce 8- and 9-level content will, inevitably, have a 10 moment. Folks who consistently produce 7- and 8-level content will never hit a 10.

When your company is having honest discussions about doing good work, you're about to make a great product. In fact, that's where Mahalo and ThisWeekIn.com are right now—and it's awesome. Folks can taste how close they are to the 9 or 10.

Being EXCELLENT at consistently producing GOOD product is OKAY.

Being EXCELLENT at producing EXCELLENT product is EXCELLENT.

Google is excellent at producing good product, but it is not excellent at producing excellent product, like Apple. Which proves that you can have a big business by being excellent at good, but to be loved you have to be excellent at excellent.

Does that make sense?

Bottom line: not everyone is going to create a 9 or a 10 every time they build something, E.S.J. (except Steve Jobs). But if you're not in the 8 or better range consistently, you don't have a place in startup land. Sorry.

To be honest, this is why I haven't written a book yet.

I think if I wrote a book three years ago it would have been a 6 or 7. If I wrote the book last year it might have been a 7 or an 8. Every month my friends send me their 6, 7, and 8 books and I read the first chapter, put it down and say, "They should have waited."

I'm waiting for next year or the year after, when I've got enough in me to write the 9 or 10 book.

Writing, like product design, is an iterative process. The more you do it, the better you get. Writing emails to my readers and watching how you respond has made me the writer I am today—which is to say one that doesn't suck, but one that is not going to write a 10 book yet.

Books and movies need to be 9s and 10s or they really should not be produced. It's too much commitment for the creator and the audience. Of course, Hollywood's monopoly on films lets them make 10 returns on 7 or 8 films. *Mission Impossible 4* is a solid 8 and *Avatar* was a 7—but they made absurd returns due to the rigged machine Hollywood has built.

What I've learned from self-analysis is that I know I can get you guys 8, 9, and sometimes 10 emails. How do I know this? Because I watch how often you forward, tweet, like, and reply to each one.

That's why you guys typically get my emails in bunches. If 50 or 100 of you write back "good one" or "best one yet," I get motivated and I write more.

1,200+ of you tweeted the "Cult of Amazon Prime" (*http://blog.launch.co/blog/the-cult-of-amazon-prime.html*) story.

I hit the 10 mark on that bad boy—and frankly, I thought it was an 8.5.

If my email can do that regularly, that's when I start writing the book. If I can put together three 10s in a row, yeah, it's time to write a book. I'm not there.

Being self-aware enough to rate yourself on a brutal scale of 1 to 10, and then figure out what it will take to move slowly up the leaderboard, is critical to being an entrepreneur.

Most folks in the world can't handle this level of scrutiny.

Bottom line: if you can't get past a 7 or 8, you should really quit the samurai/startup business. The world doesn't need you to make products. Stop. Quit.

And remember, if you are not a samurai, you are a rice picker.

Nothing wrong with picking rice, someone's got to feed the samurai I guess.

69

Once You Take Money, the Clock Starts Ticking

Chris Dixon

One of the interesting things about having been investing in startups for a number of years is that at any moment you can get an inside peek at startups at a variety of different stages. In the course of a few weeks, I might talk to people who are ideating around new business ideas, people raising seed rounds, people raising later (VC) rounds, people whose products are blowing up, people whose products are struggling, people getting acquired, people leaving acquirers to start new companies, etc. Sadly, there are also usually a few companies that are struggling and facing the serious possibility of running out of money and being forced to shut down.

One side-by-side comparison struck me recently. Company A is just now raising a seed round. The money they raise will last 12 months (personally, I strongly recommend raising 18 months' (*http://cdixon.org/2011/12/06/always-have-18-months-of-cash-in-the-bank/*) worth of runway—if you have the option to do so). Company A was also, in my opinion, not ready to raise money (they needed to work on their plan and team more). Company B raised a seed round about 10 months ago and is now struggling to raise more. Company B had the option to raise more money back then but chose to only raise 12 months' runway in order to minimize dilution. Company B also made the mistake of having a large VC invest $100k in the round (a meaningless amount to a large VC). The large VC has since said it won't support the company (despite the fact that the company made pretty good progress on the business), creating a massive signaling problem (*http://cdixon.org/2009/08/14/the-problem-with-taking-seed-money-from-big-vcs/*).

In the current "frothy" environment, where seed investors are aggressively offering money to entrepreneurs, it is easy for an entrepreneur to think, "Well, if I'm getting offered money this easily at the seed stage, I'll get offered money easily later." In fact, once you take a professional investor's money, the attitude of investors (both insiders and outsiders) changes dramatically: you've gone from planning mode to operations mode. When you do planning, research, experimenting, etc.

403

without having raised money, investors think you are prudent (I recently interviewed the Warby Parker founders for TechCrunch (*http://techcrunch.com/2012/02/24/founder-stories-warby-parker-less-than-1-of-eyeglasses-were-sold-online/*) and they said they spent 1.5 years planning/researching before they raised money). When you do it with other people's money, and don't make what they perceive to be enough progress, the investors can quickly lose faith.

The obvious lesson is well known by experienced entrepreneurs. Don't raise money until you are ready, and when you do, raise enough to have a good shot at reaching "accretive milestones" so you can raise more money, become profitable, or whatever your goals might be.

70

The Series A Crunch Survivor's Guide

Jason Calacanis

I got a ton of feedback on my email from Christmas Day titled "There Is No Series A Crunch (*http://blog.launch.co/blog/there-is-no-series-a-crunch.html*)."

If headlines, and people's attention spans for them, allowed for more complete arguments, the headline could have been expanded to: "There Is No Series A Crunch for Startups with These Characteristics...."

Besides, headlines are best when they seduce you with only partial information. What's the fun of getting all the facts in one line and moving on with your life (like we're doing with the LAUNCH ticker (*http://launch.co/*))? ;-)

Much of the feedback I've gotten came from both sides of the table: founders and investors, and of course some bloggers and "social media experts." Of course, social media experts should be renamed "people who talk a magnitude more than their experience entitles them to," but I digress.

This is specifically to founders who are not able to raise a Series A. If you're an investor, you can't read this.

OK my founders, time for some #realtalk. If you can't raise a Series A, you've learned it's probably because of some combination of the following:

1. Your team lacks a track record.
2. Your product execution is not competitive with other products investors are seeing.
3. You lack product traction.
4. The market you're addressing is not big or "important" enough.
5. You're fishing in a recently poisoned pond (e.g., the deal space pioneered by Groupon).
6. Your valuation doesn't match reality.

7. Your burn is unjustified, scary, or lacks discipline.

8. You lack clients.

How many of these problems do you have? Well, I can tell you that almost every startup I angel invest in has the majority of these issues at any given point in time. They're supposed to, after all, as you can't have a huge win if you're not willing to take a huge loss. In order to slay the dragon, you have to be willing to have the dragon eat you.

Heck, my four startups (Silicon Alley Reporter, Weblogs Inc., Mahalo, and ThisWeekIn) have had all of these qualities at different points in time. And that's great, because none—yes, none—of these things are permanent.

We can even solve for your lack of a track record.

There are lots of little hacks to make these things work, and I'll give you each of them now.

1. Your Team Lacks a Track Record

No track record, no problem! You have three ways to fix this.

First, you can hire folks who have a track record. How do you do this? You look at the successful version of yourself from the last cycle and hire from them. Building a next-generation LinkedIn? Well, find the folks who built LinkedIn or Spoke, or who worked at a major HR consulting firm, and hire them.

Then you bring them to investor meetings and have them answer the question, "Why did you join this company after having been at LinkedIn?" Just say in a meeting, "Hey Roelof, this is John Doe and he spent four and a half years working in sales and he is now joining our startup for half his pay rate... John, can you tell Roelof what attracted you to our project?"

Second, if you can't afford these folks, make a "working advisory board." A working advisory board works like this: two-year deals, a half to full point depending on the person (sounds rich, I know), four people, and a standing monthly phone call (say 10 calls a year).

On that call you give them a quick update on the state of the business and then just tell them your biggest challenge and listen. They should speak for 50 of the 60 minutes, and your management team should shut up and just listen. Afterwards, your team should talk for another hour about what folks said, and if it applies. This will cost you 2 to 4 points, but it will give you a deep bench that actually adds value and whose members earn their shares in your startup.

Finally, you can take the "connect the dots" approach, which is to give an update on key metrics every 60–90 days to investors you've met with before. Nothing pleases an investor like passing on an investment, being proven wrong by the team, and being able to correct that error by buying shares. Mark Suster has the definitive pieces on betting on lines, not dots, on his excellent blog (*http://www.bothsidesofthet able.com/2010/11/15/invest-in-lines-not-dots/*).

2. Your Product Execution Is Not Competitive with Other Products Investors Are Seeing

This is so easily solved it's silly. Investors, advertisers, and partners love shiny new objects—so give them some!

First, go find a domain name you can buy that is 50 times better than the stupid, unprofessional one you sometimes have to live with when you're on a budget. For example, if you were building a bookmarking site and had del.icio.us, you would find out if *delicious.com* was available and get the price. Say it's available for $250k. Great! Now you can bring that fact to rich investors, showing you know how to invest money wisely. For bonus points you could make a deal for $1k to have the option to buy the domain for the next six months at that price—showing you know how to make deals and put together a frugal plan.

Second, take your ugly-ass site and hire a real designer—a world-class one— to refresh it. Just a one-page refresh and you're done. Redoing your entire site might cost $10k or $20k. One page of your site? Maybe three to five days and $3k.

Language: "Hey George Zachary, you've seen our crummy-looking MVP, but I wanted to show you our new design and, well, boy... it's really exceeded our expectations. Here it is. Oh yeah, we have a killer domain and Twitter handle we're buying... you're not going to believe this, but we have *inside.com* and @*inside!*"

Sound crazy? Well, I can tell you that when I started explaining what my new project was and a) showed the iPad Mini design of Inside, b) told the story of how I got the *inside.com* domain (after 10 years of trying) for $60k, and c) said that I now had the @*inside* Twitter handle, folks immediately started saying stuff like, "This is your best idea ever—and I've heard ideas from you for the better part of two decades, Jason."

Design = credibility.

Branding (e.g., domains, Twitter handles, etc.) = credibility.

3. You Lack Product Traction

This is the hardest thing you've got on your plate. Hands down. The demo day "pump and dump" big metric push, where startups would buy traffic to build a hockey stick-ish chart, is coming to a close. Everyone knows how easy it is to buy $0.35 clicks and move the needle—but that's as intelligent as putting lighter fluid on rocks.

What you want in the startup space, and on any good fire, is a solid and small base of kindling. Get a core group of users who love your product and with whom you regularly communicate. It might be only 10 or 50 people, but having this inside group and understanding what they're thinking and how they're using your product shows you understand the important organic steps of building a world-class brand.

If the founders are talking to the first 100 customers of Airbnb, Yammer, or Business Insider, they're going to know—in large part—what the next 1,000, 10,000, or 100,000 will experience.

Language: "Hey Fred Wilson, thanks for taking the meeting. As you can see we have an awesome advisor team, an option to buy a great domain name that you could make happen, and a killer new design. Most importantly, we did a Google+ Hangout with our top 10 users, and here is a copy of the video. Wait 'til you hear how excited they are about the product!"

Roll video.

You see what we're doing? After only doing 1, 2, and 3, you've moved from "Series A roadkill" to the "for consideration" folder of a VC's Gmail.

4. The Market You're Addressing Is Not Big or "Important" Enough

Many times a market doesn't even exist until someone makes something so compelling that it does. For example, the collaborative consumption movement—led by Getaround and Airbnb—has created demand for a product that didn't exist before: renting your car and your couch.

There was no way to figure out the "size" of this market, except maybe to look at hotel rooms. However, it seems that Airbnb is not always replacing hotel rooms, but rather inspiring folks on a budget to take more trips—and perhaps longer ones?

Same with Getaround. Folks might simply stay in the city and see a movie, but if a $30/day car is available, why not take a wine trip?

What was the market for apps before smartphones? Zero. Point. Zero. Sometimes markets manifest by the will power of product geniuses.

@*Jack* brought POS services to farmers' markets, where cash was king. Those vendors never thought they would have a service like @*Square* because a) the iPad didn't exist and b) the software didn't exist.

At least that's one way to get past the "too small a market" objection. Another is to say that you're going to expand into other markets—but I suppose that is obvious.

5. You're Fishing in a Recently Poisoned Pond (e.g., the Deal Space Pioneered by Groupon)

What happens when you have a flash sale site after the fall of Groupon and Living Social? How do you get folks interested? Metrics, product, passion, and performance—at least, that's what worked for Jason Goldberg from Fab (*http://fab.com/*). Listen to this episode of TWIST (*http://www.youtube.com/watch?feature=player_em bedded&v=BU_L1UyAhMI*) where he talks about Fab's founding.

Also, remember that video services were DOA in 2000, but YouTube made them work due to Flash video, syndication, and falling bandwidth costs. What technology and market forces solve for previous failures?

Do you even know? You need to.

6. Your Valuation Doesn't Match Reality

Perhaps the biggest part of the Series A crunch is great expectations. If you've got a bunch of the problems on this list and folks don't think the "risk and reward" are in balance, why not increase the reward?

Everyone is looking to do a $15m to $20m post in their Series A. Why not raise a $2m Series A at a $6m to $7m post if things are so bad out there? Undercut the market, get the best investors possible, and prove that you deserve to survive winter.

Investors love a great deal, and the valuations are just brutal out there for investors.

7. Your Burn Is Unjustified, Scary, or Lacks Discipline

You need to look at your burn every month and ask yourself what expenses are pushing the business and product forward and which ones are legacy. Most entrepreneurs are slow to cut and fast to add costs—when they should be doing the opposite.

I've always tried to run my startups with 18 months of cash/burn in the bank. This has worked exceptionally well for me because it keeps me focused on the product, not the cliff. Having enough time to build intelligently is critical. Can you share office space? Can you rent extra desks for $500 each? Can you shut down some servers? Can your accounting person be three days a week?

Now, VCs are not going to care so much about this issue, but your runway is your chip stack, and as any poker player knows, it *sucks* to be short stacked. VCs will appreciate efficiency, but they're not going to make an investment decision on it, unless it is really scary or shows you lack discipline/intelligence.

8. You Lack Clients

Clients who love your product are the quickest way to close an A round. Cultivate deep relationships with them and get them to take surveys and share that data with your potential investors.

For example, asking them how much they would pay for your product if they built it themselves, what their total spend is in the category, and how much more they would pay for your product are all great questions for your future VCs to see.

It also shows you're not afraid of engaging clients deeply.

That's all I've got off the top of my head.

PART XIII

Management and Career Advice

71

Selling or Funding a Startup? Tips on Surviving Technical Due Diligence

Karl Treier (http://bit.ly/onstartups-selling-funding)

Be Better Prepared for Technical Due Diligence

I have been on the receiving end of several technical due diligence assessments instigated by VCs (pre-investment) or acquirers (pre-purchase). I have also been the inquisitor on a few occasions. So I thought it might be worthwhile to write this post to share my thoughts on this process and hopefully help companies better prepare for this event.

The first thing to recognize is that the assessor is not there to catch you out, trip you up, or somehow prove you are incompetent, nor is it likely that he's there to try to steal your job—so first and foremost, don't be threatened or intimidated (it's not the Spanish Inquisition; after all, "Nobody expects the Spanish Inquisition!"). It is, however, extremely likely that he is, or has been, an entrepreneur and empathizes with you, so be cooperative and cordial (maybe even downright friendly). The assessor will understand the challenges and the realities of startup, rampup, and speedup life and will not be expecting perfection. I personally would love it if every entrepreneur could get funded, or exit with an acquisition that gets them the rewards they have worked so hard to attain, but the reality is different. Remember, however, the assessor is contractually obligated to do a thorough evaluation and report honestly any deficiencies; to not do so would risk a lawsuit for negligence. Also keep in mind that the purpose of an outside individual doing this, rather than having the investors or buyers just deliver a survey to you for you to complete, is that they are evaluating you and your team, how well you think on your feet, how you engage, and your thought processes. So expect it to be an interactive conversation, more than an outright quiz or exam, which would be painful and boring for both parties.

In my opinion the primary purpose of the assessment is to evaluate four facets of your business from a technical standpoint: vitality, scalability, maintainability, and continuity. Vitality, really? I'll admit no one has asked me to go assess the vitality of an organization, but I'll explain in the next section why I use that word, because I think it fits perfectly with what I'm looking for. I'll begin each of the following sections with the *dictionary.com* (edited) definition of the word, so you see just how well they fit the goals of the assessment. I'll also provide a narrative of the objective of assessing that characteristic of the business, and a list of questions you just might get asked.

Vitality

vitality [vahy-**tal**-i-tee]
   noun, plural -ties

1. exuberant physical strength or mental vigor: a person of great vitality
2. capacity for survival or for the continuation of a meaningful or purposeful existence: the vitality of an institution
3. power to live or grow

So what am I looking for when I assess the technical vitality of an organization? Really, I'm looking to see first and foremost if the technical lead or founder is still excited about the business. Does she have a real vision of where to take the product next? Is he a fountain of ideas? Sometimes the original technical founder(s) may have left, so is the replacement a caretaker, or does she have her own ideas of where to take the technology and business? In my opinion this is a very important thing to assess. The best and fastest-growing software companies in the world have great technology leadership. You can't build great software companies with only MBAs at the top. Yes, you need the MBA types, but you also need the engineer types that can see emerging technologies and see how they can be applied to the product to further the business. The truth is that great technical leadership also attracts great technical talent, which is essential to the vitality of the company, and essential to ensuring that all the other bases we will discuss below are covered. Here are some questions you might get asked that really assess the vitality of the organization:

- Do you have a clear vision for where you want the product to be in one month, or six months?
- When you advertise a programmer vacancy, how many applications do you get?
- How many people have left, and how many have joined in the last year?
- Do you have people working for you now, who worked for you elsewhere in the past?
- How do you capture user feedback about the product, and who sees it?
- How many releases have you had in the last year?
- What keeps you awake at night?
- Do you make interviewees write code?

Scalability

scalability (ˌskeɪləˈbɪlɪtɪ)
   noun

1. the ability of something, esp a computer system, to adapt to increased demands

This one is pretty obvious, though any assessment of scalability extends beyond the system itself to include the technical organization. The answers to the first two questions below will indicate how the respondent thinks about scalability, not just from a technical perspective, but an organizational one also:

- What would you have to change to accommodate 10, 100, or 1,000 times more users?
- What would you have to change to accommodate a million users?
- What do you monitor?
- What metrics do you use to determine if you are not scaled appropriately?
- What aspects of the system do think might not scale well?
- Where are you hosted, and why?
- Do you use any third-party services, and if so what happens if they go down?
- Can you show me a network diagram?

- What single points of failure exist?
- What keeps you awake at night?
- How many open features/user stories are there, and how old is the oldest?

Maintainability

maintain [meyn-**teyn**]
 verb (used with object)
 maintainability, *noun*

1. to keep in existence or continuance; preserve; retain
2. to keep in an appropriate condition, operation, or force; keep unimpaired
3. to keep in a specified state, position, etc.

Maintainability is a favorite assessment topic of investors and buyers alike. They usually either are paranoid that existing staff will head for the hills post-acquisition (or incoming staff will discover a plate of spaghetti code), or want to turn a non-profitable company into a profitable one by eliminating "engineering," or worry that a potential future investor might discover a huge plate of spaghetti code during their due diligence and not buy. In all the above scenarios there is all too often distrust of the engineering types by the MBA types, and so they want to know if the code maintainable. Usually it is. You might notice many of the questions below originate from Joel Spolsky's 12-point test (*http://www.joelonsoftware.com/arti cles/fog0000000043.html*), which I think it's OK to plagiarize because they are just common sense:

- Do you use source/version control?
- Do you build on check-in, daily, weekly, whenever?
- Do you require comments on check-in?
- Do you create unit tests?
- Do you have code reviews?
- What development methodology do you use?
- Can you deploy a build to staging or production with one click?

- Do you have dedicated testers?
- When do you deploy?
- Does the software automatically notify you of errors?
- Do you have a bug tracking system?
- Could you walk me through some code?
- How many defects did you close last month?
- How many open defects are there?

Continuity

continuity [kon-tn-**oo**-i-tee, -tn-**yoo**]
noun, plural -ties

1. the state or quality of being continuous
2. a continuous or connected whole

This is typically the area where the greatest weaknesses appear in the assessment, particularly with younger companies. There is an assumption that the data center will always be there, and that nothing can go wrong; that the world will always stay the same. Even everyday occurrences like a few inches of snow (or feet, depending upon where you live) can cause serious disruptions that should be planned for. So, many of the questions below are aimed at ascertaining if the technical lead lives in a utopian world where nothing goes wrong, or if he allows his utopia to be tainted by a touch of realism:

- Do you have a disaster recovery plan?
- Do you have a business continuity plan?
- Is there any part of the system that is understood by only one person?
- Is your version control system backed up? Where, and how often?
- If the database server exploded, how much client data would be unrecoverable?
- If a 747 crashed into the data center, how much client data would be unrecoverable?

- Does your staff have laptops?

In Conclusion

Please don't take this as an exhaustive list of questions. Quite frankly, the role of the assessor is to think on their feet and open up the questioning to explore avenues of weakness and strength. But what I do hope is that this post gets you thinking about how you would answer these questions, and what questions might get triggered based upon your answers.

Have you been on either side of the technical due diligence process before? What were the lessons you learned?

72

Playbook for Incoming MBAs to Start a Company out of School

David Beisel

Like a lot of students, I went into business school a decade ago with a set plan to start a company straight after graduation, by cofounding an Internet startup (...again). During the following two years I did a number of things that prepared me for that endeavor, but in retrospect, I also completely missed out on a number of opportunities and valuable resources immediately in front of me that I didn't recognize at the time. My alternative working title for this post was: "Eight things I kind of knew and only mostly followed as an entrepreneur during b-school." My own circuitous path toward graduating a couple of years later intentionally without a job (see bullet #1) eventually led me on to the venture capital investing side of startups, but I still regret not fully taking advantage of the two years that only a business school environment (and calling card) can provide. Recognizing that the academic year is starting now for MBAs (as well as all other entrepreneurial-minded students, for that matter), I wanted to articulate a set of recommendations for b-school students looking to start a company immediately after graduation:

1. **Commit to graduating without a job**. It's a challenging leap of faith to take, but entrepreneurship requires a full, all-in effort. If there's an irresistible urge to hedge a bit in exploring alternative paths or engage just a bit in on-campus recruiting for traditional roles, then it's better to fully pursue one of those routes (at least for now) than be distracted by an entrepreneurial pursuit that won't materialize.

2. **Master the coursework basics, but then develop soft skills rather than specialized ones**. Part of the benefit of a generalized MBA program is developing a broad fundamental skill set across many areas of functional expertise, from finance to marketing and everything in between. After those core skills are

developed, however, it's more advantageous to spend additional class time developing higher-level "softer" skill sets that will be used throughout the entrepreneurial process rather than deeper point-solution "hard" expertise that can be hired or learned on the job as needed (e.g., take Interpersonal Dynamics, not Global Financial Reporting.)

3. **Take classes from the best "star" professors.** You're paying quite a bit of money for this education, and the different between star instructors and the solid overflow ones is step-function, not incremental. For example, Irv Grousbeck and Mark Leslie at the Stanford GSB fundamentally changed my thinking about life and business, and unsurprisingly Felda Hardymon has the reputation for doing the same at HBS. Regardless of the school, there are always the premier professors. Use your entrepreneurial drive to go around "the system" to get into those instructors' classes—beg, borrow, and steal to do so. Camp out at their offices. Or just show up for the classes and literally take the course twice, once with the star (unofficially) and again with the "standard other" instructor (officially). It's worth it. Really.

4. **Go outside the business school to meet cofounders.** Business schools are very insular islands, but they're surrounded by an ocean of students in all disciplines. Your developed skill set won't be much different from your immediate classmates', but it certainly will be different from that of someone in engineering or computer science. "Recruit" your cofounders there; it's more difficult, but that's the point. Diverse thinking will create better thinking.

5. **Go off-campus with your student ID.** Your "student" calling card immediately disarms and can open all sorts of doors that won't be as inviting the second you have a diploma in hand. Proactively and persistently reach out to people directly who could add insight and credibility, as well as potentially initiating a process for company-making deals, for your startup. In our NextView Ventures portfolio, Eliot Buchanan (founder/CEO of Plastiq (*https://www.plastiq.com/index*)) was the master of this approach and was able to bring on high-profile partners (think Mastercard) to his business before even graduating from undergrad!

6. **Immerse yourself in a domain to develop authentic ideas.** Rather than whiteboarding different potential business ideas, think about your own previous work experiences and try to solve problems for constituents in those businesses that you know firsthand. If nothing comes out of that exercise, spend time truly immersing yourself in a specific industry or domain.

7. **Do what your classmates are not.** MBAs are notorious for sheep-herding toward a particular category of startups (recently, daily deals and new online e-retailing). Aim for the upper-right quadrant on the consensus/non-consensus vs. right/wrong 2×2 matrix (*http://techcrunch.com/2011/08/20/don%E2%80%99t-follow-the-crowd/*) and develop a (hopefully correct) thesis that's not following a common assumption.

8. **Take a summer internship to hone expertise or a functional skillset, NOT for résumé padding.** Once you start a company, nobody will care what you did for 10 weeks one summer. Really. But the chance to just drop into a company and an industry for a couple of months, without any strings attached, can help develop real knowledge and facilitate connections. For example, in the NextView Ventures portfolio, Fred Shilmover worked at Salesforce.com (*http://salesforce.com*) before starting SaaS-based InsightSquared (*http://www.insightsquared.com/*) straight out of school... and now Salesforce.com (*http://salesforce.com*) is an investor in the company, too.

9. **Find yourself.** Taking two years out of the workforce before fully pursuing an entrepreneurial endeavor grants a luxurious amount of time for self-reflection. Utilizing this time to better recognize and appreciate not just your strengths and weaknesses, but also your underlying motivations and intentions, will help prepare you for the many challenges of starting a company.

73

Manage Your Tech Career

Andy Rachleff (https://blog.wealthfront.com/)

It may sound strange for the CEO of an investment management firm to say this, but managing your career well is much more important than managing your investments well.

Good investment management—using low-cost ETFs and low-fee advice—can mean higher returns in your investment portfolio. Over time, that might add up to a lot of money—maybe hundreds of thousands of dollars on larger portfolios. But the economic rewards that follow from good career decisions in the technology industry are potentially much larger.

Today, Wealthfront (*https://www.wealthfront.com/*) is launching a Startup Compensation Tool to help our clients with that part of their financial lives: their careers. The Tool offers data on the tech startup job market, including cash compensation and equity packages for a range of jobs, so that you can maximize the return on your career.

We've licensed data typically used by Human Resources departments and made it available for free—one more example of how Wealthfront is democratizing access to sophisticated financial advice and information.

I'm not suggesting money should be your first concern when you think about your career. People do the best work, and have the best chance of great success, if they do what they love on a day-to-day basis. The data in our Tool supports that idea —take a look at the way individuals with expertise in their fields earn as much as or more than managers in their fields (filter by engineer—hardware or software— on all job levels, and you'll see what I mean). A top-level scientist (an architect, in the Tool), for instance, earns as much as the person who manages the scientists, and a top-level engineer earns as much as a person managing engineers.

So, work at what you love—and then, maximize the return on your work. To do that, you need access to good information.

How to Use the Tool

You can use the Tool to give you context about the tech startup job market, specifically around equity compensation. This information isn't available anywhere else. It can help you evaluate job offers and make counteroffers. I hope the Tool also helps you think about your career path broadly, including considering what kind of company you want to join and in what position.

When I was a venture capitalist, one of the first things I discussed with my CEOs was setting a budget for salaries and equity, using what we knew about typical pay at companies in the Valley. For each position and at each level, there's a range of compensation and, of course, a mean.

The CEO decided where his or her particular firm would fall compared with other firms. For instance, would the company pay in the 60th percentile for salaries, and in the 40th percentile for equity? (That would be typical for an already successful company, which is likely to pay higher-than-average salaries and offer lower-than-average equity. Never would a company offer both above-market salaries and equity.)

That leads to my first suggestion for managing your career well: *pay the most attention to the quality of the company when you are deciding where to apply or which job offer to accept.*

Find the Right Company (or Pie)

Choosing the right tech startup (*https://blog.wealthfront.com/choose-right-job-company/*) to work for is the single most important factor for maximizing the return on your career. Choice of company trumps position, salary, and even the size of your equity package. A small equity stake in a big success is exponentially more valuable than a big equity stake in a failure or a minor success.

I illustrate the importance of growing the size of the pie to one's share of the pie to my entrepreneurship students at the Stanford Graduate School of Business by reminding them of the formula for a circle's circumference versus its area. The formula for circumference (a proxy for share of pie) is linear ($2\pi r$), while the formula for area is quadratic (πr^2).

The single most important factor in a company's big success (growing the size of the pie) is the size of the market the company ultimately addresses. Other signs of a future big exit that pays off for employees: a scalable business model and an unfair advantage (such as intellectual property, a unique business model, or a proprietary relationship) that allows a company to earn high margins.

Those things might not be obvious from the get-go because so many successful technology companies pivot. Sometimes, the best clue to a company's future success is the team's ambition. The team will work on a big problem because that's what's important to them. I can't think of a better example than my colleagues at Wealthfront, many of whom joined us because they wanted to work on an important problem: democratizing access to sophisticated financial advice.

Get What's Fair, but Don't Negotiate Too Much

You're talking to a great company, and they're offering you a job you love. Now it's time to figure out how you'll be compensated.

If the company asks you to name your salary first, ask them what they believe is fair. You can use our Tool to determine where the offer falls in comparison with the market. (The mean cash compensation across all tech startups in all the markets was $112,000 in 2011, according to our data.)

If at some point during the negotiation you're asked to name an amount or an equity stake, you can use our Tool to decide on reasonable numbers. Don't ask for an amount that is far above the average; the company most likely won't break its budgets to hire you, and you will have damaged the relationship right from the beginning.

If you're going to ask for a reasonable increase in the offer, ask for more equity. Getting another .1% can lead to a hell of a lot more money than another $10,000 of salary. (Our data shows that in 2011 the mean equity compensation across all tech startups across all maturities in all the markets was .072%.)

Based on my experience, most companies will offer you a fair wage and a fair equity package. Those that don't are those you don't want to work for.

The Bottom Line

Managing your investments well is important. Wealthfront manages portfolios of ETFs for our clients at a fee of only .25% a year. Over 20 years, the money you save on our fees relative to traditional advisors' could save you as much as 60% of your initial investment. That's a lot.

Managing your career well is even more important, because the stakes are so much higher.

When technology companies win, they win big. There's no way to predict exactly how much you'll make if you work for one of those winners when it goes public, but I can give you a sense of the value. Consider: the typical successful public technology company generates revenue of $500k per employee, and is valued (that's its market capitalization) at 5 to 10 times revenue. To find the value per employee, we multiply the revenue per employee by the typical market capitalization/revenue ratio. We can then multiply that number by .15—the percent of shares that employees, excluding executives, typically own.

It's a rough calculation, but it gives us $375,000–$750,000 for the typical employee in a typical IPO. That's more than three to six times the average pay at a tech startup ($112,000 in 2011, according to our data).

With any luck, and if you join a tech startup in the early years, the payoff can be much larger.

Wealthfront can help you understand what you deserve to earn, when you should sell the options you receive, and how you should invest the proceeds. Over time, you can expect us to create more tools and publish more research to answer financial questions for people who work at technology companies.

74

Hey Entrepreneur—
Please Get an MBA

Mike Gozzo (http://gozman.wordpress.com/)

A few years ago I was working in a job I loved with a company (*http://matrox.com/imaging/en/*) that was doing highly sophisticated technical work (i.e., not what most consumer web companies do). I loved my technical role and the challenges and freedom it afforded me, but I felt that there was a whole other side of the world that I didn't understand.

I enrolled in a part-time MBA program in a well-ranked (*http://johnmolson.concordia.ca/en/component/content/article/96-jmsb-news/2362-jmsb-moves-up-in-worldwide-rankings*) business school and got to work on case studies, networking, and all that good stuff on nights and weekends. My relationships became tired and strained, and I literally sweat through managing both a technical career and a demanding academic curriculum. It took me some time (almost five years!), but I graduated with an MBA.

If you were to listen to some startup types (*http://naysawn.com/hey-entrepreneur-please-dont-get-an-mba/*) (or worse yet, your early-stage VC investors), you'd skip grad school and stick to ramen in your garage while trying to nail a huge viral coefficient and plastering whiteboards with agile index cards and a huge-ass lean canvas. After all, the only things that matter to your business are your user acquisition techniques and the number of people on your LinkedIn that are wearing hoodies in their profile pictures, right?

This is why, if you're serious about being an entrepreneur, an MBA will give you an extra edge.

1. What You Actually Learn

MBA programs vary from school to school, but you can be sure that by the time you're out you'll be conversant in a range of topics. You'll know enough of everything business-y to be dangerous. Need to read a financial statement? Set up a pricing plan? Motivate your employees? Understand a VC's game plan when he offers you a term sheet? Understand why you're bleeding your seed money like a hunted seal? An MBA will teach you the fundamental theory that lets you do all of these things.

You will study almost every industry on the planet. During my MBA, we covered companies from Google to Avon from a variety of perspectives. Think that Avon has nothing to teach you about startup marketing? Think about how they built the *ultimate* affiliate program and drove millions in revenue through user acquisition before Zuck was even born. There are lessons in these companies and industries that are begging to be applied to the Web and "disruption."

Sure, you could teach yourself all of this by reading book after book (in fact, you will read a great many during your MBA), but you likely won't be talking about this stuff over beers with your colleagues who share a range of experiences from industries unlike your own. I'm blessed to have people from Montreal to Mumbai in my MBA network that have built web startups, run construction firms, brought pharmaceuticals to market, and kept steel mills running. The kind of perspective on strategy you get when combining these disparate points of view is as humbling as it is eye-opening.

2. Tuition Costs

Tuition costs can be prohibitive for an MBA. I was lucky that in Quebec we pay the lowest costs for tuition in North America. My entire MBA cost under $10,000 (including books), thanks to massive government subsidization (tuition for international students would be many times greater).

To make an educated decision about whether or not the tuition is worth it MBA style, you need to figure out the ROI. Thing is, it's hard to put a precise dollar amount on the return you'll get from your degree in the context of your first tech startup.

This will vary from person to person, but try to think long term and consider the extra edge in terms of your career flexibility (what if this bubble bursts?) and your ability to communicate with stakeholders outside of Silicon Valley and Hacker News.

3. Time Commitment

MBA programs suck up your time. There's no escaping it. If you want to do well, you need to work hard, attend a ton of group meetings, and write a heck of a lot of PowerPoint decks. However, in a startup, you won't have it any easier. An MBA is a great way to teach you how to find balance between your work and your personal life.

While studying I made some awful decisions that really put a damper on my interpersonal relationships. I was performing well at the office, was above average at school, and failing with loved ones. I quickly learned how to balance it all and launched a startup (*https://www.theappifier.com/*). By the time I graduated, I had been on TechCrunch, been through an accelerator, had a product in market, had revenue, and was interviewing my first employee. I actually didn't attend convocation because I was prepping for an investor pitch. I also did this while caring about my family and building strong ties.

If I can do this, so can you.

4. The Wrong Network

I love YC (*http://ycombinator.com/*)'s model and their alumni network. I'd love even more to be plugged into it. That said, how much disruption can you really create when everyone in your circle has the same worldview?

MBA schools will lead to your network being chock-full of mid-level executives across a range of strange and traditional industries, but these people will challenge you to think about fundamentals of your business and ask you the tough questions that only an outsider could see.

Some of the best advice I've received on raising capital and managing competition has come from a guy who works in Saskatchewan modeling the financials around wheat production. He also made an introduction that led to a term sheet.

5. Many MBAs Choose Not to Start Businesses (and Who Gives a Shit?)

Think about it—relatively few people start businesses.

You start a business because you're passionate about a problem and want to resolve it your way.

MBAs learn how to do it the traditional way: market studies and business plans (think Lean Startup, but with a 30-page report stuck to it). Many simply don't find the opportunity or don't want to shoulder the risk. Web startups aren't for everyone, even if software is eating the world.

My Suggestion

Follow your heart. If you want to be an entrepreneur, go out and be an entrepreneur. If you want an MBA, get an MBA. These two paths are complementary, not disparate, and you can do both.

Most importantly, remember that education is not about top 10 lists, how-to guides, or viral blog posts. Real education opens your mind to the world around you and helps you really understand the *why*. Remember that blindly executing is the fastest way to run off a cliff.

75

Why I Left Consulting and Joined a Startup

Michelle Wetzler (https://keen.io/blog)

Whether you're a technology consultant or you're in a startup, there's a good chance we have something in common. I call it career commitment avoidance.

The #1 reason I chose consulting as my first job after graduation was that I didn't want to decide where I would work, in what industry I would work, or even what I would really *do* on a day-to-day basis. I wanted to do a lot of things, and picking a single one of them just seemed too limiting.

With new projects, new clients, and the expectation that employees will "grow into" whatever role they get next, consultants never really have to decide who they're going to be in life, and that can be very liberating.

Like many others entering this profession, I figured after a couple of years I would gain the perspective I needed to hone in on my dream job. Years later, that still hadn't happened.

I started revising my notion of a dream job. I realized the right job for me isn't one job. It's a career that changes a lot, where I get to learn new things all the time. I began to wonder if consulting was the dream job. Maybe the reason I'd stuck around for so long was that consulting is the combination of so many things I want in a career:

1. **Learning a lot, fast.** When your clients are paying $XXX/hr for you to be there, they expect you to know stuff. A lot of stuff. On top of absorbing obscure technical know-how for each of my projects, I learned how to be accountable and manage a team.

2. **Emphasis on people and teams.** I worked on teams of 2, teams of 20, and multimillion-dollar teams of over 100 consultants. Working on a consulting project is truly a bonding experience. Since most people on the team fly in to work for the week, you're not just doing hard work together. You're also eating every meal together, getting shit-faced together, and living in the same hotel. You spend more personal time with these people than with your spouse. What's the #1 reason consultants give when asked what they like about their job? "The people."

3. **Merit-based compensation.** Some people would hate it, but knowing that I would be ranked against everyone else at my level, then recognized and paid accordingly, was motivating for me (I'm a little bit competitive).

4. **Work hard, play hard.** That's such a clichéd phrase, but there are some really intense people in consulting, and it can be energizing to be around them. They run marathons, go snowboarding on weeknights, run charity events, and more —all on top of working inhuman hours. There were times when I would work 13-hour days, party until 3 a.m., then do it again the next day. Seems a bit crazy now, but it wasn't a drain. It was fun.

So why did I quit a great job and join a startup for less pay, less job security, and significant risk to the relationships I have with my fiancé (Keen's CEO) and best friends (everyone else at Keen)?

Mostly, I was growing tired of implementing <some old-school technology> to solve <some generic enterprise problem>. I'm a builder at heart, and I wanted to contribute to Creating a Thing, not just bolting together boring software other people had halfheartedly built 8 years ago.

Figure 75-1. Crying at the bottom of the shower

There are also some, um, less pleasant aspects of being a consultant. Unless you are really lucky, you will at some point wind up on a project with asshole executives and a commute that makes you hate life (see Figure 75-1). Some people say these projects build backbone. I think the only good thing about them is that they are catalysts for a career change. It was one of these projects that finally changed my thinking from "I need to figure out what to do with my career" to "I need to make a change right now." I quit my job and started looking for the next great thing.

That's how I wound up here at Keen. And guess what? Startups share many of the qualities I love about consulting:

1. **Learning a lot, fast.** Here are just a handful of things I've learned in the past few weeks:

- How startup financials work, so I could comprehend seed round financing and negotiate my own salary and equity compensation
- Our system architecture and associated vocabulary (JSON, REST, Flask, Mongo, map reduce, etc.)
- How to create my first Ruby program, and integrate it with Keen
- What differentiates our company from other players in the analytics space
- How to get strangers on the Internet (and at conferences, meetups, and parties) to talk to me about analytics (we call this customer development)

You get the picture. In a startup, you get to be involved in all kinds of aspects of the company, and there's always more to learn and build.

2. **Emphasis on people and teams.** While people are important in a consulting firm, they're absolutely critical in a startup. With an industry average of a 20% turnover rate, consulting just doesn't offer the same level of quality you can get in a six-person startup, especially when it's six people who took great risks based on their faith in each other. The team at Keen is the #1 reason I joined the company.

3. **Merit-based compensation.** My equity stake and the small size of our team means my work directly contributes to the value of the company, which in turn contributes to my own personal net worth. In short, I can enjoy the company's successes as if they were my own successes, because they are. That's a rewarding feeling, and it definitely outweighs the salary cut I took to join Keen. Besides, I'm smart enough to have figured out that making anything over a certain amount of "comfortable income" contributes very little to my overall happiness.

4. **Travel.** Travel is one area where startup perks are not going to compare to consulting, but startups offer significantly less pain in this area. I don't get to fly much for work these days, but I also don't have to spend two hours a day driving to a client's office. My daily commute is now measured in steps, not hours.

5. **Work hard, play hard.** There's this perception about tech startups that the employees are working all night, sleeping under desks, pooping in socks, and bleeding code. Startup pace is supposedly so fast you can't even imagine it. People say things like "a year in startup will advance your career 37 years!"

I've worked around the clock before. One time, Kyle literally spoon-fed me dinner while I coordinated a critical go-live issue. Later that month, a lead told me that the overall productivity *and health* of our Mumbai team were declining because people kept coming to work sick. But perhaps the most eye-opening experience came when one of my direct reports *asked my permission to eat dinner.*

That isn't cool. It's fucking embarrassing.

Consulting firms say they value "work-life balance," but the truth is that consultants themselves tend to be workaholic types, especially senior leaders. No matter how many vacation days, flexible work schedules, or company wellness policies are offered, there are folks who are going to work as much as possible. In projects where this is taken to extremes, you get consequences like the ones I just described.

That's why it's a huge relief to join a team that values a sustainable pace. The Keen founders have a term for it: "rested racehorses." We are an elite team that can run fast, but we don't sprint every day. We need to be rested so we can sprint when it's truly important.

Finally, I want to circle back to the original lure of consulting—the lack of commitment to a "job." Startups take this freedom to the next level. There is a strong culture of making it your own way, building your own brand, and focusing on whatever you feel is important. After spending a certain amount of time around entrepreneurs, you begin to wonder where you ever got the idea of a "career," an "employer," or a "profession." This is a much more creative and opportunistic lifestyle.

If you're stuck in the consulting rut, consider joining a startup. Just like consulting firms, startups value smart, hardworking generalists who can learn quickly. You'll have significantly more ownership of the business, the product, your day-to-day activities, and your career path. You'll have the opportunity not only to build a great team and product, but a great company. So, what's stopping you from making the switch?

If you're thinking about a consulting career or joining a startup (I would highly recommend either!), I'm happy to help in any way I can.

About the Editor

Tom Eisenmann is the Howard H. Stevenson Professor of Business Administration at the Harvard Business School. He studies processes for launching new ventures, with a focus on the lean startup approach. Professor Eisenmann is Chair of Harvard's MBA Elective Curriculum—the second year of the MBA program—and Faculty Co-Chair of the HBS Arthur Rock Center for Entrepreneurship. He also is course head of "The Entrepreneurial Manager," taught to all 900 first-year MBA students, and faculty co-leader of the Harvard Innovation Lab–sponsored New York City Winter Break Trip, in which students from across Harvard explore entrepreneurship in cultural industries. In recent years, Eisenmann has co-led four Winter Break trips to Silicon Valley, and he created two MBA electives: "Launching Technology Ventures," which examines challenges that entrepreneurs encounter when starting and scaling new ventures; and "Managing Networked Business" (now called "The Online Economy"), which surveys strategies for platform-based businesses that leverage network effects.

Eisenmann received his Doctorate in Business Administration, MBA, and BA from Harvard University. He spent 11 years as a management consultant at McKinsey & Company, where he was co-head of the Media and Entertainment practice during the early 1990s. Eisenmann is a director on the boards of Harvard Business Publishing and Harvard Student Agencies.

Colophon

The cover and body font is *ScalaPro*, the heading font is *BentonSans*, and the code font is *TheSansMonoCd*.